AF543365

ANGAMI SOCIETY
AT THE BEGINNING OF THE 21st CENTURY

ANGAMI SOCIETY
AT THE BEGINNING OF THE 21st CENTURY

Edited by
Kedilezo Kikhi
Alphonsus D'Souza
Visakhonü Hibo

AKANSHA PUBLISHING HOUSE
NEW DELHI-110002 (INDIA)

AKANSHA PUBLISHING HOUSE
4649-B/21, Ansari Road
Darya Ganj, New Delhi - 110 002
Ph.: 23263193 / 9811582579 / 09435116718
Telefax: 011-23263193
Email: ektabooks@yahoo.com
www.akanshapublishinghouse.com

Angami Society at the Beginning of the 21st Century

@ Editors

First Published 2009

ISBN 978-81-8370-178-5

[All rights reserved. No part of this publication may be reproduced or transmitted, in any form or by any means, without prior permission of the editors. Any person who does any unauthorized act in relation to this publication may be liable to criminal prosecution and civil claims for damages.]

PRINTED IN INDIA

Published by Akansha Publishing House, New Delhi and Printed at Aryan Enterprises, Delhi.

CONTENTS

Al[illegible]ther factors, these processes [illegible] le[illegible] the economy, agrarian struc[illegible] re[illegible] most fundamental change [illegible] no[illegible] of agriculture, as the mainstay of the village ec[illegible]aditional agriculture meant primarily [illegible] foo[illegible] for domestic consumption is becoming [illegible] or[illegible]n the introduction of cash crops. [illegible] fields are ea[illegible]terted into construction sites for commercial pur[illegible]ots of forest are being planted with commercially val[illegible]es. Such changes in the use of land [illegible] that la[illegible] no more as a form of property but as a commodity tha[illegible] be sold and bought or leased out for a rent [illegible] cash.

[illegible] commodification of land indicates a new pattern of la[illegible]s. The concept and practice of absolute [illegible] b[illegible]als has begun to spread. There has been a tra[illegible] from communal ownership to individual [illegible] Fur[illegible] practice of tenancy has emerged. [illegible] changes in [illegible]ations have been accompanied by a change in the ag[illegible]ructure.

[illegible]h this paper deals with the [illegible] ag[illegible]anges in Angami society, [illegible] fo[illegible]er Naga tribal societies as well. This is because the [illegible] forces of changes are at work also in other [illegible] so[illegible] Nagaland.

REFERENCES

1. [illegible] H. M (2001). *Encyclopaedia of North-East India [illegible] Nagaland*. New Delhi: Mittal Publications.

2. [illegible]thers, Bruce G. and Laura Anevich [illegible] "The [illegible] of Property Rights". *Annual Review of Sociology* [illegible] 19:23-46.

3. [illegible] of India (1991). *Nagaland State: District [illegible]* [illegible] Census Publications.

FOREWORD

Very pleased to write the foreword for the collection of diverse ideas, opinions and thoughts compiled by the painstaking editorial efforts of Kedilezo Kikhi, Alphonsus D'Souza and Visakonu Hibo. Angami Society at the beginning of the 21st century is indeed a welcome compilation as the Society is torn between modernity, tradition.

Dr Shurhozelie's describing the Ura academy and the evolution of Tenyidie is very important as it is now possible to record the oral tradition into an easily readable form for posterity. Certainly, the role of Christianity over the last 165 years and how it enabled the society to become a modern society is a turning point in the history of Angami history. This was followed by introduction of modern British model of education significantly transformed the society. The role of English language has also played its role in recording the important oral tradition but having one in Tenyidie is significant as it is the mother tongue.

The compilation has talked on diversity of topics such as communitization, role of media, the basic issue of environment depredation, health, youth and alcoholism and I hope the contributors have discussed some solutions to the various issues, especially youth unemployment.

Has education and related issues helped the society in globalisation or simply remained an examination oriented pursuit? Should we redefine the purpose of education and do we need to increase the quality and quantity of good teachers so that our youth are able to compete globally? Why only minority population pursue higher studies in Nagaland and why most of them prefer studies outside Nagaland. Is the University playing its role for what it was set up about 21 years ago? Is the youth torn between social dynamics and economic development?

I hope this compilation will trigger a whole new thinking process and ask very pertinent and basic questions on where we move from here. I wish this book will be read, discussed, action plans taken so that there will be continuous awareness in keeping pace with technological advances.

Prof K. Kannan
Vice-Chancellor
Nagaland University

ACKNOWLEDGEMENTS

At the very outset, we acknowledge the active and inspiring participation of all the learned resource persons coming from a cross-section of academia, social activists, journalists, administrators and young scholars in this ICSSR-NERC sponsored seminar on "Angami Society at the Beginning of the 21st Century: Academic Reflections on Selected Themes", the outcome of which is the present volume.

We are grateful to Dr. C.J. Thomas, Director-ICSSR, NERC Shillong and all his staff for their encouragement, assistance, and above all sponsoring the seminar. We are also thankful to the Principal and staff of Japfü Christian College, Kigwema for their hospitality and extending all possible help in making the seminar a grand success.

The editors are grateful to Dr. Shürhozelie Liezietsu, Hon'ble Minister, Urban Planning and Co-ordination, Higher Education, Economics and Statistics, Government of Nagaland and Mr. Menükhol John, Commissioner & Secretary, Family and Health Services, Government of Nagaland for delivering the Chief Guest Speech and the keynote address respectively.

We thankfully acknowledge Rev. Dr. Alphonsus D'Souza, Dr. Buno Liegiese, Fr. Melville Pereira, Dr. Walter Fernandes and Mr. Niketu Iralu for chairing the academic sessions.

Lastly we thank all the participants of the seminar for responding to our call and then attending the seminar from different places.

Kedilezo Kikhi
Alphonsus D'Souza
Kohima **Visakhonü Hibo**

LIST OF CONTRIBUTORS

1. **Shürhozelie Liezietsu**, Hon'ble Minister, Urban Planning and Co-ordination, Higher Education, Economics and Statistics, Government of Nagaland. & President, Ura Academy, Kohima, Nagaland.
2. **Walter Fernandes**, Director, North Eastern Social Research Centre, Guwahati.
E-mail: walter.nesrc@gmail.com
3. **Alphonsus D' Souza**, St. Joseph's College, Jakhama.
E-mail: alphonsusds@gmail.com
4. **G. Singaiah**, Professor and Head, Dept. of Management, North Eastern Hill University, Tura Campus.
5. **Niketu Iralu**, Trustee of Friends, Moral Re-Armament & Member, International Council of Initiatives of Change. Email: niketuiralu@gmail.com
6. **Thepfulhouvi Solo**, Retd. Principal Secretary, Forest, Wildlife & Environment, Government of Nagaland.
E-mail: Angami_t@yahoo.co.in
7. **D. Kuolie**, Reader & Head, Department of Tenyidie, Nagaland University.
8. **Buno Liegiese**, Reader, Department of Education, Nagaland University.

9. **Rusovil John**, Member Secretary, Nagaland Pollution Control Board, Government of Nagaland. E-mail: npcb2@yahoo.com
10. **Niu W. Kuotsu**, Principal, Sazolie College, Jotsoma.
11. **Sedevi Angami**, MS, CIHSR, Dimapur.
12. **Ketshukietuo Dzüvichü**, Principal, Oriental College, Kohima. E-mail: atshu.dzuvichu@yahoo.com
13. **Viraho Hibo**, Vice-Principal & Head, Department of Education, Japfü Christian College, Kigwema. E-mail: visakhonu99viraho@gmail.com
14. **Chandan Debnath**, Lecturer, Dimapur Govt. College, Dimapur & Research Scholar, Dept. of Business Administration, Tezpur University, Assam. E-mail: debnath@tezu.ernet.in
15. **Christina Kekhrieseno**, Lecturer, Wankhao Govt. College, Mon.
16. **Kevizakie Rio**, Lecturer, Government Higher Secondary School, Kohima.
17. **Melville Pereira**, Research Scholar, JNU, New Delhi.
18. **Visakhonü Hibo**, Head, Dept. of Sociology, JCC, Kigwema & Research Scholar, Department of Education, Nagaland University. E-mail: visakhonu99viraho@gmail.com
19. **Kedilezo Kikhi**, Lecturer, Department of Sociology, Nagaland University. Email: kedithejakikhi@yahoo.co.in

INTRODUCTION

This volume of essays on Angami Community brings together diverse opinions and multiple interpretations on selected themes by various scholars and learned persons from inside and outside. Angami, a major community in Nagaland, has extensively been studied by many scholars in recent times; but not a common platform for a common reflection on the research findings. The focus of this volume is mainly on the problems and issues faced by the Angami community at the beginning of this 21st Century ranging from language, politics, media, education, environmental depredation, health, youth, unemployment, social dynamics, development, old age, gender issues and the like.

The resource persons had done thorough research in their entrusted specific issues, had not only highlighted their main findings but came up with fruitful arguments. We believe this volume will serve as a benchmark for the community and a roadmap for the community in this 21st century. The participants felt this retrospective exercise of pausing together, looking back into the past and deliberating for the future is a must exercise for every other Naga community. The book is a must read not only for the academicians but for all those who want to engage in live debate on the issues, discuss and address it, rectify and march ahead. It will also be a beneficial reading for the public leaders, church leaders, politicians, bureaucrats, policy makers and planners, research scholars and the students alike.

I

The first section of essays entitled "Tenyidie Language" deals with Ura Academy and the scope of the vernacular language as an academic discipline. Shurhozelie Liezietsu in his paper gives a description about the history of the Angami language and how the American Missionaries started teaching vernacular language 'Tenyidie' at a small mission school. His paper elaborately deals the formation of various committees at various stages for the development of Tenyidie language culminating into its present status. He also states how Angami Literature Committee was renamed Ura Academy as a literary society. He mentions Ura Academy has made considerable progress in various fields. Today, Tenyidie is taught not only at schools and colleges but even taught at the post-graduate level. Tenyidie is the first Naga language to be introduced at the University level. Through this paper he calls upon the people especially the educated to realize the importance of learning Tenyidie. He also states the Academy encourages development of dialects (Kicha die) like Chokri, Kheza, Zemi, Liangmai, etc. but recommends that while developing these dialects, one should take care of the aspect to link up with Tenyidie at the higher level.

D. Kuolie's paper highlights the importance and scope of Tenyidie as a mother tongue (first language). The function of mother tongue is highlighted as a medium of learning, thinking and creativity. MT is also taken as the chief means for quality education. In the context, Tenyidie is treated as the main issue for the Tenyimia community with special attention towards academic importance in favour of the general mass of the community. He argues the scope of Tenyidie is as vast as the language of English in academic field. The difference is a matter of status, richness of its literature, speakers/readers. The paper highlights literature development has endless horizon and every talented one can play according to one's choice. By establishing rich literature, various disciplines of study can be established. He further argues if literature of all discipline of study is developed in Tenyidie, our future generation will find greater scope and opportunity for their well being in all sphere of life.

II

This section entitled "Angami politics" deals with the present Naga political situation vis-à-vis the role played by the Angamis in the Naga political history particularly by A.Z. Phizo.

Niketu Iralu in his paper "The Kingdom of God and Our Crisis" reflects the Naga political crisis as the outcome of poor response to the challenges. The subsequent response of all Nagas to the same crisis of opportunities and challenges has produced the society we have today, 'over ground' and 'underground'. He questions have not extensive portions of the Naga homeland become a nightmare with Dimapur heading the list? He argues that we need to assess ourselves correctly and know exactly who and how much we are, and how far we have come on our journey. He calls upon the Nagas to thank all those who by their diverse contributions have achieved for us what we are today, no matter how humble that may be, and learn to build on the foundation we have inherited, without coveting what we don't have and are not entitled to have yet".

He states the moment we each obey God, unity, reconciliation, forgiveness, goodwill, co-operation, and all else will automatically appear in our land. Unification will be part of the package without our doing anything to achieve it as it is always a by-product of the other deeper things. If we Nagas with God's grace and mercy will decide to help one another to rise to what we all are meant to be, we will make it.

III

The next section deals with traditional learning systems and modern education, communitisation of elementary education, youth and problems. Alphonsus D'Souza's paper points out that tribal student have learning styles that differ from those of non-tribal students. The study talks about the tribal societies particularly of the north-east, having rich traditions and well established traditional processes and institutions for transmitting knowledge and skills. The languages of these tribes had no script till the advent of modern education. Therefore, traditional method of imparting knowledge had to be through oral explanation and activities. Incorporating such traditional processes and practices into the modern system of education will make education an enjoyable and enriching experience for tribal children and students. At the same time, it will probably make them more confident to face an increasingly globalised world.

Buno Liegise in her paper makes an attempt to assess the impact of communitization process on the government elementary schools in Angami villages which was introduced in the year 2002-2003. She states communitization of elementary education in Nagaland is by far the most significant decision taken by the government of Nagaland in the field of school education. To her it is a bold step as 'communitization' of any institution of the government means transferring ownership to and the responsibility of its management with the community. The study also highlights the major programmes and activities of the VECs and the problems faced by the VECs and a list of suggestions for improvement of the communitization process. Communitization process is at a crucial juncture. And Angami villages are in the phase of rejection of the old and experimenting with the new.

Viraho Hibo's paper on "Educational Achievement and Aspiration of the Angami Students: A Study of Two Colleges" compared the performance of Angami students at matric exam and the consequent following exams. He studied the students by categorizing them into educated families and uneducated families, boys and girls - by using various indicators like aspiration and achievement. The study findings include amongst others - students from educated families have relatively higher aspirations; boys have higher aspirations than girls but the performance of girls have been better. Hibo in his paper talks about Angami parents giving too much importance to matric exam alone. The study revealed that there is no competitive spirit among the Angami students. English language is an important aspect which determines the educational achievement of students in addition to hard work. Therefore, both spoken English and written English should be given equal emphasis. He stressed there is a need felt that Angami students at the college level (BA level) requires proper guidance from both parents and teachers.

Kevizakie Rio's paper "Education as an Industry: Impact on the Angami Society" focuses on the enterprise of providing for education by the private sector to those who are ready to pay at much higher rate for the services that otherwise (and conventionally) are imparted at a very cheap rate by the system of education run by the government. He calls the system of private enterprises imparting education to students in the state as an 'industry' because like any other enterprise, it is mainly undertaken to earn income and profit. However in general private institutions strive hard to impress their clients and exhibit remarkable salesmanship to attract them whereas the institutions of the government sector have no incentives or urge to do so. Therefore he states, it is obvious for parents of the students to send their children to such institutions with good prospects though the costs are high.

Kedilezo Kikhi's paper addresses amongst others questions like – i) do the educated youth of the state possess the necessary requirements to get a job? ii) 'Who' do the educated unemployed blame for not getting a job? It is understood from this paper that the problem of unemployment among the educated youth is one of the gravest that the state faces today. It has invited the anger of youth and they are increasingly indulging into illegal, anti-social and other violent and criminal activities too. And this can be read as an expression of their distrust to the system. The deprivations in the matters of recruitment further generate socio-economic problems like corruption, nepotism, favouritism, etc. Kikhi argues the problem of unemployment among the educated youth is a serious problem, which needs timely attention and solution. Unemployment should not be viewed as a 'residual' problem to be tackled after the other problems have been solved, but as a 'primary' problem. It calls for determined efforts and appropriate policies, plans and programmes, so that our educated young men and women can become job creators and not job seekers.

IV

This section entitled "Issues on Environmental Depredation" deals with the ecological status of the Angami land and the problems of pollution in the region. Thepfulhouvi Solo has in his paper elaborated that Angami region is one of the richest biological diversity in the world and is part of one of the Biological Hot Spot of the world. He talks about different species of plants, shrubs, grass, etc and stated for instance there are 7 different rhododendrons in the area. Thus the area provides food for the animals, birds, and insects every season of the year. He mentions Angami area is one of the richest in wild vegetables; there are some 125 different kinds of edible wild leaves in Angami area. The world is stagnating on the list of vegetable species domesticated thousands of years ago. Modern man has not added much new species in the list of vegetables his ancient forefathers have domesticated and some of the wild vegetables found in our jungle could very well be domesticated to add to the worlds. And as for the varieties of medicinal plants in the wild, the possibilities are perhaps beyond imagination. Solo states the relationship between plants and animals 'ecology' is very delicate, subtle and important. One of the most important wealth of the Angami is the biological wealth of its jungle. But he argues in his presentation the ecology is preserved luckily not by Angamis but by mountains and remoteness.

Rusuvil John in his paper stressed that the waste disposal in Nagaland is unscientific. For instance, he stated the people of the land are not aware that bio-medical waste is hazardous. The surface water of the state is unprotected from untreated industrial effluents and wastewater, runoff pollution from chemical fertilizers and pesticides. He stressed that Nagaland has no sewage system as yet. The use of pesticides in our wet paddy fields needs special attention, because of the fact that fishes, snails and small water creatures serve as delicacies and may get into the food chain. John has highlighted encroachment into roads and public drains causes traffic congestions, clogging of drains and flash floods. In many rural areas open latrines are common even today. Our system of burying the death in the residential areas may affect the ground water sources. He states with modernization many of our homes have become comparable to those of the Europeans in terms of luxury and cleanliness. However, as we step out of our homes we are confronted with heaps of unattended waste dumped by us into the streets. The attitude of "not in my compound is ok" has to change. The problem of pollution can best be mitigated not by rules but by creating awareness and concern among the people.

V

The fifth section deals with the issues of health. Sedevi Angami in his paper analyses the health status of the Angamis in particular and the Nagas on the whole. He points out in his paper the most common and peculiar diseases of the Angamis as TB hepatitis, Drug resistant TB, Hypertension,

Renal stones, stomach cancer, etc. The paper critically evaluates the whole functioning of the health administration in the state and list out practical suggestions for improvement and solutions like - the necessity for research cells, mass vaccination, PPP model centres, health education in the curriculum, proper networking and planning committee, etc. He states if these suggestions are adopted, then it can make dramatic changes in the health of our state in the next 10 years. But it will require a bold and necessary decision and the willingness to change and try out something new.

VI

This section entitled "Old Age and Gender Issues" discusses the problems of the aged and gender related issues. Ketshukietuo Dzüvichü in his paper examines the socio-economic and health problems of the aged among the Angami Nagas. The paper analyses their age and marital status, educational level, living arrangement and occupation. The study reveals that the Angami aged still enjoy higher status in the society. On the economic status, self sufficiency in terms of food availability which is the top priority in an Angami society is prominent but in terms of income, most of them are in the lower income group. The study on the health problems of the Angami aged of Nagaland reveals that majority of the aged suffer from one or a combination of ailments but many of them either regard themselves to be in excellent condition or are indifferent to their health or consider it as common in old age. Despite of all ailments and handicaps, the medical facilities available for the aged are inadequate and many aged are compelled to seek help from private practitioners in spite of their poor economic status.

Visakhonü Hibo in her paper "VDB and the Role of Angami Women" gives a description about the introduction and instant success of VDB in Nagaland initiated by Shri A.M. Gokhale in 1976. She critically argues on how women are handicapped by the system in this male dominated society. She took case studies at Viswema Village and shares the prospects of women in the future if properly re-structured. She states in her paper, Angàmis from time immemorial had been following the patrilineal/patriarchal system of governance. In this context it is not Angami man who is refusing to admit women at the decision-making bodies but it is the traditional way of life that is still taking time to shift to modern concepts of accommodating women even in a modern and recent construction like the VDB. Many a time, women themselves feel it is inappropriate to be part of the bodies that plans and does the decision-making, especially at the village level, not knowing that they are making their daughters go a few more years backward which in turn will have a very negative impact on the overall societal progress towards positive changes.

Niu Whiso Kuotsu in his paper addresses the challenges that faced the Angami Men in this 21st century. He argues that the journey to modernity will be neither smooth nor promising unless we also learn to solve and handle our own affairs responsibly and competently. The rapid changes have generated new problems, new demands and new challenges revealing our unpreparedness and inadequacies in coping with the requirements for modern development, management and governance. To him, some of our major inadequacies are work ethic and dedication, competence and efficiency, integrity and justice – resulting in corruption, nepotism, tribalism and factionalism – and clarity of vision in formulating polices and plans. These challenges are faced by the whole state and the Angamis also share the challenges with other tribes. In his paper he talks about one more challenge faced by the Angamis as a tribe and that challenge is the decline of their power and influence due to the decline in the quality of their performance in various fields. So although the Angamis had played a leading role in the past in moulding the history of the Nagas, now they are being gradually relegated to a secondary role in almost everything.

VII

The last section entitled "Social Dynamics and Economic Development" analyses the various changing processes of Angami society and the consequent developmental activities. Walter Fernandes in his paper talks about the dichotomy of tradition and modernity in Angami community. He argues what does globalisation mean to the Angami tribe? He deals with the main features of globalisation which has to be understood as a different process from modernisation and its interaction with the Angami community. The study shows that the Angami have had very little experience with globalization till now but have interacted with modernisation. The Angami have got more benefits of modernisation than the remaining tribes where studies have been conducted. They have thus, laid a foundation for dealing with the processes of globalization. Fernandes cautions the benefits of globalisation may reach a few and the majority may feel mainly its negative impacts. It can weaken their egalitarian culture and take them towards greater inequalities and class formation.

Cristina Kekhrieseno in her paper "Changing Land Relations and Angami Society" deals with the changing land relations in a tribal society, namely the Angami society of Nagaland. The paper highlights the three basic types of land in an Angami village, namely, i) terrace fields, ii) *jhum* fields, and iii) forest. It also deals with land disputes and ownership of land. Land owned by an individual can be of two types, namely, ancestral land and personally acquired land. Ancestral land is inherited from one's ancestors, while personally acquired land is acquired through purchase or exchange or received as a gift. Such individually owned land, whether ancestral or acquired, can be of any type. In practice, individuals own all the terrace fields, while fields used for shifting cultivation and forests are mostly communally owned. Communal ownership of land is vested with the lineage, clan or village. Such land can be fields used for shifting cultivation, forests, water channels, streams and rivulets. Such land is known as *kayie* (inherited) land. This paper also deals with the unique nature of agrarian changes in Angami society as seen in the emergence of absolute property, tenancy, and the various factors responsible for these changes.

Chandan Debnath and G. Singaiah in their paper define culture of a community as repositories of human knowledge conditioned by the dominant expectations of people, time and situations. This essentially means no culture is static, values and beliefs change to accommodate newer expectations and need. In the light of the above understanding, he argues how culture as such is considered to be a constraint in the path of development? Therefore the alternative being, underdevelopment is more an effect that can be attributed to human inefficiencies. It is similar in nature to a journey which lacks direction and priorities. When a society lacks confidence in its own cultural and economic strengths there is a tendency to replicate the approaches and means of others. They state in their paper such form of development lack collective appreciation and often the means used to carry out the same is a top down approach. The problems get compounded in a society which has very low power distance, believes in equity and participation, and group problem solving. Will such an approach work? Collective societies place great importance to consensus and participation. They conclude development is a participative exercise which involves common strength, combined resources, collective wisdom to make it effective. Anything which calls for common strength, resources and wisdom has its source in the culture of the people.

Melville Pereira in his paper, while affirming the need for modernization of customary law, argues that codification, instead of reforming the customary law, may sound a death-knell to its very existence. To him a better alternative could be documentation of these age-old laws by a representative body of the tribal community, which includes men and women across age-groups. The documentation process could be widely discussed and debated in the tribal community, paying attention to issues of gender justice, common property resources and strengthening of self-governing institutions. Pereira in his paper has also suggested a road map for the future - like statewide awareness drive through seminars and workshops by a competent body, documentation of customary laws by all tribal groups, etc. He desires that Naga culture and customary law becomes part of curricula in the school syllabus as well as in legal studies of the state. This is necessary he argues because of the disappearance of the *morung* system. Customary law needs to be made gender sensitive in keeping with the requirements of human rights issues.

Kedilezo Kikhi
Alphonsus D'Souza
Visakhonü Hibo

Kohima

1

URA ACADEMY AND THE EVOLUTION OF TENYIDIE

Shürhozelie Liezietsu

Legend says that God gave a script to our ancestors on a hide which was eaten by dog and, therefore, our ancestors lost their script. J.H. Hutton also makes a reference to this legend vide page 291 of his book, "*The Angami Nagas*". The cultural life, the religious practice, the village administration system, etc of our ancestors were systematic and of very high standard. It is difficult to believe that our ancestors maintained such high standard of organized society without having some kind of civilization at one time or the other. It is hoped that research in this field may reveal interesting discoveries about the originality of our people in due course of time.

For many years, our forefathers lived without any contact with the outside world. After the British set up their permanent headquarters at Kohima in 1878, the first American missionary C.D. King arrived at Kohima on 25th February, 1881. He started a school in 1882. For the first three years, Assamese was said to have been taught in that small mission school. C .D. King introduced teaching Tenyidie in 1884. After C.D. King, Dr. Sidney W. Rivenburg came to Kohima and worked among our people for many years. The Kohima Mission School soon became very popular and many people sent their children to study in this school from almost all over Tenyimia areas including Semas of Pughoboto area. Those who studied in this Mission School learnt to read, write and speak Tenyidie very well. But when they went home they started writing in their own village accent and pronunciation. Therefore, the educated class could not communicate in writing due to different spelling patterns based on their own local pronunciation, for example: *chülie* (Tenyidie); *tshülie* (Kohima group); *shülie* (Khonoma group); *thul* (Southern Angami group); *thiyi* (Eastern Angami group); *chünyie* (Tuophema group), etc.

While observing this difficulty, Rev. J.E. Tanquist thought it necessary to garner public opinion to make decision for the common spelling pattern based on Tenyidie books written and translated by the missionaries. He, therefore, convened a meeting and constituted Angami Literature Committee in 1939 with Lhoulienyü Suokhrie as its Chairman, George W. Supplee as its Secretary, other members were Rüzhükhrie Sekhose, Krusiehu Belho and Neingulie Keditsu. This committee was approved by the Deputy Commissioner of Kohima at that particular time, C.R. Pawsey.

We have found that this committee worked very hard from 1939 till 1948, the year the Indian government expelled George W. Supplee from India on suspicion for Naga political problem. During this ten years period, the committee finalized the basic structure of spelling and word division in Tenyidie, thus laid the foundation of Tenyidie of its standard form.

The progress of development of Tenyidie was not very satisfactory for some years due to political disturbances in Nagaland. Though literatures do not grow under disturbed condition, yet some of our elders did their best to promote Tenyidie even under disturbed condition. In 1954, the Angami Vernacular Text Book Committee was constituted with Dr. Üzielie Peseyie as its chairman and Rüzhükhrie, Zhavise, Krusiehu and Neiliehu as members. This committee in consultation with the Angami Literature Committee selected text books for use in schools. In the meantime, an Advisory Text books Committee for Naga Hills was also constituted with Deputy Commissioner as its chairman and Deputy Inspector of Schools, Naga Hills as its secretary. Other members were Assistant Inspector of Schools, Naga Hills, Shillong, Nihoi Jakhalu and Dr. Neilhouzhü Kire. In 1954, one of the resolutions of this committee says, "resolved that the Registrar Gauhati University be moved to recognize the two major Naga Hills dialects, Angami and Ao as suitable text books are now ready for Matric Course". We fully acknowledged the efforts put in by our elders in promoting Tenyidie even during the worst period in Nagaland.

On 23rd May, 1970, a group of Angami contractors and leaders had a picnic at Northern Angami Hall at Chüziema. The meeting decided, among other things, to reorganize Angami Literature Committee and nominated the following persons: Rüzhükhrie Sekhose, Shürhozelie, Kezhagwelie Peseye, Beilieü Shüya and Dr. H.V. Sakhrie. The committee was also empowered to co-opt another four persons. Therefore, this newly constituted committee in its first meeting on June 9, 1970 co-opted the following persons: Mr. Zhavise Vihienuo, Rev. Tsolie Chase, Neiliehu Belho and Mr. Vikeyieu.

One of the first programmes taken up by this committee was organizing a Tenyidie Seminar for language teachers in Kohima area from 9-11 March, 1971. Teachers from many schools participated with enthusiasm.

In 1971, the Angami Literature Committee took a major decision that the activities of the committee should cover not only development of literature but also the socio-cultural aspect of Tenyimia people as a whole. It was therefore, decided to change the name of the committee from Angami Literature Committee to URA ACADEMY. Accordingly, preparations were made and Ura Academy was inaugurated on 6th November, 1971 by the then Chief minister of Nagaland, Dr. Hokishe Sema. It was raining the whole day and the old people who came to grace the function interpreted rain on that day as a good omen.

Ura Academy is primarily a literary society. The Academy is committed to working for preservation and perpetuation of Tenyimia culture in the present Tenyimia society which is undergoing great flux in lifestyle and culture. The poetic and philosophic aspects of Tenyidie, traditional garments, traditional ornaments and armours, folk dances and songs of Tenyimia people and all positive practices of our culture, such as, the practice of courtesy in speech, of giving honour to one another and to the elders in particular, etc. It is committed to work for the welfare of the people in various fields of human development.

There is a Board of Directors represented by various Tenyimia groups such as, Angami, Chakhesang, Pochury, Rengma, Zeliang, Mao, Maram, Poumai. Under this Board, there are many different divisions to look after various aspects of development in the field of literature, academic qualifications, social education, socio-cultural services, publications, women and youth welfare, etc.

During the last three and a half decades, Ura Academy has made considerable progress in various fields. It has published several hundred books on different subjects. Tenyidie was given recognition by NEHU in 1988 to be introduced in the Pre-University level. It was first introduced in Kohima College in 1988 and upgraded simultaneously in a proceeding manner from pre-university to degree level and to honours course. Tenyidie was introduced in the post-graduate level in 1997 under Nagaland University. The department has produced more than 40 post-graduates so far. We have Tenyidie subject in Kohima College, Phek College, Pfütsero College, Baptist College, Kohima Science College, and Dimapur College. The subject is now manned by qualified Lecturers. It is always our appeal to the colleges in Tenyimia area to introduce Tenyidie as a subject. More than 40 dissertations were completed by our students, the list of which is attached as annexure 1. These dissertations covered a wide range of Tenyimia life and culture.

One of the Academy's annual features is holding Tenyimia seminar in which language teachers are invited to attend. Writers, educationists, public leaders and subject experts of different lines of teaching are invited to address the seminar. Besides this, it also hold meetings with area and village representatives occasionally in order to create awareness for all round development covering a wide range of subjects like agriculture, horticulture, fishery development, cattle farming, forestry and other eco-based subjects.

Ura Academy publishes a monthly journal entitled URA DZE which carries important information on the activities of Ura Academy. Poems – old and modern, stories, dramas, and other literary pieces are the regular features of this journal.

Ura Academy celebrated its Golden Jubilee in 1989 (1939-1989). To commemorate the Jubilee, Jotsoma village arranged a very good monumental stone which was pulled by Kohima village youth in traditional gate pulling style on 6th November 1989 with much gaiety. In the evening, the inaugural function was held at Khuochiezie where thousands of Tenyimia people from all walks of life attended the function with great enthusiasm. The highlights of the inaugural function were presentation of cultural dances, recitals, presentation of classical as well as modern music. The function was a grand success which continued the next day at BE School auditorium with technical sessions, exhibition and, of course, a big feast.

The history of the evolution of Tenyidie is simple. In 1972, Ura Academy had taken decision to adopt words accepted by Tatar Hoho of the Federal Government of Nagaland like *eno, eli, enoli, ahng, kilonser*, etc. We have published those new words in Ura Dze and asked people to practice using them. We were aware that language can be developed only through usage but it cannot be imposed on the population. After this first list published in 1972, we have decided not to coin new words.

The standard of Tenyidie which is in use now is based on the spelling and word division pattern framed by the first Literature Committee. We have updated few only to clear confusion between words like *chü* and *cü*; *tse* and *tshe*; *pfe* and *pfhe*; *pfü* and *pfhü*. For this decision we have consulted the Central Institute of Indian Languages, Mysore. We have also consulted the work of Robbing Burlings, a linguist from Pensylvania University who came to Assam in the fifties and studied Garo language. During his stay in Assam, he met Dr. K.S. Tseikhanuo and recorded some Tenyidie words from him. After some time, he produced a leaflet containing Tenyidie-English in which he uses words like cü (*ch*ü); *cie* (*chie*); *pfe* (*pfhe*), etc. his work was found to be in agreement with the recommendation of the CIIL, Mysore. Hence we have decided to change the spelling pattern much against the wishes of the people at the initial stage. But now younger generation is no longer in confusion to read Tenyidie. I would like to go one more step further, that is, the *Bible* in Tenyidie (Ketholeshü) is most widely read by the people. It was written before these changes in the spelling pattern were affected. Therefore, the old spelling pattern continues even after 37 years without any revision which creates confusions as of old. We hope the *Bible* (Ketholeshü) will be revised soon with the present standard Tenyidie to enable our people to read with more interest.

Tenyidie is the first Naga language to be introduced at the University level. We encourage development of dialects (Kicha die) like Chokri, Kheza, Zemi, Liangmai, etc. But we recommend that while developing these dialects, one should take care of the aspect to link up with Tenyidie at the higher level. Take for example; the Rengmas have two distinct dialects. With the development of the two dialects, young Rengma people cannot understand one another. The only alternative for them is to converse either in English or the so called Nagamese. If so, we are going backward rather than going forward.

Therefore, one of our prime concerns is to create awareness among the people to realize the importance of learning Tenyidie. If the educated group, like the group which gathered together here today, gives some importance to Tenyidie, our objective can be achieved without much difficulty. The elderly people from Rengma area, Pughoboto area, Chakhesang area, Sopfümia area and Zeliang area can speak Tenyidie very well. Tenyidie is spoken in the Pochury areas of Myanmar even today. To perpetuate this trend, little attention is demanded from all of you.

Annexure 1 – List of M.A. Dissertations

1. Ako Savi	A Study of Tenyimia Classical & Modern Poetry
2. Buno	Literary Assessment of Early Tenyimia Writers
3. Medongulie	A Critical Study of Literary Work of Shürhozelie

4. Neikhotsonuo	A Thematic Study of Tenyimia Poetry
5. Thejazeü	The Stylistic Study of Tenyimia Poetry
6. Neilalie Yaotsu	Myths & Legends of Tenyimia
7. Menguzeü	Festivals of Northern Angami
8. Nüyelü Keyho	Ancestral Culture of Chokri Area
9. Pudenü Thaprü	Major Festivals of Tenyimia
10. Akhrieü	Festivals of Western Angami
11. Metuo Liezietsu	Process of Ritual in Religious Culture of the Northern Angamis
12. Vizomenuo	Ancestral Culture of the Angamis
13. Zacivelü	Process of Ritual in Religious Culture of Chokri Area
14. Sepole Hesuh	Influences of Tenyimia Culture on Behaviour and Attitude of the People
15. Mhalezolie Kire	Language and Media in Tenyimia Group
16. Mhasivilie	A Study of Dialectical Variation of Northern Angami
17. Neichüpe	A Study of Dialectical Variation in Kheza Area
18. Vimedo Keyho	A Case Study of Tenyidie Teaching at Secondary School Level in Kohima District

19. Neizovinuo	The Role of Women in Tenyimia Society
20. Lhouvisalie	Politics and Leadership in Traditional Tenyimia
21. Keduolhoulie	Formation of Tenyidie Questions and Negations
22. Khriekethozo	The Study of Social Structure of Tenyimia
23. Kekuodenuo	A Study of Traditional Law of Inheritance of Tenyimia Society
24. Virielhou Rieu	Tenyimia Tradition of Work Culture & Economy
25. Kevise Khalietsu	The Traditional System of Education in Tenyimia Society
26. Neilatuonuo	Poetic Work of D. Kuolie
27. Vipinuo	Ancient Diplomacy & Inter-Village Relations
28. Petekhrieo	A Critical Study of Tenyimia Classical Poetry
29. Poseyi	Dialectical Variation of Chokri
30. Neitsoü	Ancestral Culture of Kheza
31. Kezhavino	Religious Philosophy of Tenyimia – A Case Study
32. Nourhetuonuo	The Festivals of Southern Angamis
33. Neilazoü	Economic Products of Tenyimia & their Usage

34. Nouneseno Mor	The Festival of Rengma
35. Dziesevituo Sachü	Art & Craft of Tenyimia Community
36. Khrüvolü Keyho	The Technique of Traditional Agriculture of Tenyimia
37. Vevotalü	Ancestral Culture of Pochury
38. Neizevonuo Suokhrie	A Stylistic Study of Tenyimia Literature
39. Ruokuovotso	Poetic Work of Medo
40. Kenilel Kevin Rote	Artistic Technique of Shürhozelie
41. Neiphrezonuo Mepfhüo	Ritual Process in Religious Culture of Mao Naga

2

THE SCOPE OF TENYIDIE AS AN ACADEMIC DISCIPLINE

D. Kuolie

[*This is a concept paper, an awareness projection in form by taking the ground realities of language in general, its acquisition and learning process. Language is classified into first language or mother tongue (MT) and second language. The function of mother tongue is highlighted as medium of learning, thinking and creativity. MT is also taken as the chief means for quality education. In this context, Tenyidie is treated as the main issue for the Tenyimia community with special attention towards academic importance in favour of the general mass of the community.*

The scope of Tenyidie is as vast as the language of English in Academic field. The difference is a matter of status, richness of its literature, speakers/readers. If we consider Tenyidie as a separate identity in itself, the demand is to enrich its literature in all field of study. Literature development has endless horizon and every talented one can play according to one's choice. By establishing rich literature, various disciplines of study can be established. For instance, in the field of 'performing art' we can develop script writing for dramatic performances. If literature of all discipline of study is developed in Tenyidie, our future generation will find greater scope and opportunity for their well being in all sphere of life.]

Introduction

Universally, life is a process with full of activities, both physical and mental. All our experience, daily activities and future planning are unique features in life. How we store such variety of features is basically abstract in nature. Our brain has unlimited capacity to store such features in the form of memory which is a mental power. But our mental power functions well in a universal medium what we called language. Language in terms of competence and performance of a person has two primary layers – First Language and Second language. The first language is acquired and the second language is said to be learned. The first language or mother tongue (MT) is the most effective medium of human thinking process. Virtually, man's thinking process depends upon the extent of concepts that he/she acquires. In our context, Tenyidie is the medium of thinking for the Tenyimia community. Mother tongue has the greatest potential of creativity. To supplement the points, let us refresh our memory by referring to four significant statements given by (a) Kothari Commission (1964-66) that a child who receives education through mother tongue will be better in understanding the concept than a child who receives education in other languages. (b) Mahatma Gandhi remarked, "The motivation towards learning and the progress of an individual can be achieve through mother tongue only". (c) Comparing mother tongue with breast milk Tagore says, "No milk can be substituted to the breast milk of the mother to the child. Like that, other languages cannot be a substitution of the mother tongue to the student in the process of learning". (d) The Supreme Court of India observed that there is a language conflict in the students when they are taught the subjects through a language other than their native language, and suggested to eliminate this mental tension among the pupil whose home language is not taught as first language.

Linguists treat all languages equal because each language provides the best tools to describe the centre and thought of respective ethnic group of society. Irrespective of number of its speakers a language provides its best service to its community. To refer to our topic, we can rightly claim that Tenyidie can serve Tenyimia community as the easiest medium of learning, the highest degree for creativity, the most effective medium of thinking, the shortest route to acquire knowledge and application. For the reason, to discuss its scope as an academic discipline is worth sharing.

However, before we begin the deliberation, allow me to highlight a precise note on the definition of *'academic discipline'* so that we can have a clear view while entering into the discussion of the scope of Tenyidie. In a simplest sense, an 'academic discipline' is a line of study in the realm of knowledge acquisition/learning process. In the realm of human knowledge language has no boundary. An academic discipline is usually identified from a number of disciplines of studies or bifurcated from another study discipline which is/ are allied in nature. An academic discipline of study is objectively study to increase or extend the benefit of knowledge towards prosperity where mankind is central to its usage and utility. To prove as an academic discipline let us see the enclosed chart.

Scope of Tenyidie for Quality Education

If we take the view of the psycholinguists, mother tongue is the easiest medium of learning and there is potentiality of learning any degree of knowledge. The Nagas emphasized too much on English for learning neglecting too much of our own languages. This attitude in educational policy or in learning process results a false pride in the mind of our students. We let our children labour too much on English language in the form of their intellectual exercise but provide no space to think or to act for any creative works either physically or mentally. We left no chance to the mass a chance to improve their knowledge even through passive learning. We have, in the year 2001 general census provisional report, 17.74% of Nagaland population live in urban areas and 82.26% in rural areas. The destiny of the mass in rural areas will be permanently doomed from further intellectual development. Let me refer to Melvin J. Fox, who in his *Language and Development* (1985) states,

> Shifting the objectives for education from schools for an elite to learning for the mass of citizens of all ages necessitates indigenous approaches to goal-setting; as well as to curriculum preparation, teacher training, educational planning, research, evaluation and testing, if imported models identified with 'modernization' are to be effectively replaced.
>
> Participation of the people at all levels in all spheres of activity is indispensable to both development and nation building, and this participation can only be achieved through local/regional languages.

The Nagas claimed to have 66.6 % literacy rate (2001 Census). But how many of those literate be competent in English? Perhaps, not even 20 % of the literate class has competency in English language. It is apparent that many of our graduates cannot speak or write English correctly. If so, it is hard to expect the students who left their schooling below the Secondary rather to say than Elementary, to be competent in the language of English. We have so many drop-out students in a series, i.e. from class VIII, IX, X, XII and so on. The average of HSLC results shows hardly 50 % success every year. The year 2007, 15589 students sat for the HSLC examination. The published result revealed 7964 students passed showing 51.09 %. 80 - 90 % of failed students in HSLC examination are found to be in science and mathematics. This indicates their lack of language power (English) as there is no facility to learn the concepts of those disciplines of study. As a result, we keep on filtering students at every stage since the beginning of their schooling. Those drop-out students, (if BA/B.Sc/B.Com is taken as the base level) probably will cover 70 – 80 %. But we never attempt to formulate any policy for continuous education, particularly for the general mass. Our school curricula provide no pragmatic approach to the learners for value education. We talk much about QUALITY EDUCATION but we hardly pay any heed to pave the way for the future generation to avail such value education. We allow our children to labour too much on English language, which means we are letting them to cultivate English culture and mentality. But we are growing more unemployed youth as no work culture is imparted in school text books. Because of such underlined factors our education produced many deviating personalities.

Some major behavioural trends are the following:

a) Those who are learned but without mother tongue since their formative stage of learning are finding difficulty to adjust themselves in the traditional/native society.

b) Those educated class cannot read the Bible in village churches and remain lip-tight when the congregation started singing hymns in Church services. Their feeling of superiority complex from the common fellow beings leads them to dissociate from their parental society. In many cases, such class of people hardly show respect for the elders.

c) When they don't learn the ancestral and moral values of honesty, truthfulness, hard labour, obligation to one's traditional society, the cult of corruption in public offices is fast developing. Perhaps, there may be no solution of such unethical life in our society unless our true culture is revived, studied and practiced. The revival is possible only when we allow our children to study those human values and responsibilities through our respective mother tongue.

d) A highly learned man develops on personal capability to contribute towards betterment of his fellow beings/ society/ common mass out of his acquired knowledge in term so knowledge sharing, economic development, science & technology promotion, etc. In other words, they are literate of their own mother tongue.

e) Any under-educated youth becomes the burden of the family or society as they don't have quality education for application or acquire any work culture during formative stage.

f) It results in producing high rate of educated unemployed youth.

Scope of Tenyidie as Storehouse of Culture

Tenyimia community has rich heritage. Any heritage, tangible or non-tangible takes change with passage of time. However, language serves as the storehouse of that culture. Language and culture are like the two faces of the same coin. Language stands as the strongest fort tom preserve the culture. However, certainty depends on the development of literature of that language. As such, literature serves as the field of learning, reviving and promotion of that culture. Likewise Tenyimia literature serves as the ground for cultural study of Tenyimia group of society. By doing so, Tenyidie serves as the chief source as well as medium of transmitting our ancestral values such as honesty, dignity of labour, hard labour, sacrificial services, politeness, hospitality, etc. An ethnic group is also identified by its language and culture.

Language signifies culture and cultural practices manifest social group in continuity. For instance, our traditional song or folksong has its typicality in world music. Our folksong, particularly group song has seven parts of voice combination – (i) *nuosenuo*, (ii) *puonuo*, (iii) *thepfularei* (all female voice), (iv) *thenularei*, (v) *kege* or *thepfularei*, (vi) *puokrü* and (vii) *krüde* (all male voice). I shall claim that our folksong melodies are a significant identity.

Potentiality of Tenyidie for Economic Development

The land of the Nagas is unique with full natural blessing—from mystic to scenic beauty; from freshness of air to its purity of water resources; richness of natural vegetation and other natural resources to the healthiness of her inhabitants; its temperate climatic condition to the suitability of harmonious society that nature bestows upon us; is a heaven to the people if one can fully access the value of the land. Comparatively, the land and its resources within Tenyimia area appear to be better than other hilly regions occupied by other Nagas.

Our land is also very fertile that variety of crops can grow in our land. Following the 2001 general census, 82.26 % lives in rural areas where no one can be said to be landless labourer. In the field of agriculture and allied disciplines we have no literature in local languages. The intellectuals or planners ignore the indigenous methods of cultivation and encourage high-tech application which is not suitable to our land. Also there is always a gap between the architect and the workers in execution. Our people have physical and natural resources but lacking in determination, technical skills, proper planning and production-cum-commercial coordination. If proper guidance through promotion of mother tongue is given, the mass might be gear up to full activity. A motivated personal can learn immense knowledge that ideas from such provided literature and apply it for any growth.

Conducting workshops/seminar in local languages in village itself might lead to development of exercisable education to the general mass in terms of economic progress.

Two important points on Scope of Tenyidie

The scope of Tenyidie can also be highlighted with the given two important proposals:

a) Extension of facility for Tenyidie scholars – State Level Educational/Eligibility Test Examination. NU has approved in its Academic Council and Executive Council.

b) URA Academy and Tenyimia Central Union have been jointly pursuing a proposal to the Government of India for INCLUSION OF TENYIDIE IN SCHEDULED – VIII OF THE CONSTITUTION OF INDIA. The aim of this venture is to create a wider facility for job seekers through competitive examinations at National and State levels in Government and public sector services.

At present, I am urging the Government of Nagaland, to adopt a policy on education, mainly focus on conceptual learning facility to the children of Nagaland. *That is, to adopt Mother Tongue as a compulsory subject replacing the so-called Alternative English subject for all levels of schooling.* Implementation will generate job opportunities, research facilities, and revival of traditional values and practices, strengthening Christianity, increasing economic activities, etc. and to march forward for transforming our society towards better living.

CLASSIFICATION CHART

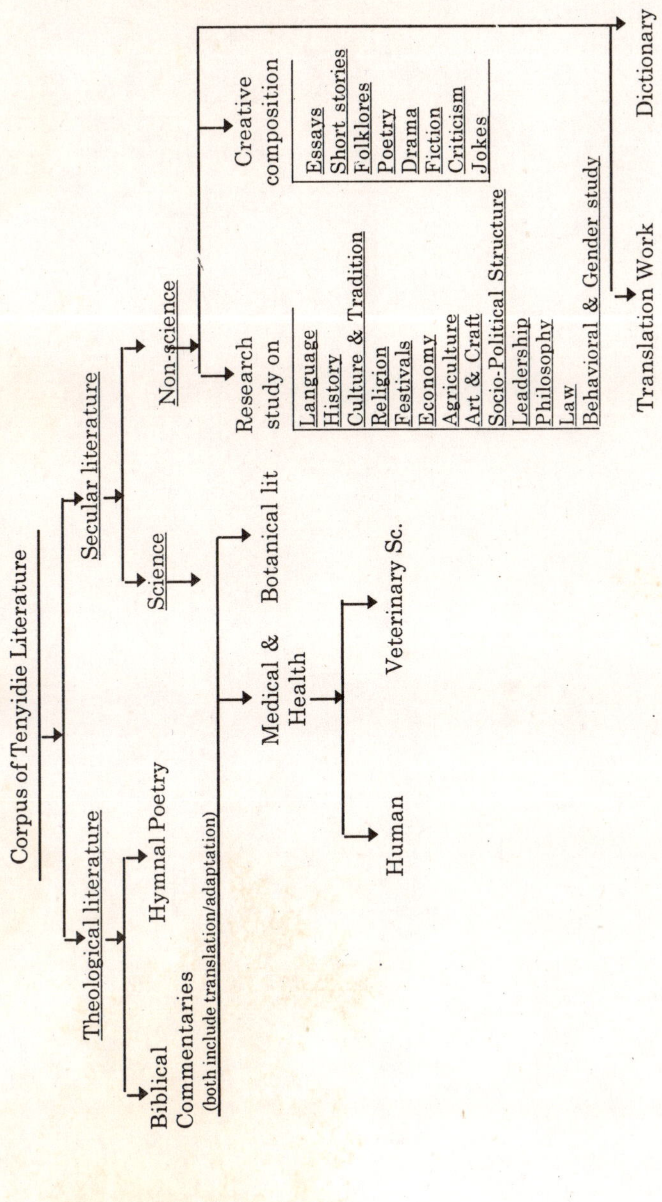

Section II: Angami Politics

3

THE KINGDOM OF GOD AND OUR CRISIS

Niketu Iralu

It seems we can safely say human aspirations and dreams are from our Creator. And He allows, indeed expects us to struggle hard for them. But what seems to be absolutely clear from the histories of all peoples, nations and civilizations is that unless our struggle builds His kingdom on earth, because we obey him not ourselves, we always end up building our own kingdom which turns out to be Satan's hell on earth as it must be in hell? Our own Naga struggle has also amply demonstrated this unchangeable truth of history.

W.H. Auden thus described the situation in Europe just before the 2nd World War II broke out:

> "In the nightmare of the dark
> All the dogs of Europe bark,
> And the living nations wait,
> Each sequestered in its hate".

Is this not our situation right now? Have not extensive portions of the Naga homeland become a nightmare with Dimapur heading the list? Why, Oh, why?

The factions of the Naga struggle, their tribal umbilical cords uncut and poorly concealed, have for so long barked at one another through our newspapers, carrying out mutual assassinations, ceaselessly collecting taxes, each group sequestered in their hates and their respective camps. The rest of us wait and watch helplessly not knowing how to transform the barking into honest conversations and dialogues to evolve the solutions we need. Because we ourselves, the non-combatants, are still so used to our traditional securities of our tribes we are tentative or not transparent in our interactions with one another so that our reaching out to one another across the divides of distrust, uncertainties and ill-will to create the envisioned Naga identity is desperately ineffective. We wonder meanwhile just what the brains in Delhi paid to plan an end to "the Naga nuisance" must be doing? Does anyone in Delhi realize that even a sparrow does not fall without God seeing it and India should be more careful about consequences?

Arnold Toynbee said

> **"All of history can be written in two small words: Challenge and Response... Each society progresses to the extent that it meets its challenges".** The quality of the response decides the quality of the outcome.

The Naga struggle was and is the honest, honourable response of the Nagas to challenges of a changing world impacting them. The struggle has caused so many things to happen so quickly. We underestimated how Delhi would interpret our being made a part of India at the eastern fringes by the British against our wishes when the bureaucrats would eventually discover the stand the Naga pioneers had taken. Before we realized just what was happening the struggle gave birth to the State of Nagaland. To the majority of the Nagas it was an illegitimate birth. The State was Delhi's response to the challenge the crisis the Nagas presented to the newly established Indian Republic. *B.K. Nehru*, speaking from his experiences as Governor of Nagaland, said the State was a mistake, too hastily conceived and born. Delhi was desperately keen for its child to succeed. However its boundless generosity and permissive discipline spoiled the child. But today Nagas are prepared to do anything, even to the extent of trying to force God to enable them to get near to the child in order to get some of the things Delhi sends to keep the child going. The fact is both Delhi and we Nagas need the State equally today, pending a settlement.

Those who stepped out and acted, some of them genuinely seeing it to be the best and right thing for the Nagas in the given crisis, and enabled Delhi to create the State, suddenly found themselves in positions of embarrassing power and support with unlimited funds available to play their roles as Delhi's allies. The opportunities and challenges that confronted them were unprecedented and thoroughly unfamiliar. Thus the response of Delhi to the Naga crisis turned out to be a greater crisis for the Nagas which they had not anticipated. Here we seem to have a perfect instance of a Toynbean situation of Challenge and Response?

The quality of the response of Naga politicians and bureaucrats to this new crisis from the start to this day, and the subsequent response of all Nagas to the same crisis of opportunities and challenges have produced the society we have today, 'over ground' and 'underground'. And we know what that society is like.

Here I am not judging or condemning the response of the politicians and bureaucrats down the years, nor the response of our people to the changing situation. We cannot really condemn one another because the response of the vast majority of Nagas to the State has clearly shown what the quality of our response to a Naga republic would have been had our freedom fighters succeeded in to '60s in pushing the huge Indian army to Khatkati in Assam?

The point I am trying to understand for myself in order to try to bring it into discussions and questionings among Nagas is that we need to assess ourselves correctly and know exactly who and how much we are, and how far we have come on our journey. This boils down to something like this - "We are not more than what we are. Let us not fret or complain about this which we cannot change. But thank God we certainly are not less than what we are! Let us also thank all those who by their diverse contributions have achieved for us what we are today, no matter how humble that may be, and learn to build on the foundation we have inherited, without coveting what we don't have and are not entitled to have yet".

Unless we make such an unquestionable, truthful assessment and build our future together with passionate care and concern for one another instead of heartless selfishness and indifference, we are doomed to drag one another down to a black hole similar to those in outer space which pull everything into themselves including light. And the economic principle to guide us in building the society we need is this: "There is enough of everything in the world for every one's needs, (opportunities, loans, subsidies, lands, timber, water, etc), but not for everyone's greed. If we will learn to care enough and share enough, everyone will have enough". Do our limited resources and fragile ecosystem allow anything less demanding than this today?

Now to come to the kingdom of God: what, where and when is it anyway? To try to answer these questions is to immediately discover that we are looking at something much more than church buildings and increasing the size of the congregations inside them, important as that is to start with. We realize that we are looking at the actual place we give God in our lives, how we treat one another, really, how we respond to situations. We realize that by our response to our conscience and soul, our connection points with our Creator, we are either building God's or Satan's kingdom right now, and that is what, when and where the kingdom of God is, not something we go to after we die.

Only with such a concept of the immediacy of the kingdom of God and of Satan directly resulting from our choices and actions, our religion makes sense and the changing of our daily situations and the shaping of our future possible. Otherwise we live as selfishly and thoughtlessly as we like, create a hellish society for everyone, and expect the government, the UNO or someone else to come and solve the problems we have created. Even building churches with ill-gotten money where devout Christians may pray to God to save our society does not work. The kingdoms of God and of Satan are the immediate consequences of our thoughts and actions.

Dorothy L. Sayers clarifies this point:

> **"War is a judgment that overtakes societies when they have been living upon ideas that conflict too violently with the laws governing the Universe. Never think that wars are irrational catastrophes: they happen when wrong ways of thinking and living bring about intolerable situations".**

Haven't we created intolerable situations for one another? Doesn't Sayers' observation explain the protracted, low-intensity, hellish war that the divided factions of our struggle and the shameless exploiters of our crisis have brought upon the hapless Nagas today?

C.S. Lewis put the total context of all crises such as ours this way:

> **"There is no neutral ground in the universe. Every square inch, every split second is claimed by God and counter claimed by Satan".** It is against this reality that we have to judge our thoughts and deeds and their consequences whoever we are.

If Lewis is right then is there any act of selfishness, pride or revenge that is not important or just a personal matter?

A careful analysis of our crisis produces the following conclusion. It sounds controversial but it is not really: God and Satan are indeed the culprits responsible for the turbulence of our crisis! Their titanic contest to win us to their sides to use us to build their rival kingdoms on earth is causing the shaky Naga boat to rock and sway violently. They are not at all hiding their fierce contest in order not to disturb us! If this is so then Nagas are not really enemies of one another but fiercely fought-over precious goods!

God wants us to give our best to one another to help and inspire one another to do the right best thing for the common good, instead of provoking one another to do the worst, as we are doing at Satan instigation. The no- holds-barred battle God and Satan are waging in all of us is the reason why we are producing conflicts in just about everything we do, showing who is winning and guiding us? The moment we each obey God, unity, reconciliation, forgiveness, goodwill, co-operation, and all else will automatically appear in our land. Unification will be part of the package without our doing anything to achieve it as it is always a by-product of the other deeper things.

Dostoyevsky's insight into this eternal contest explains it all. He said

> "On earth God wrestles with the Devil and the battle ground is man".

If we Nagas with God's grace and mercy will decide to help one another to rise to what we all are meant to be, we will make it. If instead we will obey ourselves, nothing in heaven or on earth can help us to win.

4

TRADITIONAL LEARNING SYSTEMS AND MODERN EDUCATION

Alphonsus D'Souza SJ

[This paper deals with the problems a teacher, especially one coming from a non-tribal background, faces while teaching tribal students. It points out that tribal students have learning styles that differ from those of non-tribal students. It offers the theory of multiple intelligences as a suitable framework for understanding the learning styles of tribal students. Then it argues that the learning styles of tribal students are based on tribal learning systems. Finally it suggests that beneficial practices of traditional learning systems should be incorporated into the present educational system for a development of the various intelligences of tribal students.

The material presented in this paper is based on the personal experience of the author and on the conclusions of a recent study by Hector D'Souza of St Paul Institute of Education. This study (D'Souza, Hector 2006) is at the stage of final reporting.]

The Problem

A teacher, coming from a non-tribal background, beginning to teach a class of tribal students, faces some peculiar reactions from the students. In the first place, he generally finds that the tribal students are silent most of the time. He finds that they remain silent even when he asks them questions on something that he has explained. If he is a good observer, he notices that students quietly consult one another rather than seek clarifications from him. Gradually the teacher also notices that the students like to write notes. He also finds that tribal students have fantastic memory power to remember what they write, that they are capable of memorising what they have written even if they have not understood much of what they have written. In course of time, the teacher also notices that even the study habits of the tribal students are peculiar. Instead of studying regularly, they prefer to study only when they have to face an examination.

When he deals students of this type, a teacher may come to different conclusions. It is possible that he may consider tribal students as deficient in some intellectual abilities. In fact, some non-tribal teachers dealing with tribal students have come to such a conclusion. For instance, some have said that tribal students cannot really do well in mathematics and science because they cannot grasp abstract concepts. Unfortunately this view is often accepted by the tribal students themselves who say that they cannot study mathematics. But such an understanding, whether by the non-tribal teacher or the tribal students themselves, is fundamentally flawed. It confuses difference for deficiency. Tribal students are different, not deficient. Tribal students are different because their learning style is different.

Theoretical Framework: Multiple Intelligences and Learning Styles

Even when a teacher is ready to accept that tribal students

could have learning styles of a different type, the teacher is still not sufficiently open to deal with tribal students. The most basic problem is the concept of "intelligence". The widespread belief is that intelligence is a fixed innate quality that is unevenly distributed in a population. It is believed that intelligence can be measured in terms of IQ scores. This belief often leads a non-tribal teacher to consider his tribal students as having average or below average intelligence. Therefore, while recognising the reality of different learning styles among the tribal students, it is also necessary to discard the traditional concept of intelligence in the light of the theory of multiple intelligences.

Theory of Multiple Intelligences

The theory of multiple intelligences was developed by Gardner (1983) who broke away from the prevalent theory of intelligence. In the place of the single quantifiable intelligence, he argued that there were different types of intelligences. He identified eight types of intelligence. They are: 1) linguistic intelligence, 2) logical-mathematical intelligence, 3) spatial intelligence, 4) bodily kinesthetic intelligence, 5) musical intelligence, 6) interpersonal intelligence, 7) intrapersonal intelligence, and, 8) naturalist intelligence.

Originally Gardner identified only seven intelligences but in 1996 he added the eighth, namely the naturalist intelligence. He also considered adding such other intelligences as the spiritualist, existential and the moral, but ruled them out because they did not satisfy the criteria that he had enunciated.

The theory of multiple intelligences has been criticized by psychologists and educationists. The most common criticism is that the theory is based on Gardner's intuition rather than empirical data, and that the intelligences are just other names for talents or personality types.

Despite various criticisms, during the past twenty years, the theory of multiple intelligences has been used by a large number of educators with a great deal of success. There are several schools and institutions which espouse it as pedagogy. Many books and educational materials exist to explain the theory and to show how it may be applied in the classroom. One such work is that of Campbell and others (1999).

Given the situation in Nagaland, it may not be possible to espouse the pedagogy based on the theory of multiple intelligences. But it does indicate to us the need to break away from the unidimensional concept of intelligence. It also challenges us to give adequate importance of other types of intelligences which are more common among tribal students than we are ready to accept. If we do so, we will more easily accept that tribal students have styles of learning that differ from those of non-tribal students.

Learning Styles

It is generally believed that every individual has a favourite method of learning. Based on this assumption, the idea of individualized "learning styles" originated in the 1970s, and gradually gained popularity. The learning style of an individual is the method of learning particular to an individual and is presumed to enable that individual to learn best. Various instruments have been designed to identify different learning styles. One such instrument is that of Dunn and others (1984).

A large number of models of learning styles have been proposed. Each of these models consists of at least two different styles. One such model identifies three basic learning styles, namely, visual, auditory and kinesthetic learning styles. Visual learning occurs through images, demonstrations and body language. Auditory learning occurs through hearing the spoken word. Kinesthetic learning occurs through doing, touching and interacting.

It must be accepted that the theory of different learning styles is also criticised by psychologists and neuro-scientists as having no scientific basis. Extensive criticism is found in Coffield and others (2004). Nevertheless an understanding of their learning styles has been found to be effective among the students for enhancing their performance. Similarly educators who have adapted their teaching methods to the learning styles of their students have found that their teaching has led to better performance by their students.

In a non-tribal context, learning styles are seen as the way individual students prefer to learn. But in multi-ethnic contexts, educators in the USA, Canada and Australia have found that learning styles are strongly influenced, if not determined, by their culture. As Gay points out,

> By the time children begin their formal school career at 5 years of age, they already have internalized rules and procedures for acquiring knowledge and demonstrating their skills. These cognitive processing protocols are learned from their cultural socialization. They may be refined and elaborated over time, even superseded on occasion for the performance of certain tasks. But the core of these culturally influenced rules and procedures continue to *anchor* how individuals process intellectual challenges for the rest of their lives (Gay, 2000:150).

Unfortunately, hardly any research has been done in India on the learning styles of tribal students. For example, the work edited by Verma (2004), despite its title claiming to provide information on current research on learning styles does not deal with the learning style of the tribals. Similarly, Roy (2007) claims to deal with Ethno-Pedagogy but actually is concerned with the status of tribal teachers in Bengal and Assam. However, there is some interesting material in Slattery (2006) who proposes cooperative learning as a method for teaching Mathematics to tribal children. Though his project is aimed at the tribal children of Jharkhand, we can draw some lessons from him.

When this author began teaching tribal students in 1995 in Nagaland, he encountered the problems mentioned above. He found that the learning styles of his students were different from those of the non-tribal students. Therefore, to identify the learning styles of his students he administered a simple test found in McGrath, (1996). He was surprised to find the vast majority, about 85%, of the students were visual learners and adopted concrete and active approaches to study. This conclusion made him realise that the learning styles of the tribal students generally had a cultural basis, and that they were derived from the traditional methods of learning and socialization.

Tribal Learning Styles and Traditional Learning Processes among the Tribals

The study of D'Souza (2006) deals with the traditional learning institutions and processes found among the tribal societies of the North East in general and in the Angami, Dimasa, Garo and Rongmei tribal communities in particular. We shall make an extensive use of the findings of this study.

An important feature of these tribes is that their languages had no script till the advent of modern education. Therefore, traditional method of imparting knowledge had to be through oral explanation and activities.

> In the traditional system, the methods of oral explanations were of two types. In the first type, the elder took the initiative and taught what he or she thought was important. Story telling and singing folksongs belonged to this category. In the second type, the elder answered the questions posed by the learner. It can be presumed that a tribal youngster would be as curious as any youngster and would ask questions to satisfy his or her curiosity.

> The second method of imparting knowledge, and particularly the skills, was based on activities. The elder performed the activity, and the learner observed, as in the case of performing a sacrifice or weaving a cloth. But in the case of common activities, the elder either led by example or guided its performance. In this activity based learning, the elder taught by example more than by words.
>
> An important feature was the extensive use of memory to store knowledge acquired through hearing and seeing. It is amazing to find that tribal students have fabulous memory power. However, this capacity for memorising is based on visual and auditory perceptions. It is not surprising therefore that tribal students are mostly visual learners (D'Souza 2005: 70).

In the traditional system of learning, the institution of *morung* or bachelors' dormitory played an important role. However, Hutton (1969: 49) mentions that among the Angami it was not as prominent as among other Naga tribes. Nevertheless, it did play a significant role. It provided a place for the peers to interact. But more importantly, it provided a space where the elders and the youngsters could interact for the purpose of the transmission of tradition, knowledge and skills. It is in the dormitories that the elders would communicate the folklore, arts and crafts and the skills required for war. It is not surprising therefore that it was in the dormitories that the weapons of war were stored and the trophies displayed. Thus the institution of morung or dormitory may be considered the backbone of traditional learning system. The institution of morung has greatly declined in recent times due to various factors. Among those who accepted Christianity, the church began to replace it. The church became the centre of activities, including modern education. In places where Christianity was not accepted, the modern school played a similar role to some extent. Hence, the present church based youth organisations and the various student associations may be considered as continuing some of the functions of the traditional morung. It is interesting to note that nowhere in India are there so many youth organisations and student associations as in North- East India (D'Souza 2006: 67).

According to D'Souza the following were the basic features of the traditional learning systems.

1. The traditional learning system was community based and strongly social in orientation. It aimed at the formation of the younger generations to assume adult roles in their societies rather than the development of the individual as such. It sought to impart knowledge and skills that were required for the well being and perpetuation of the community as a whole.

2. The knowledge and skills that were imparted were of a practical nature. Only those skills that were considered necessary were imparted. It was, in other words, not a quest for knowledge as such, but the transmission of knowledge and skills with a practical and utilitarian purpose.

3. It was a general training of the individual aimed at the formation of all skills, rather than the formation of specialists. It was general education in a strict sense.

4. The method of imparting knowledge and skills was through oral narration and physical activities. It stressed physical experience rather than mental abstraction. Therefore it was strongly activity based. These activities were usually done in a community setting that emphasised on cooperation rather than competition. These methods were enjoyable, not dull and boring.

5. The elders played the important role of teachers. The elders could be older siblings, parents and others. But

they were men and women of knowledge and experience, concerned with the welfare of the community as a whole.

6. The peer group or friends also played an important role in the processes of socialisation. It was within the peer group that an individual learnt to work together. It was through this cooperative learning process that an individual acquired the practical skills required for cooperative living.

In brief, the traditional processes of teaching and learning in the tribal societies were based on activities and practical experience, aimed at the formation of young men and women to assume adult roles for the welfare of their communities. This stands in sharp contrast with the system of modern education and the teaching learning processes adopted in the modern system (D'Souza 2006: 71).

Traditional Learning Systems and Modern Education

Modern education was introduced in the North East after the establishment of colonial rule. With all its shortcoming and deficiencies, it has come to stay. In fact, it may be considered necessary in the globalised world. Therefore, it is impossible, even inadvisable, to return to the good old days of the traditional system of learning and socialization. But what can be done is to incorporate some of the methods and values into the modern system so that tribal students derive the maximum benefit from modern education.

The theory of multiple intelligences should also broaden our views about education. It should make us realise that intelligence is not unidimensional but multifaceted. It should enable us to appreciate the different types of intelligences found in tribal students. In any case, the acceptance of the theory will certainly change our ideas about the modern system of education.

With regard to learning styles, tribal students are predominantly visual learners. They also prefer to learn by doing. Recognition of this fact will lead us to adopt teaching methods that involve much more than the traditional lectures or even the chalk and talk method. Written handouts, suitable reading material and extensive use of the library should be a part of our teaching. Besides, given the preference for learning through activities, various types of project work should be made a part of the educational system.

Given the important role played by peer groups in tribal communities, it is highly desirable that cooperative learning rather than competitive learning is encouraged. This implies that group work and common project work should find an important place in our teaching methods.

Conclusion

Tribal societies have rich traditions and well established traditional processes and institutions for transmitting knowledge and skills. Incorporating such traditional processes and practices into the modern system of education will make education an enjoyable and enriching experience for tribal children and students. At the same time, it will probably make them more confident to face an increasingly globalised world. As D'Souza (2002) and many others has said, we need to think globally but act locally.

REFERENCES

1. Campbell Linda, Bruce Campbell and Dee Dickinson. 1999). *Teaching and Learning through Multiple Intelligences.* 2nd edition. Allen & Bacon : Boston.

2. Coffield, F., Moseley, D., Hall, E., Ecclestone, K. (2004). *Learning Styles and Pedagogy in Post_16 Learning. A systematic and critical review.* London: Learning and Skills Research Centre.

3. D'Souza, Hector. (2002) "Tribal Learning in Nagaland : A

Perspective" in C. Joshua Thomas & Gurudas Das (eds) *Dimensions of Development in Nagaland* New Delhi : Regency Publications.

4. D'Souza Hector (2006). *Tribal Learning Processes in North Eastern India..* Draft of the Report. Phesama, Nagaland : St Paul Institute of Education.

5. Dunn, R., Dunn, K., & Price, G. E. (1984). *Learning style inventory.* Lawrence, KS, USA: Price Systems.

6. Gardner, Howard. (1999) *Intelligence Reframed: Multiple Intelligences for the 21st Century,* New Yrrk: Basic Books.

7. Gardner, Howard (1983) *Frames of Mind: The Theory of Multiple Intelligences.* New York: Basic Books.

8. Gay, Geneva. (2000). *Culturally Responsive Teaching - Theory, Research & Practice.* New York: Teacher College Press.

9. Hutton, J.H. 1969, (1921). *The Angami Nagas.* Bombay: Oxford University Press.

10. McGrath, E.H. (1996). *Basic Managerial Skills.* New Delhi: Prentice-Hall of India. Pp.87-88.

11. Roy, Rajarshi.(2007). *Ethno-Pedagogy: Education of Tribes, Teachers' Training and Juxtaposition of Status.* Delhi: Shipra Publications.

12. Slattery, Robert. (2006). *Can Tribals Learn Maths? A Cooperative Research Project.* Hazaribagh, Jharkhand: Masi Marsal School, Charhi.

13. Verma B.P. (Ed) (2004). *Current Research in Learning Style.* New Delhi: Mittal Publications.

5

ANGAMI VILLAGES EXPERIMENT WITH COMMUNITIZATION OF ELEMENTARY EDUCATION IN NAGALAND

Buno Liegise

Introduction

The educational landscape of the villages in Nagaland does not look half as attractive as its geographical and cultural landscape – the majestic mountains and cascading hills, the clear springs and gushing rivers, the rolling stretches of paddy fields and gardens of many varieties of organic vegetables and fruits. The village 'kharu' (village gate), 'thehu' (morung) 'kichüki'(dormitory)- all signifying the culture of the people, their intelligence and creativity, their level of hard work, discipline and determination to say the least. Sadly the schools provide no match to such rich community life of the people in the village.

Schools in the villages, particularly the Government schools, lag behind in many respects - amenities and facilities, discipline, teaching and learning experiences, school maintenance to cite a few. Many schools lack a stimulating environment, they do not have a library or laboratory, no playground to call its own, no basic health care units, no clean drinking water supply and some schools do not even have toilets for the boys and girls. The site of some schools is also not appropriate for children's free play. It is a shame to the State and the nation as to why children in the Government schools should continue to perform poorly in education.

Such a pitiful condition of schools do not auger well for a people who prides itself of its cultural heritage and traditions. A Naga village may not possess much 'hard power' of capital, infrastructure or economy but it has immense 'soft power'. It is a treasure trove of precious culture, tradition and values. There is much to learn from it. Community living practices - of sharing with the poor and the destitute, of respect for the parents and elders, of helping the sick and the aged, of performing social works together and celebrating festivals with much grandeur. In an Angami village, social groups formulated on the basis of age, for example, the 'thesü' 'kikra' and 'peli' undertake many developmental activities. Works taken up by any of such age-based social groups are performed with high level of motivation and pride. Besides, an Angami village can still boast of its pure air, unpolluted by what is called green house gas and its water source is clean and uncontaminated as yet.

If only such potentials of the village physical environment and the cultural values of the rural folks can be adequately harnessed, an Angami village can be the destination for any world class educational institutions in the 21st Century.

Communitization of Elementary Education in Nagaland

Introduced in the year 2002-2003, subsequent to the enactment of Communitization of Public Institutions and

Services Act, 2002 (Act No.2), Communitization of Elementary Education in Nagaland is by far the most significant decision taken by the Government of Nagaland in the field of school education. In a sense it is a bold step as ' communitization of any Institution of the Government means transferring ownership to and the responsibility of its management with the community' as stated in *A Handbook of Communitization of Elementary Education, Directorate of School Education*, August 2002-2003. In the first year only 205 Government schools were communitized on voluntary basis. However by the year 2004 all Government Primary Schools and Government Middle Schools were brought under purview of the Act. Hence today all Government elementary schools are owned and managed by the community, so to speak.

Features of Communitization Process

- Village Education Committee (VEC) is a pivotal organ in Government elementary schools- primary and middle schools.
- It is empowered to disburse the salary of the Government School employees.
- It ensures discipline among teachers.
- It grants casual leave and recommends other types of leave to Government.
- It can select and/or recommend appointment of substitute teachers against long term vacation.
- It has been given the power to operate the principle of 'no pay no work' and utilize the amount deducted for school repair after obtaining prescribed formalities.
- It obtains funds for purchase of textbooks, furniture, and repair of school building.
- It has the responsibility to motivate village community

to contribute in cash and kind or labour for the development of the school(s) and engage local craftsmen etc. on voluntary or on payment of token honorarium for teaching in school(s).

- It is entrusted with the responsibility for universal enrolment and retention of all children up to age 14 years.
- The Government remains the final authority. It issues directives to VEC which is binding on the VEC.
- The Government provides all finances to VEC and reserves the right to withdraw some or all powers from the VEC in case of misuse or mismanagement.

Source: *The First Year of Communitization of Elementary Education in Nagaland, 2002-2003.*

The present study makes an attempt to assess the impact of communitization process on the Government elementary schools in Angami villages.

Objectives of the Study

1. To make a general assessment of Government schools in the Angami villages.
2. To find out the changes brought about in the Government schools as a result of the communitization process.
3. To examine the problems faced by the Village Education Committee and the Head teacher/ Teacher-in-charge.
4. To offer some suggestions for improvement of the Government schools in the context of the Communitization process.

Sample of the Study

Eight Angami villages (Rüsoma, Meriema and Kohima

village from the Northern area, Kigwema, Khuzama from the Southern area, Khonoma and Jotsoma from the Western area and Tsüü from Chakhro area) were randomly selected and within it nineteen Government schools - primary and middle schools, included in the sample - 19 head teacher/ teacher-in-charge and 8 VEC Chairman/Secretary.

Definition of the terms used

Communitization: transfer of ownership and management of the Government elementary schools - primary and middle schools, to the Community.

Angami village: a village where majority of the population belongs to the Angami tribe.

Tools used

The study is descriptive in nature. Two sets of structured interview schedules were used. One for the Village Education Committee Chairman/ Secretary and the other for the Head teacher/Teacher-in-charge.

Analysis of the data was made on the basis of the responses given by the respondents which are given below.

Findings

The findings of the study are given in table 1.

Table 1 reveals that a Government School was established way back in the early 1900, hence a century old. Three schools were over seventy-five years, while most of the schools were around forty years or so. Only one school was established in 1993. Formal system of education reached the Angamis early as compared to some other Naga tribes. The pioneers in the field of education in the Angami region were the American missionaries, Rev. Charles Dewitt King (1879) and Rev. S.W Rivenburg (1885), and later Rev Supplee. Their remarkable contribution led the Angamis to understand and appreciate the value and significance of formal education.

The table also shows that some schools are understaffed while a few others are overstaffed. While it may be mentioned that the number of students in the government schools seem small, two schools having only 32 –36 students, all school have more than 5/6 different classes, the Government primary schools have classes A, B, 1 to 4, while the Government middle schools have classes 5 to 8. In the present sample only one school (No.14) had both primary and middle schools under the same roof.

Table 1
Profile of the Government Primary/Middle Schools

School/Est Yr.		No. of ST	No. of TE	Educational Qualification					Trained
				UM	MT	PU	GR	MA	
1.	1988	40	05	1	1	3	-	-	05
2.	1963	51	13	-	-	2	11	-	10
3.	1960	81	07	2	1	3	1	-	07
4.	1981	55	03	1	-	1	-	1	03
5.	1922	85	07	-	4	1	1	1	07
6.	1981	69	06	1	1	3	1	-	06
7.	1900	36	08	-	-	3	5	-	08
8.	1966	72	07	-	-	4	2	1	07
9.	1970	85	09	-	1	4	3	1	08
10.	1959	41	06	-	-	1	5	-	06
11.	1959	54	07	-	5	1	-	1	06
12.	1952	32	06	-	-	4	2	-	05
13.	1964	41	07	-	-	2	3	2	06
14.	1968	403	32	-	5′	8	17	2	30
15.	1949	169	16	-	4	5	4	3	15
16.	1927	54	08	1	2	3	2	-	06
17.	1993	114	03	-	-	1	2	-	03
18.	1929	80	05	1	1	2	1	-	05
19.	1967	90	07	-	-	2	2	3	07

Many of the teachers had pre-university education, most were graduates, and a few had masters' degree. It may be said that the educational qualification of the government school teachers were good. Besides, most of the teachers had undergone the trainings given by the Directorate of School Education and the State Council of Educational Research and Training on the 'New Pedagogy'. A few of the teachers (5) had Bachelor in Education (B.Ed) degree as well.

Table 2
Areas of Improvement after Communitization In Teacher and Student Performance

There is Improvement in the Following Areas	*VEC* Yes	No	*HT/T-I-C* Yes	No
1. Teacher Regularity	8 (100%)	-	19(100%)	-
2. Teacher Sincerity	-do-	-	-do-	-
3. Teacher Performance	-do-	-	-do-	-
4. Student Enrolment	-do-	-	-do-	-
5. Student Attendance	-do-	-	-do-	-
6. Student Retention	-do-	-	-do-	-

The above table 2 pertains to the impact of the communitization of elementary schools in the Angami villages under study, which indicates that there has been a definite improvement in the teachers' and students' performance in the schools. The positive unanimous response of the VEC chairman/secretary of all the villages and the head teacher (HT)/teacher-in-charge (T-I-C) of the Government schools that the level of regularity/attendance and sincerity of the teachers and students were improving is encouraging. However, they were guardedly optimistic regarding the broader impact of the communitization experience. They also mentioned that the improvements registered need to be sustained and further improved.

The retention rate had improved. All remarked that the drop-out cases had significantly lessened. In most villages, the VEC members indicated that universalization of elementary education had been achieved - that all children between the age of 4 to 14 years were in school. This, in itself, is a remarkable story to tell. However, whether this momentum can be sustained, is the real question to ask and as such proactive measures must be taken to further strengthen the process.

On Midday Meal, all the schools indicated that they receive supply of items like rice, dal, channa, maggi, potatoes etc and some amount of money. It was stated that there was serious problem with certain raw items supplied to the schools some years ago, like rotten potatoes and low quality rice, but in the same breathe it was mentioned that quality is slightly improving in recent times.

Where *Textbooks* were concerned, all the Government schools were in receipt of textbooks. Only a few schools indicated that they were receiving the supply on time and most of the schools were not getting the textbooks and exercise books on time. Procuring books late hampers teaching – learning process.

Free *school bags* are given to the girl child in the Government primary schools, but do not quite come as a huge help. Education is an uphill struggle for the rural girl child in particular.

Most head-teachers indicated that *salaries* were obtained on record time, which is highly appreciated by Government school employees.

Even so, in this way, encouraging stories are emerging in certain corners of the Angami region. Below is a case in point - Illustrative Case Study.

A List of Some Major Programs and Activities of the Village Education Committee

- Inspection of Government schools.
- Provide motivational talks and advices.
- Conduct VEC meetings three/four times annually apart from emergency meetings.
- Operate 'no pay no work' policy.
- Insist teaching in English in schools.
- Contribute desks and benches.
- Assist in civil works.
- Organize parent- teacher meetings.
- Repair school building/furniture.
- Take initiative to organize co-curricular programs, e.g. sports & games, free music classes by some VECs.
- Raise funds to meet urgent needs of schools.
- Take up school problems with Higher Government Authorities, especially cases of transfer-with-post and appointment of substitute teachers.
- As a result of increased awareness, student unions of some villages organized free tuitions/study programs for the poor and the backward children.

It must be noted that VECs of some villages were not functioning actively as others. There were some feeling expressed in certain villages that the members of the VECs should be selected with great care as much of the work for improving the schools depended on the sincerity and effectiveness of the VEC.

List of Problems Faced by the VEC

- The problem of staffing pattern. Some schools lack teachers while others have excess. Example - three teachers cannot effectively manage a GPS having five/

six different classes. Also some balance of male and female teachers may also be maintained as far as possible. One school had all male teachers while another had mostly female teachers.

- Schools lack basic facilities like a typewriter, not to talk of computers.
- Funds for civil works do not come on time which results in tremendous difficulty. Periodic supervision of construction works should be carried out by the concerned authority.
- Much time is consumed in conducting /attending meetings within and outside the village and in assisting the civil works. It is too much of a sacrificial work.
- No fund for VEC/school office maintenance. No fund for hospitality. Whereas there were many visitations of Government officials and guests for different kinds of school works. Providing refreshments become a strain to the school/VEC.
- No travel allowance or any type of allowances for the VEC chairman. It becomes almost impossible for the VEC to function effectively in the absence of any fund for executing its duties and responsibilities. A day trip to the headquarter/town, where the offices and bank are located, would cost anything between Rs 200/- to Rs 300/-.
- A grave problem of the VEC is its conflict with the Directorate of School Education in cases of transfer with post and appointment of substitute teachers. The voice of the VEC is often sidelined and not listened to, which is a violation of the very spirit of the Communitization process.
- The negative attitude towards the Government schools still looms large.

- Poor parental response to school education has a practical problem. Most parents are illiterate / uneducated and are not able to assist their children in their home study. Some are not in a position to provide basic study material/environment.
- Poor transport and communication facilities in the villages.

Suggestions for Improvement of Communitization Process

The Village Education Committee has a vital role in the management of the Government primary and middle schools in the villages. In villages where the VEC is sincere and executing its duties with a sense of purpose and vision, there is clear evidence of schools doing better than before the launch of the Communitization process. However, there is also the tendency of VECs to remain passive for more reasons than one. The selection of the VEC members, particularly the Chairman, must be made with due care. The person must be ready to afford time and commitment to participate in the VEC programs and activities. Members must be able to work without fear or favour for the education of the children and the welfare of the community.

Since the responsibility entrusted on the VEC is immense - management and coordination of various developmental works of the school(s), it is only reasonable to allocate some fund for office works and maintenance. A decent honorarium may be given to the chairman of the committee. This will upgrade the status of the chairman, and demand for accountability from the person can also be made.

Training and capacity building of the VEC members and other personnel involved must continue. To transfer power and responsibilities to the community without adequate training and education may not yield the desired result. VECs must be encouraged to creatively device ways to involve the larger village community participation. For instance the social age-based groups may be drawn in to help in developmental social works, organize cultural and musical programs to raise fund, explore local resources and indigenous methods for classroom teaching-learning, and organize meaningful refresher courses and training programs for teachers by inviting resource persons within the community. The 'thehu' which is a traditional institution for holding social discourses, may be used as a platform for addressing educational matters vis-à-vis the communitization scheme.

Concerned Government departments must continue to provide education and training programs for teachers, particularly for upgrading knowledge in specific subject content. A critical review of the training packages/'New Pedagogy' may also be helpful, keeping in view the needs and conditions of the rural folks.

The communitization process is at the nascent stage. Directorate of School Education and other higher Government offices should take extra care to respect and uphold the rules and regulation and policies laid down by it. Trust and confidence of the community must be nurtured and strengthened. Violation of the spirit of communitization will only dissipate the enthusiasm and goodwill obtained so far.

In this context reasonable queries and resistance from the VECs against any form of corruption and violation of rules can actually serve as a check on the different branches of the Government to ensure that rights are duly protected and usher in a greater sense of transparency and accountability in governance. Hence, the VECs must be listened to.

Monitoring and supervision must be activated. Nothing can take the place of timely monitoring of civil works and administration and academic programs. Clear guidelines, instructions/directives must reach the schools/VECs on time to enable them to respond effectively. Delay and/or late receipt of information from Government department(s) appear to be a huge hurdle.

There is also a need for relevant bodies/organization and civil society to address many challenges faced by the schools in a systematic, analytical, dispassionate and an easily understandable manner. In this context, there must be a platform where academics and intellectuals of every village come together and act as a moral force in bringing about better school education for the people in the villages.

Many Angami villages are inching ahead in achieving universalization of elementary education, while this, in itself, is encouraging; there is the need to take proactive measures to further consolidate the progress made thus far, to sustain children's interest in education beyond this stage of education and also to improve the quality of education.

It may be stated that communitization process was launched to change the sagging image of the Government schools and restore it a respectable place so that people will begin to view it as vibrant institutions in the service of the society. And perhaps there is hope as claimed by a head teacher '... we are hopeful that more and more children will come to our school in the future'.

Communitization process is at a crucial juncture. And Angami villages are in the phase of rejection of the old and experimenting with the new.

Illustrative Case Study

Situated at seven kilometers from the Capital Kohima, Rüsoma's response to the Nagaland Government's program of Communitization of Elementary Education is an interesting story to share and, perhaps, learn from.

The Government elementary schools at Rüsoma including two Government primary schools and one Government middle school were among the first schools to be communitized in the year 2002. The community leaders studied and discussed the new scheme carefully and concluded that the community would stand to gain by supporting the program. The Village Education Committee (VEC) was constituted and, in this way, the journey of communitization began.

Theirs is a story of the community uniting and moving forward. The young and the old came together to rebuild the Government schools. With the help of a vehicle jack they lifted the verandah of a school, which was literally falling apart. They cleaned the school building and compound, painted the walls and renovated the classrooms. All such works, simple as it might appear, required some hard cash which led to some concerned community leaders run around enlisting support from the wealthier families of the community. This fund raising drive to meet the urgent needs of the schools began one day when the principal of a District Institute of Education and Training generously contributed Rs 2000/- towards the improvement of school, during a training program. Today even the village folks realize and understand that it is for them to do even more! Unlike in the past, parents too are coming forward to strengthen the process in more ways than one – contributing free services and /or donations to help tide over rainy days, participating in parent-teacher meetings and sharing ideas, providing raw materials and the like.

More and more teachers are going for trainings and as a result, teaching-learning process is becoming more interesting. Teachers have become more regular at work. Student enrolment, attendance, retention and performance are also stated to have improved. The number of students in the Government Primary School, Thepezou was 13 before communitization, today it stood at 90. While in the Government Primary School, Bawe there were 37 students in 2002, today there are over 80 students. There is not only more enrolment of students in the schools but there is less number of dropouts. Above all, the most gratifying piece of information is that students were performing better, some obtaining first division in the Board Examinations, which was unheard of in the past.

With the Government schools improving and attracting more students, and the community calling for unhindered support to the process of Communitization of Elementary Education, two private school authorities closed down their schools (Christian English School and AG English School). Hence, since 2007 there is only one private school (St Joseph's School) standing in the village under the aegis of the Rüsoma Catholic Church, which is faring quite well and offers a healthy competition to the Government schools.

REFERENCES

1. *Handbook on Communitization of Elementary Education.* Directorate of School Education, 2002.
2. *The First Year of Communitization of Elementary Education in Nagaland, 2002-2003.* Government of Nagaland, Department of School Education, Kohima, 2003.

6

EDUCATIONAL ACHIEVEMENT AND ASPIRATION OF THE ANGAMI STUDENTS: A Study of Two Colleges

Viraho Hibo

Introduction

Hutton wrote that the Angami Nagas were very polite and hospitable (Hutton, 1968, p. 39). These traits of the Angamis could be taken as a compliment on one hand but on the other hand these are the traits that make the tribe in question to become too adjustable to both positive and negative actions and thought patterns. It has also a bearing on the Angami students' performances and achievements. Many of them, like their elders, are "Jack of all trades, master of none" type of students. This all-rounder feature of the Angami students makes them adjustable in almost all circumstances, situations and geographical locations but effects their academic achievements and aspirations when compared with the mainstream society. Many of their counterparts, especially in South India, are master of one trade mostly. If they want to excel in their studies, they will put 90% plus of their time, energy and money into it. So also if they are interested in any particular games or sports, they will streamline their all in all in the field chosen and will excel in it. The main aim of education is for an all round development of the individual but for the Angami students, other aspects of their lives becomes more important and thus their academic achievements and aspirations are also fairly low. The situation is not helped and rectified by the older generations because the trend of the lifestyle of students has not changed much and therefore no anomalies are seen by them. The Angamis stresses a lot of importance to marriages, funerals, and other social gatherings. It is never desirable to be termed as an anti-social animal because prestige and honour will not follow your house-hold. These social obligations also cost the students highly in their academic performances and their aims in life, if any.

Meaning of Education

Education is a never ending process. It can be broadly made to accommodate both formal and informal education. Education is the most important invention of mankind. It is more important than his invention of tools, machines, space craft, medicine, weapons and even of language too was the product of his education. Man without education would still be living just like an animal. It is education, which transformed man from a mere 'two-legged animal' into human. It helps us to behave like a man and prevents us from behaving an animal (Dash, 1996, p-1). The imperative character of education for individual growth and social development cannot be challenged. This realisation is making all modern nations, especially developing nations to give priority and heavy investments into the educational sector. The basic meaning of education remains the same but like any other aspects in the society; education is also undergoing a lot of changes. Education is an active and dynamic process.

It is much more than mere schooling, memorizing or learning a prescribed syllabus. Therefore, J.S. Mackenzie rightly says, Education is a process that goes on throughout life, and is promoted by almost every experience in life. When the learner comes in contact with any real situation in life, he utilizes all his past experiences that are relevant to it and gains new experiences. Therefore education is considered by the educationists as an active and dynamics process.

The concept of education is dynamic. It has passed through many ages and stages in the process of evolution and at every stage it has a different meaning according to the existing social conditions. The concept of education is still in the process of evolution and this process will never come to an end. New times will always demand a revision of the prevailing educational ideals. Great educators in the past explained the term 'education' as the art of 'leading out'. Their explanation was proved by the derivation of the term education –'E' means 'out of' and 'duco' means 'to lead.' Thus education is to draw out rather than to put in. The whole aspect of education-intellectual, moral and physical consist in leading out the innate knowledge, virtues, powers and potentials of the individual. In the Latin dictionary we find the word 'educere' which means 'to lead out' or 'to draw out'. According to this view, the main purpose of education is to lead out or to draw out rather than to put in. There is yet another view according to which the term education comes from the Latin word 'educare' meaning 'to educate', 'to bring up', 'to nurture'. In other words, it means that the child is to be brought up according to certain aims. It is again believed that the term education is derived from the Latin word 'educatum' which means the act of teaching or training, thus we find that according to Latin words, 'educere' and 'educatum', education is external in nature. It is imposed on the child from outside. So it is impossible to draw out unless something is put before hand. Thus education is both acquisition of knowledge or art of teaching and the development of skills, attitudes, habits etc. The individual should be trained through the experiences of his life, so that the best in his life can be achieved.

Formal Education

Formal education is the education which is provided in the educational institutions according to a particular pattern. In the school, the educator educates the educands, according to a specific programme while aiming at a particular goal. In this formal kind of education, the time and place of teaching are fixed, and the educand has to arrive at the place and at the specific time to receive education. The length of such education is also fixed in terms of years. Both the kinds of education mentioned earlier can be included under the formal classification because both are often provided in schools and colleges. The advantage of the formal kind of education is that it can be scientifically and consistently provided to a large number of children simultaneously. The objectives of this education are also determined beforehand. Although, education in one form or the other continues as long as a person lives, education in its more common meaning start at the age of four or five and continues to the age of twenty-five. At this stage, the individual passes through a succession of institutions of primary, secondary and advanced education in the form of schools, colleges and universities. Through this various stages of learning, the individual receives formal education, provided on a pattern determined by a syllabus which itself is framed with a view to achieving certain fixed targets.

The Educational Achievement of Students

> *Educational Achievement:* It is the performance of a student in the college subjects. It is operationally defined as the average of percentage of marks obtained by a student in his or her annual examination, mid-

term, autumn exam and winter exam, conducted by the individual colleges.

According to Wily and Andrew, one of the main purposes of measuring the achievement of pupils is to ascertain the degrees to which the educational objectives of the school/college are being realised (Wily, 1955, p- 174). The results of the measurement of achievement, taken at intervals over a period of years, provide a continuous means of evaluating the students' growth and help to determine the effectiveness of the curriculum in meeting the individual needs. The normal pattern used by teachers is to use marks to record the evaluation of the students' level of academic achievement. These marks are based on the internal exams too but relies more on examinations. The marks represent the proficiency possessed by the students in school/college/university subjects.

To see, evaluate or check the achievement of the students, examination is one of the techniques. An examination is a systematic test of knowledge or skills carried out under the authority of some public body or conducted by the teachers themselves. Examinations, in one or the other form, have been in existence from the distant past. Examinations have stimulating effect both on the pupils and on the teachers by providing well defined goals and objectives of education. It may have different motivating factor for both the teachers and students. To the teacher, examination is the time when response from one's teaching can be judged positively or negatively. To the students too, the examinations provide a goal towards which they can strive and advance towards attaining that goal in a given time. This requires a continuous steady and constant effort on the part of the students. The student is judged through external and internal exams. The exam results also give judgments of failure or success in one's performances which is recognized by all. Examinations help in evaluating the achievement of the students. It also indicates the strong and the weak points of the student in different subjects which motivates or warns the student concerned. Examination also helps to measure the efficiency of the teacher, thereby, raising the standards of education. Examination is also a process that helps in selection of students through competition where teachers and parents can observe the performances of their pupils and wards. It also can help measure some personality traits like the student level of consistency, determination, obedience, humility and so on. Therefore, an examination is a necessary tool.

The achievement of the students depends on themselves as have been observed. Some students are too casual in their studies not giving any efforts; some study at the eleventh hour (during exam); while some are too irregular in the class; these are some of the poirts which hamper their studies.

> *Educational Aspiration:* Educational aspirations reflect a cognitive type of motivation of the individual. Frank defines it in terms of the level of future performance in a familiar task which an individual, knowing his level of past performance in that task explicitly undertakes to reach. James Drever explains it as a frame or reference involving self esteem or alternatively as standard with reference to which an individual experiences, that is, he has the feeling of success or failure. Thus, the term educational aspiration, involves the estimation of his ability for his future performance.

Findings from the Two Colleges

The final year students of St. Joseph's College, Jakhama and Japfü Christian College, Kigwema were taken as the sample for the study of educational achievement and aspiration of the Angami students. 42 Angami respondents were randomly chosen for the study. The students were studied as two categories. One group comprised of students who belonged to under- matriculate and illiterate families (family A). The other comprised of students who are from matriculate and above families (family B). For the convenience of the study, "Family A" is referred as an uneducated family and "Family B" is referred to as an educated family. The overall achievement of the Angami students was found to be quite low; the average achievement in BA I & II was only 47.6%. The target set for BA III exam was only 53.5% which indicates that they are aiming only for a few increase in their marks at the same division. Out of 42 students, 21 students are girls and 21 students are boys. 22 students are from uneducated families and 20 are from educated families.

The study revealed that students from educated families performed better than students from uneducated families and even their targets were found to be higher than their counterparts. It is also found that the children of educated parents are brought up from private schools whereas most of the students from uneducated families were from government schools. The higher average performance of students belonging to educated families may be attributed to their better schooling and family background. However, at the college level where they enjoy more freedom, their low performance and low target, in spite of their potential, indicate their lack of determination to improve or compete though they have a consciousness that they should not fail in their exams. At the college level, children from educated families with regards to their academic achievements are also not much higher than the achievements. This shows that family and schooling backgrounds do not matter much in their performance at the college level. The general low performance and target also speaks of their lack of seriousness, determination, vision and zeal to strive forward in life.

The study reveals that up to the secondary level, the Angami students were able to score First Division marks, where about 12% of the students secured first Division in their HSLC exam and in HSSLC exam about 14% secured First Division again. However, at the BA I & BA II, only one girl managed to get First Division marks, which is only about 2 %. This might be due to the lapse in the supervision of the parents at the BA level. At the college level, it also is the individual's performance without the help of private tuitions. The academic achievement of children belonging to both educated and uneducated families are almost at par with each other. The girls from uneducated families achieve better than all the others but they are not as ambitious as the children from educated families. The boys from uneducated families perform the lowest. This may be due to undue respect from their parents as also freedom from any type of advices. The overall performance of the girls was also better than the boys but the target of the boys was found to be higher than the girls.

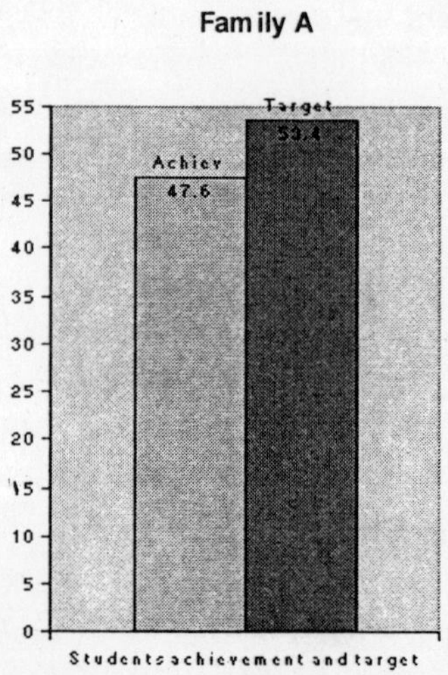

Figure 1

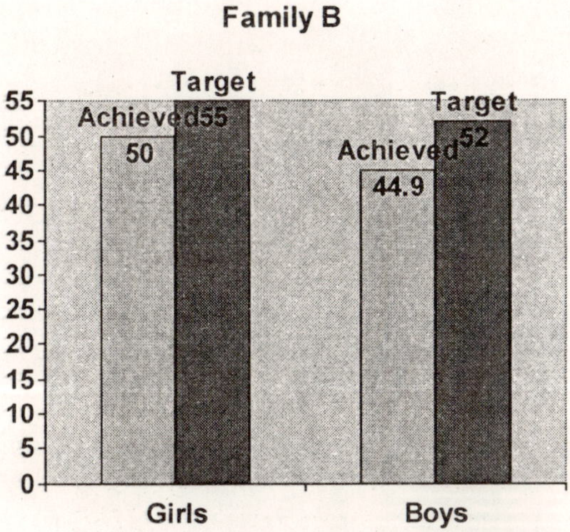

Figure 2

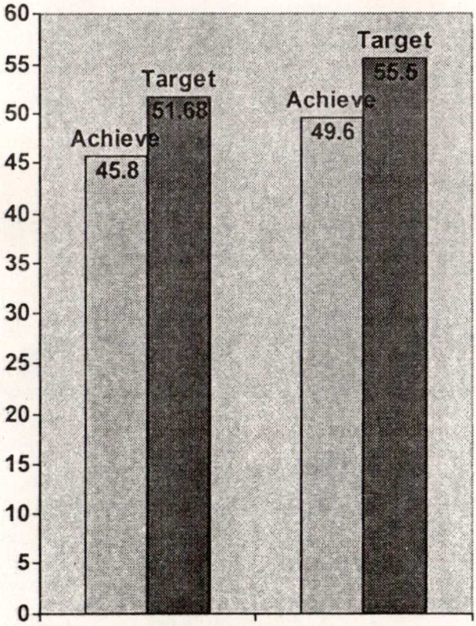

Figure 3

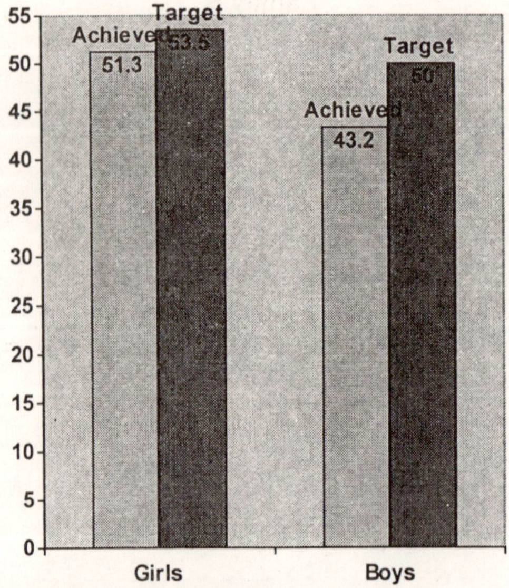

Figure 4

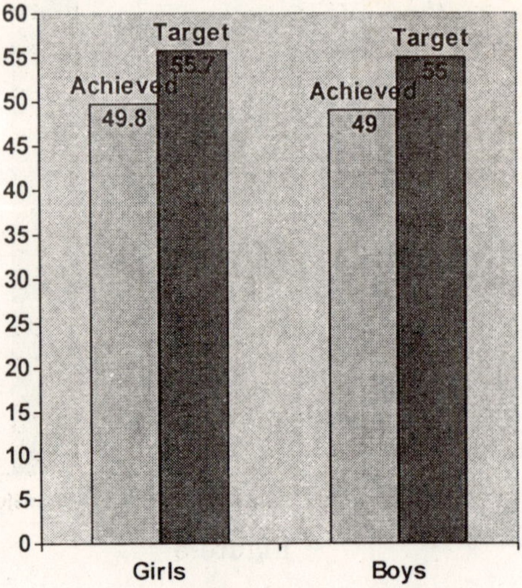

Figure 5

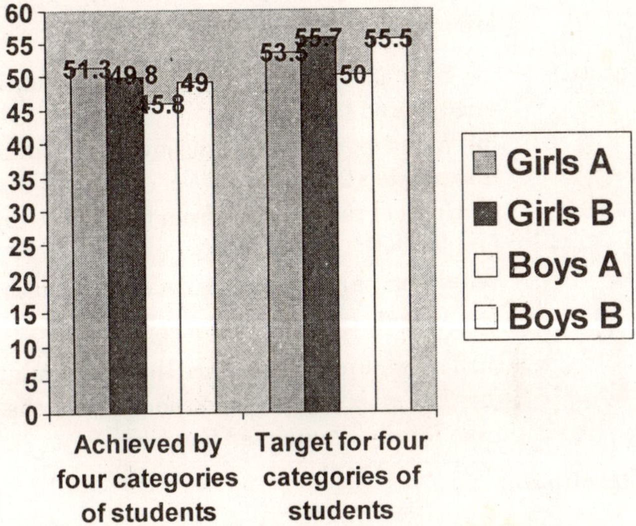

Figure 6

Figure 1 The achievement is about 47.8 % and target is 63.4%. It means both achievement and target are low.

Figure 2 (a) Girls do better than boys.

(b) Girls are more ambitious than the boys.

Figure 3 (a) Students from family B/educated families do better than students from family A/uneducated families.

(b) Students from family B/educated are more ambitious than students from family A/ uneducated families.

Figure 4 (a) Girls do better than boys.

(b) Girls have higher academic targets.

Figure 5 (a) Girls do better than boys.

(b) Girls target is higher than boys.

When achievement is compared with target, boys are found to be more ambitious than girls.

Figure 6 (a) Best performers are girls from family A/ uneducated families.

(b) Worst performers are boys from family A/ uneducated families.

(c) Highest target- girls from family B/educated families.

When comparism is made between achievement and target.

(a) The best performers are the least ambitious.

(b) The most ambitious students are the boys from family B/educated families.

Conclusion

Parents after matriculation loses interest in the performance of their wards, maybe H.S.L.C. exam is taken in a very competitive spirit even on parents to parents' levels. For the science students H.S.S.L.C. is given much attention by parents but arts and commerce students do not get that much of attention. The majority of parents literally stop overseeing the performance of their wards.

Perhaps they are considered grown up or perhaps their wards performances no longer get social applause or credit as in the H.S.L.C. exams.

Angami students are not bothered whether about their weak and strong points involving different subjects. Even when they get low marks or high marks, they get no special messages to improve or target higher marks in exams. When the examination is not taken seriously by teachers and students alike; than the standard of education falls.

Examination helps to measure the efficiency of the teacher but usually when students fail in bulk, the students get the entire blame. When it is supposed to be shared on a 50-50 basis by both teachers and students or perhaps parents also should be blamed to some extend, or better still, it should become the norm that students should visit libraries, make their own preparations and struggle to excel in their educational achievements. This also will ensure that they will mature in their academic growth in an adequate manner.

The study also revealed that there is not much competitive spirit amongst the Angami students studied.

English language is an important aspect which determines the educational achievement of students in addition to hard work. Therefore, both spoken English and written English should be given equal emphasis. Proper educational background, especially at the early years of schooling should be given special importance. This will also result to the decrease in the memorizing culture of the Angami students. It has also been observed that students who had their schooling background from some private schools who emphasize on teachers being properly trained had an impact on higher educational achievement even in the later years. This also proves that teachers should be properly trained. An issue also is raised to teachers of higher education as to whether we are adequately trained for teaching students' in spite of our Master Degrees, M.Phils, PhDs. etc.

There is a need felt that Angami students at the college level (BA level) requires proper guidance from both parents and teachers. A healthy competitive spirit should be imputed in them so that their educational aspirations is raised which will automatically leads to higher educational achievements. The reason that makes the girls perform better in the educational achievements may also be attributed to the sense of responsibility assigned to them from a very young age. The Angami patrilineal system is found to favour boys from a very young age by excusing them from almost all domestic chores. They are not trained mentally to look into the nitty-gritty of everyday life which in turn might be also responsible for making them to neglect their studies on a daily basis. They are lower in their educational achievements as compared to girls but are higher in their aspirations. Therefore, boys need to be given more responsibilities from childhood. At the same time, girls need to be imputed with a sense of higher ambition in order to raise their aspiration level.

REFERENCES

1. Agrawal, J. C., *Landmarks in the History of Modern Education*, Vikash Publishing House (P) Ltd, New Delhi, 1993.
2. Agrawal, S.P. & J.C. Agrawal, *Educational and Social Uplift of Backward Classes – Part 1*, Concept Publishing Company, New Delhi, 1991, pp. 109 – 110.
3. Angami Students Union, *Hudi Dielie*, Issue No.1, 2006.
4. Best, John W & James V. Kahn, *Research in Education*, Prentice Hall, New Delhi, 1999.
5. Burns, Robert B., *Introduction to Research Methods*, Sage Publications, New Delhi.
6. Chandra, Soti Shivendra & Rajendra K. Sharma, *Principles of Education*, Atlantic Publishers and Distributors, New Delhi, 1996.
7. Directorate of Economics & Statistics, *Statistical Hand book of Nagaland*, Government of Nagaland, 2006.
8. Downs, Frederick S., *History of Christianity in India*, Vol. V, Part 5, Bangalore: Church History Association of India, 1992.
9. D' Souza, Alphonsus & Christina Kekhrieseno, *Coping with Social Change in North – East India,* St. Joseph's College, Jakhama, 2002.
10. Elwin, Verrier, *Nagaland,* Published by P. Dutta for the Research Department, Advisors Secretarial, Shillong, 1961.
11. Elwin, Verrier (ed.), *The Nagas in the Nineteenth Century*, xford University Press, 1969.

12. Ghosh, B.B., *Studies in the History of North-East India*, North Eastern Hill University Publications, Shillong.
13. Gore, M. S., *Indian Education: Structure and Process*, Rawat Publications, New Delhi, 1994.
14. Hibo, Visakhonu, *Social Change and the Angami Nagas*, St. Mary's College, Shillong, 1992.
15. Hutton, J. H., *The Angami Nagas*, Oxford University Press, London, 1969.
16. Moore, Wilbert E., *Social Change*, Prentice Hall of India Private Limited, New Delhi.
17. Sharma, K.R., *Educational Lifestyle of Tribal Students*, Classical Publishing Company, New Delhi.
18. Sinha, A. C. et.al (ed.), *Hill Cities of Eastern Himalayas*, Indus Publishing Co., New Delhi, 1993.
19. Talesra, Hemlata, *Sociological Foundations of Education*, Kanishka Publishers and Distributors, New Delhi, 2004.
20. Ulich, Robert, *History of Educational Thought*, Eurasia Publishing House (P) Ltd, New Delhi.

7

EDUCATION AS AN INDUSTRY: Impact on the Angami Society

Kevizakie Rio

> Parents, rich or poor, rural or urban, educated or illiterate, all are consumed by a desire, stronger than ever before, to see their children avail of education and almost as if by consequence, therefore, access better lifestyles. It's an attitudinal change among parents. A refrain earlier - "What good is education"- is a rare response today. For the belief that education is benign, that it is an essential ingredient for one's well being and most certainly for one's upward mobility in the modern world seems to have permeated Nagaland's collective consciousness.

Our present study will focus on the "*enterprise of providing for education by the private sector*" to those who are ready to pay at much higher rate for the services that otherwise (and conventionally) are imparted at a very cheap rate by the system of education run by the government. As we all know, imparting elementary as well as secondary and higher education has since long been one of the most important activities of the state and in all the states of India there is a well organized system of primary and secondary schools run by the government. These schools and colleges in the government sector are almost fully supported by the state and therefore, they impart education to the students at a very cheap rate.

However, since the last three decades or so, many towns in India have experienced the flourishing of private schools and colleges of various types. It has been observed that there is an ever growing demand for private schools and colleges in almost all states in India and the enterprise of private schools and colleges has established itself so well that it has now assumed the characteristics of a full-fledged industry in the tertiary sector. Private schools and colleges are flourishing in almost all towns in India; they have come up in large numbers in the rural areas as well. The wave has been felt even in Nagaland, more so in the Angami areas.

The system of private enterprises imparting education to students may well be called an *industry*, though it is often startling because, conventionally, first, '*industry*' is often associated with '*manufacturing*' and secondly, providing for education has been the activity of the state, mainly with the widely acclaimed objectives concerning welfare and promotion of human capital for fostering development. Those who know these private schools and colleges rather closely would almost unanimously agree on considering them an enterprise, like any other enterprise, mainly undertaken to earn income and profit. These schools and colleges employ teachers at a low salary, charge substantial amount as admission and tuition fees, often provide for residential facilities to enhance profitability, and yet, at many instances, remain unmindful to providing enough facilities to students. On scrutiny, one may have only a mixed type of feelings about the academic standard of these schools and colleges. However, in general, private institutions strive hard to impress their clients and exhibit remarkable salesmanship to attract them, whereas the institutions of the government sector have no incentives or urge to do so.

Not all private institutions run and succeed only on the impression created by their skill at salesmanship. Some private institutions indeed do better than government-run institutions. Therefore, it is obvious for parents of the students to send their children to such institutions with good prospects even though the costs are high.

It is a commonplace knowledge that most parents will develop a liking to a particular educational institution which is doing well. Matters like HSLC/HSSLC/Degree results, quality of education, surroundings, extra-curricular activities and most of all the devotion of teachers towards the students count. Since many of these qualities are available in many private institutions, the parents prefer these brands (branded schools, colleges), though all private schools and colleges do not behave uniformly.

In this study, education has been given the epithet of *industry*, because it produces the manpower of different skills and efficiency for the production process of the economy. Whereas the products of other industries are valued for their usefulness in the production of final consumption, the product of education is valued for its productivity – in production process. That is why; schools and colleges may be considered as "teaching firms". Many "industrial' concepts can be meaningfully employed for the analysis of education although it has its own peculiarities.

The system of private educational organizations falls under the category of tertiary sector. It is concerned with provision of services (imparting education and allied facilities). Like in any other industry it buys factors of production such as land, building materials, study materials, etc. and further it employs teachers and non-teaching staff. Logically, a private educational institutions acts as a mill in which the customers (i.e., the parent of a child) bring in the raw material (the child), to be shaped for the future benefits. In doing so, the schools and colleges charges necessary fees for the services rendered to the child or pupil.

Evidently, profit maximization is one of the basic objectives of these privately run institutions. Unlike the government-run schools and colleges which are geared by 'duty of the state', social service, welfare or development motives and so on, a private schools and colleges attempts to maximize its profit in various ways, viz. charging higher admission fees, tuition fees, hostel rent and other donations. Apart from these objectives some of the objectives which are deemed worth mentioning are expansion of the infrastructure and also providing quality education.

In the organizational perspective, private schools and colleges may take the form of a 'sole proprietorship' in which a single individual is the sole owner of the school. The discretion pertaining to policy making lies with the owner and he alone bears the losses and takes the profit. Secondly, there is 'partnership' where more than one person is involved. Mutual consent and voluntary agreement create them. Though the joint capital is not a norm of partnership they agree to share the profit. Thirdly, there are 'cooperatives' that run the school for the furtherance of their economic interests. Many of these schools and colleges proclaim to providing maximum services to all the students' community and not to make profit. Another form of institution may be referred to as 'joint or Deficit'. Both government and private individuals have their shares in the administration of such schools and colleges.

The system of private institutions has a market structure. As an industry it falls under the purview of monopolistic competition. Schools and colleges produce more or less closely substitutable products such as instruction to pupils and examination results. One definite thing about the customers (the parents of pupils) is that they have preference for a particular variety or brand of products. These brands are close but not perfect substitutes for each other.

To summarize, the system of private enterprises catering to the demand of the clients (parents/students) for education have all major characteristics of an industry: (a) profit motive, (b) investment, (c) hiring of factors of production like skilled and unskilled labour, infrastructure like building/land, etc, (d) catering to the demand in the market, (e) product differentiation, (f) technology and innovation, (g) advertising, (h) pricing policy, (i) competition, coalition, leadership and other types of organizational manifestations, (j) location decisions and localization, and so on. Since any system that sales its product in the market and exhibits the characteristics mentioned above would be labeled as an industry, there is no reason why the system of private schools and colleges should not be labeled as an '*industry*'. Long back, *Kipgen* (1988) had noted this feature. Nevertheless, there is now a growing recognition of the system of private schooling and higher education as an alternative to state-run education system and a perspective has emerged in which they may be compared and evaluated (*Government Vs Private Schools. Delhi Times*, June 11, 2001). *Wadhwa* (2003) documents: "*The Great Indian School Bazaar is booming as never before. In a country where demand for good schools has traditionally outstripped supply, and a new generation of upwardly mobile parents want to give their children only the best, businessmen of every hue – realtors, traders, hoteliers, industrialists, NRIs, franchise chains – are setting up schools*" and "*People have realized that in these times of recession, schools make for regular, stable income*". Also, "*The Pune Zilla Parishad has received 32 applications in just the last 20 months for starting private schools*" and "The Jain Group of Bangalore plans to set up about 100 Jain International Schools in the next 10 years, each at a cost of Rs. 22 crore", etc. *Wadhwa* (2003).

Joshi (2000) envisages monopolistic competition in the education industry run by the private enterprise. *Wadhwa* (2003) quotes Shomie Das, a Dehradun-based education consultant saying: "*People have realized that in these times of recession, schools make for regular, stable income. And given our growing population, the demand for school will only increase. The land and infrastructure remain assets forever. Plus the respectability and status that come from being in the education business are intangible profits*". p. 49. *Kothari* and *Panchmukhi* (1990) point out that education influences economic development. It alters the attitude to work, consumption preferences, saving propensities, economic rationality, adaptability, innovativeness, flexibility, attitude towards family size and various social attitudes relevant from economic point of view. *Natarajan* (1990) refers to Alfred Marshal who felt that education is the most valuable of all capital that is invested in human beings and therefore considered it as a national investment. Marshall is of the view that the most valuable of all capital is that invested in human beings. He remarked that if the capital stock of the world were destroyed but knowledge of its construction and use still remained, it could be reconstituted within comparatively short period. But if stock of knowledge and skill to use it were destroyed then many ages might pass it was reconstituted- indeed it might not be reconstituted at all. This view of education business can only make private schools an industry.

Whatever might be the reasons for the observed demand for private schools and colleges and whoever is working in them on whatever terms, the following points qualify the private schools and colleges to be an object of economic analysis:

(1) It imparts education to a large number of students and thus adds to the augmentation of human capital

that has its own role with regard to the economic development of the region and nation as a whole.

(2) It provides employment to a substantial percentage of the educated population.

(3) It generates income flow that in turn generates demand for many other services and commodities and further income and employment in turn.

(4) It helps to materialise entrepreneurial and managerial abilities in many youths and helps to find the "achieving society" in the words of D.C. McClelland.

(5) It promotes development-movement upward of the whole system-in which literacy plays a great role.

Entrepreneurship among the locals to start private schools and colleges had brought a paradigm shift in the education business among the Nagas and the Angamis in particular. Kohima, being the capital of Nagaland, is the seat of Governor, the council of ministers, Secretaries and Heads of Departments, has another advantage of having government employees, who in turn bring their families to reside in Kohima and send their children to the schools and colleges.

Impact of Education

The advent of western education among the Angamis had brought about multi-faceted impact in the society. Among these, economic impact is noteworthy.

Sl.	*Status*	*No. of Students*	*No. of Teachers*	*Non T-Staff*	*Income*	*Expenditure*	*Profit*
1	Schools	24941	766	148	96172005	55654870	40517135
2	Colleges	9123	257	53	61062120	47017832	14044287
3	Total	34064	1023	201	157234125	102672702	54561422

Generalized table: Private Schools and Colleges

a) *Employment*

Private educational institutions are the employment given next to the public sectors. Since there are no big industries and investment companies in the hill state of Nagaland, private schools and colleges has come up as an alternative to give employment to the local people as well as the non-locals. The private schools and colleges gives employment to 1023 teachers and 201 non-teaching staff. Out of these total employments, a major portion of employees belongs to the Angami community.

b) *Income generation*

Private schools and colleges are income generating sectors. A quick look at the above table and it shows that annually, both the sectors are earning 157234125. The main income of these sectors comes from monthly tuition fees, admission fees and grants from the Government. Most of the private schools and colleges are profiting fairly well, though a huge chunk of these income goes to the salaries of the teachers and non-teaching staff.

Among the 10 private colleges in Angami area, 7 colleges belong to the Angamis. This shows that a major portion of college owners belongs to the local people. Though there are about 60 private schools, only 33 could be surveyed of which 23 schools belongs to the Angamis either owned individually or joint-venture or to an organization.

Further with the mushrooming of private schools and colleges, Private hostels also have come up in numbers to cater to students those who come from other districts to study in these institutions. Though these hostels are not surveyed, many owners of these hostels belong to the Angami community. Apart from that even in some villages where colleges and schools had earned a good reputation, students rent their houses in case they do not get a hostel seat.

c) *Human resource development*

One far reaching impact of education in the Angami society is the knowledge of Human resource development. Most of the traditional barriers had been broken with the introduction of western education. As people started to understand more of science and technology, their lifestyle, sanitation, health and their approach to solving problems had been changed considerably. The earlier thinking of '*What is tasty*' is now framed as '*What is healthy*'. Most of the students who have finished their studies had joined allied service or into teaching profession or occupied into some jobs which is giving a good return because of education.

In fact today's young officers and top job holders belong to students passing out from private schools and colleges. With exigencies of time, competition among different schools and colleges has become the order of the day. More efforts are put on the quality education and also quality of the students to bring impetus to the institution. All these qualities are endowed in the private educational institutions.

REFERENCES

1. Barthwal, R.R. (1996). *Industrial Economics: An Introductory Textbook.* New Delhi. New Age International (P) Ltd.
2. Basch, D.L. (1997). 'Private Experience in the Early 1990s: The Impact of increasing College Funded Grants' in *Research in Higher Education.* Vol. 38(3): 271-296.
3. Bates, L.J and R.E. Santerre. (2000). 'A Time Series Analysis of Private College Closures and Mergers', *Review of Industrial Organisation.* Vol.17(3): 267-276.
4. Burkhalter, B.B. (1996). 'How Can Institutes of Higher Education Achieve Quality within the Economy', *Total Quality Management.* Vol.7(2): 153-160.
5. Byrns, R.T and G.W. Stone. (1989). *Economics.* (4th edition). Scott, Foreman and Co. Glenview, Illinois/London.

6. Choudhury, S etal. (2003). 'Tot for the day': No work and all play' in *Outlook* (Cover Story). Vol XLIII (16), April 28th, pp. 52-55.

7. Joshi, K.M. (2000). *Higher Education: Development Issues.* New Delhi. Commonwealth Publishers.

8. Kipgen, L. (1988). *Economics of Private School Industry: A Case Study of Shillong.* M.Phil. Dissertation (Unpublished). Department of Economics, NEHU, Shillong.

9. Luenberger, D.G. (1995). *Microeconomic Theory.* New York, McGraw-Hill Inc.

10. Sema, P. (1992). *British Policy and Administration in Nagaland: 1881-1947.* New Delhi. Scholars Publishing House.

11. Wadhwa, Soma.(2003). 'Riding the Riverdale High' in *Outlook.* Vol XLIII(16), April 28th, pp. 49-51.

8

EDUCATED UNEMPLOYED YOUTH: Problems and Consequences

Kedilezo Kikhi

[Youth despite of all their energy and enthusiasm, merit and mission, aspirations and attempts, appears to be lost and deprived. In this regard, the present study attempts to deal with a few questions like – i) Do the educated youth of the state possess the necessary requirements to get a job? ii) 'Who' do the educated unemployed blame for not getting a job? iii) What are the problems faced by the educated unemployed youth and its related social consequences?]

I

Nagaland is a state having a weak industrial sector and an underdeveloped agriculture, bulk of the educated population depends on the service sector. There is no balance between the supply of workers and the demand for their services. Therefore open unemployment occurs because able and willing educated persons are in search of work, but there is no work for them. The outflow and the inflow of the state are not balanced.

Unemployment refers to a situation where persons who are able to work and also willing to work at the prevailing rate of wages, does not find work. This is an involuntary idleness leading to wastage of labour. It is not confined to any category of persons. It may be among the unskilled, high skilled and technically qualified persons. Able-bodied persons who voluntarily remain unemployed are excluded from the concept of unemployment. It has three elements: i) an individual should be capable of working; ii) an individual should be willing to work; and iii) an individual must make an effort to find work.

In Nagaland there has been an alarming rise of educated unemployed youth adversely affecting them. The total number of unemployed, which was 22,069 in 1991 on the live register, had risen to 37,090 in 2000, which is a percentage increase of 68.06 and had further risen to 49,960 in 2006 with a percentage increase of 126.38 (taking 1991 as base). The state had 10,534 registered educated unemployed in 1991, whereas the figure rose to 22,119 in 2000 and further rose to 31,277 in 2006.

In the present context, people are confused as what to fear? And whom to fear? Some people fear i) unemployment, while there are others who fear ii) the unemployed youth. The educated unemployed are a dangerous person. He can become dangerously vocal and influential to give constant threat to the security and stability of the state. He nurses a sense of personal injury and if the grievance is long continued and the numbers involved are large, the situation can become decidedly explosive. The unemployed persons belonging to this category are 'not dumb, driven cattle', but intelligent people, and will not accept an unenviable position lying down. It also involves the waste of the best of our human resources for these educated people to remain idle (Puttaswamaiah 1977).

Today, the unemployed youth have become a problem in its own, for the society and the nation. Youth, the force and future of the nation have become the most vulnerable section of the society. They are the most neglected lot, which has lost all public sympathy. They are i) physically deprived, ii) morally depressed, iii) socially ridiculed, iv) economically dependent and v) psychologically frustrated, which only has neglect and insult in its account (Bajpai 1992). Most of the problems of the youth emanate from their unemployment and therefore, unfulfilled needs in the society. Today many problems beset the youth and these certainly need timely recognition.

Youth despite of all their energy and enthusiasm, merit and mission, aspirations and attempts, appears to be lost and deprived. In this regard, the present study attempts to deal with a few questions like – i) Do the educated youth of the state possess the necessary requirements to get a job? ii) 'Who' do the educated unemployed blame for not getting a job? iii) What are the problems faced by the educated unemployed youth and its related social consequences?

II

Earlier studies have traced the problem of unemployment back to the Industrial Revolution, and more recently due to the educational explosion. Nagas, though they were socially, economically, etc backward before the advent of the British and its administration, yet the socio-economic system was free from the problems like unemployment. An imported system of education, which is meant for supporting clerical staff to the colonial rule, is blindly followed by the country and in all its states till today (Bajpai 1992). The educated unemployment and many other related problems faced by the state today are perceived to be the bye-product of its education system.

A Babu's job became a matter of craze for the Nagas especially after the statehood (1st December 1963). The present young generation got mainly enchanted to the mirky lights of electronic gadgets. The present youth are no more interested in the paddy fields or in jhum fields or in any manual labour. Education has developed a kind of complex with the educated youth. Moreover, the parents of the state expect their wards to get white collar jobs after education. And therefore irrespective of the economic background the parents send their children to schools and colleges, which finally create a large army of educated unemployed youth in the state. And unfortunately many of these educated unemployed youth have lost the dignity of labour, though are ready for manual jobs in case of no other alternatives. Generally youth should have high ambitions, but in the state general goalessness is more visible among the unemployed youth. Very few educated youth plan and prepare for the future. There are instances where the youths fight for few available opportunities without any proper preparation and planning. Many youths even fail to read their own capacity and ability, having ambitions that can never be fulfilled. Many educated youth in the state lack adventurism usually expected of them, rather they appear to be over-submissive, frustrated and an idle lot of Luddites.

The unemployment of the educated youth is not only a problem of theirs, but has become the problem of the family, the society, and the nation at large. After spending the hard-earned money of one's parents and about two decades of precious time, the educated youth finds himself at the crossroads. He is desperate for any kind of job but finds no one to buy him. And thus, every educated youth is humiliated in two ways: i) Firstly, he can not contribute anything to the familial economy because he could not work during the course of his study. ii) Secondly, his two decades devotion to education is a waste without any fruits.

The educated unemployed also find himself answerable to the aspirations and expectations of the family. He is answerable to the family, who has spared everything on him, who has invested on him its sweat earned income/money with a hope that he would emancipate the family from all socio-economic curses after his education. Subjected to all this, and particularly to the parent's expectations, the educated unemployed youth find himself guilty. The study reveals that few of them do not wish to go home and do not even wan to meet their friends. He keeps avoiding everyone; he does not want to meet anyone, as he does not have the courage. He feels like a 'death sentence' or a poison has been put under his throat when somebody ask him "what are you doing now-a-days?" A few of them has to work in unfavourable, inferior conditions and thus develops many psychological and health problems. The queues of educated people looking for jobs are growing longer day by day.

Colin (1972) lists seven features of bereavement of unemployed youth:

1. Realisation of loss
2. Alarm reaction
3. Urge to search for and find lost object
4. Anger and guilt
5. Feeling an internal loss of self or mutilation
6. Identification with symbols of a job
7. Pathological variations of a grief

Bajpai (1992) have lined down the following nine problems faced by an unemployed youth.

1. Loss of trust and support of the family
2. Financial hardship
3. Psychological problems like frustration, loss of self-esteem and self-confidence, depression, anxiety and the feeling of self-contempt.

4. Adjustmental problems – intra-personal and inter-personal, with family, peer groups and society.
5. Rejection by society
6. Mal-nutrition and ill-health.
7. Favouritism and corruption in the matters of employment
8. Problems related to sex and marriage
9. Problems related to identity formation.

These problems may be present individually, successively and collectively. Douglas and Driscol (1973) have identified four stages that an unemployed person experiences: i) there is initially a period of relaxation and relief after completion of one's studies. ii) After a rest period, the person will enter the period of concerted efforts where he will energetically look for work.

iii) When these efforts do not pay off and the person is still unemployed a period of vacillation and doubt sets in and mood changes occur. iv) If this continues long enough and the person does not gain employment, he or she enters the period of malaise and cynicism.

Likewise, the educated unemployed youth of the state suffers from many (most) similar problems discussed above. In a nutshell, the unemployed youth of the state are faced with the following problems:

1. With high expectations from their wards, the parents send them to school, college, and university despite of many financial barriers. But the hopes of the parents seem belied. The parents, who expect a lean of support from their child, realize him as a burden over the family, even after completion of studies. Therefore, the educated youth appears to be in 'loss of the thrust' of the family, by being unemployed.

2. The unemployed youth develops a feeling of frustration, a feeling of self-contempt, guilt and looses self-confidence on the non-fulfillment of his family expectations. Though he highly regards his parental feelings and expectations, he finds himself incapable, despite his best efforts.
3. The unemployed youth fails to adjust with his friends, his family and the society. Many of them incur inter-personal conflicts due to which he either becomes idle or a rebel.
4. Due to his rebelling nature he faces dejection from the society, friends and even family members. He looses respect and sympathy of the people.
5. The educated unemployed feels deprived due to corruption, nepotism, and favouritism in the matters of employment. Their sentiments are grieved because of the biased method of selection. This has developed anger and guilt in the minds of the unemployed youth.
6. Due to overwhelming frustration and the feelings of worthlessness, it often leads to mal-nutrition and ill-health of the youth.
7. The unemployed youth faces financial hardship. He wants to be independent but at the same time could not even meet his basic personal needs.
8. The unemployed youth suffers from identity formation and as a result identifies oneself with symbols of a job though they remain unemployed.

These are some of the striking problems faced by the educated unemployed youth pertaining to the state of Nagaland. Some of these problems are further elaborated in detail below, in the form of the attitudes of the unemployed youth towards various social aspects.

III

In continuation with the discussion of the problems a few questions are asked to study the attitudes of the unemployed youth towards various facets of society. The questions are concerned with the attitudes of the unemployed youth in response to the various social aspects viz. the job, the present education system, the method of selection or recruitment, the employment exchange, etc. The respondents on being asked a question, will you get a satisfactory job? About 22.51 percent are confident of getting a satisfactory job, while 5.76 percent responded 'no'. About three-fourth i.e. 71.73 percent are not sure whether they will get a satisfactory job or not.

The most preferable job for these youth is government job. About 67.01 percent of these unemployed respondents has marked government job as the most preferable job, 6.81 percent preferred private jobs, while the remaining 26.18 percent preferred self-employed jobs than any other jobs.

It is true that a specific type of education makes oneself eligible for a specific job, for example, professions like doctors, engineers, etc. However, to get any kind of job appears to be everyone's ambition. The study reveals that more than three-fourths of the unemployed youth i.e. 83.25 percent are ready for any kind of job including manual jobs. In other words they are not looking for specific jobs. About 16.75 percent are not ready for manual jobs.

In addition to the above discussion, table 1 gives about the attitudes of the unemployed youth towards jobs. About 98.95 percent have agreed that work is natural and dignified and therefore every capable person should work. The educated unemployed youth want job or they want to work and they are capable. But joblessness leads to idleness, rebellious nature and frustration, which further leads to all kinds of problems. Now despite the failures, about 88.48 percent strongly agrees to keep on trying for jobs without getting easily disappointed, however only 34.56 percent are confident of getting suitable jobs. About 42.93 percent of the unemployed youth are not confident to get any suitable job even when the right time comes. These 42.93 percent have lost confidence in themselves, about the employment system. This section of the educated unemployed population feels maximum deprivation, which will slowly develop into guilt and anger.

Table 1
Attitude towards the Job

Sl. No.	*Statement*	*Responses in %*		
		Yes	*No*	*can't say/ don't know*
1.	Every capable person should work because work is natural and dignified	98.95	0.00	1.05
2.	I will go on trying for jobs without getting easily disappointed by failures.	88.48	5.76	5.76
3.	I am confident that when the right time comes everyone will get a satisfactory job.	34.56	42.93	22.51

Studies conducted earlier elsewhere (Ahuja 1997; Bajpai 1992; Puttaswamaiah 1977) has shown the youth's dissatisfaction with the present education system. These earlier studies are of the view that education itself creates unemployment. The present education system even alienates the youth from their society. These studies show that the prevailing examination system is inappropriate and therefore, passing out these examinations makes no important contribution to secure a job. It suggests – since these examinations cannot give any job and the actual test of student's knowledge is to be assessed by a competitive examination/test, there is no need for such a fake examination. But the present study reveals contradictory results.

It is observed from table 2 that an average 56.98 percent of educated unemployed youth are satisfied with the present education system. In contradiction to earlier studies conducted in other states, the educated youth of this state opines that the university courses still prepare the students for jobs (43.45 percent). In response to a question, the educated youth responded that the universities are not admitting too many students (59.69 percent) and it is not a waste to give higher education to the youth even though there are no jobs available (78.01 percent). The educated unemployed youth holds that though jobs are not offered to the students, the quality of education has not gone down. As depicted in the table, about 78.01 percent of the respondents are satisfied with the quality of education. However about 45.55 percent of the unemployed youth are of the view that the education standard has declined due to the political interference with the universities.

As far as the medium of instruction is concerned, only a meager 7.85 percent are not satisfied with the foreign medium (i.e. English), while 70.16 percent educated youth are satisfied with the English medium of instruction.

The method of selection to various jobs is not appropriate as it is biased towards the rich and the bureaucrats. The government is claiming to make policies for everyone, but about 84.82 percent respondents are of the view that these policies benefit the rich sections only.

After completing their studies, about 63.35 percent (table 3) respondents agreed that employment is a necessity whether one is rich or poor. The study reveals that the educated youth regard achievement criteria i.e. education, hard work and ability to be the most important factor for getting a satisfactory job. Factors like bribery and luck are not perceived as important and primary options. But on being denied of employment for long, under the present conditions, about 57.59 percent respondents are willing to use any means to secure a job. Corruption and nepotism in the process of selection is unanimously accepted by the respondents. Unanimously the respondents are of the view that 'money' and 'influence' has fortunately become the formula to procure a job (95.82 percent). A poor student without money and influence has very limited chance of getting a job in the present system (73.30 percent). This practice or formula of procuring a job has become the norm of the day.

Table 2

Attitude about the Present Educational System

Sl. No.	*Reasons / Statement*	*Responses in %*		
		Very Important	*Somewhat Important*	*Unimportant / Incorrect*
1.	*(It is a waste to give higher education to the youth)* when there are no jobs available.	18.33	3.66	78.01
2.	Universities are admitting too many students compared to the number of jobs available.	21.99	18.32	59.69
3.	University courses do not prepare students for jobs.	23.04	33.51	43.45
4.	Jobs are not offered to the students because of the quality of education has gone down.	4.71	17.28	78.01
5.	Political interference with the universities has contributed to the decline of standards.	45.55	41.88	12.57
6.	Education through a foreign medium prevents development of talent.	7.85	21.99	70.16

Table 3

Attitude towards the Method of Selection

Sl. No.	*Statement*	*Responses in %*		
		Yes	*No*	*can't say/ don't know*
1.	Government claims to make policies for everyone but they benefit the rich sections only.	84.82	4.71	10.47
2.	Persons who are rich should not bother about employment.	23.56	63.35	13.09
3.	In the present condition one must use fair or unfair means to get a job.	57.59	30.89	11.52
4.	The condition of the society today is such that those who have money and influence can easily get a job.	95.82	2.61	1.57
5.	Even a poor student without money and influence can easily get a job.	13.61	73.70	13.09

On being asked a question, the educated unemployed youth responded that they are not satisfied with the government i.e. the administrators and the policy makers, policy planners and the political leaders who are in power. They responded not only their dissatisfaction but also blame the government for not getting a job.

The educated unemployed youth expects some positive and concrete steps from the government to curb the problem of unemployment. Like, an industry could be governmental machinery where lots of educated youth could find solution to their hunger for jobs. But Nagaland is a poor state with no industry and the educated unemployed youth (75.92 percent) unanimously agreed to it. Again, unfortunately the state government could not maintain few small industries, which we have, like Tuli Paper Mill, Dimapur Sugar Mill that has to be closed down. The respondents (76.44 percent) are convinced that the government is not doing enough in promoting or setting up industries in the state. This is also a clear indication that the administrators and policy makers have not paid enough attention to the problem of unemployment (67.02 percent). Still more, political leaders have not shown enough courage in dealing with unemployment (65.97 percent). But against the statement – the government collaborates to keep unemployment high – is incorrect according to 68.06 percent of the respondents.

Table 4

Attitude towards the Government

Sl. No.	*Reasons/Statement*	*Responses in %*		
		Very Important	*Somewhat Important*	*Unimportant/ Incorrect*
1.	No industry to absorb the educated unemployed youth.	75.92	14.66	9.42
2.	The government has not gone far enough in promoting or setting up industries.	76.44	14.66	8.90
3.	Administrators and policy makers have not paid enough attention to the problem of unemployment.	67.02	29.32	3.66
4.	Political leaders have not shown courage in dealing with unemployment.	65.97	30.89	3.14
5.	The government collaborates to keep unemployment high.	12.57	19.37	68.06
6.	Improper utilization of funds leads to stagnation of development.	90.58	8.90	0.52
7.	The various governmental departments do not properly notify vacant jobs.	78.01	17.80	4.19

The study shows that the various funds and schemes that are meant for development and advancement of the state have been misused. For that matter about 90.58 percent of the respondents blame the government for stagnation of development due to improper utilization of funds. This directly affects the educated unemployed youth for stagnation of any society forbids employment opportunities. Again, 78.01 percent of the respondents agreed that the various governmental departments do not properly notify vacant jobs.

After World War II, in 1945 the Directorate General of Employment and Rehabilitation has been established in order to provide employment and rehabilitation to released soldiers, under which Employment Exchanges are established all over the country. In 1959, Indian Parliament passed the Employment Exchange (compulsory notification of vacancies) Act that came into effect from May 1960. The name of the Directorate General of Rehabilitation and Employment is changed to Directorate General of Employment and Training (Bajpai 1992).

Unfortunately Employment Exchanges are not serving in the manner, as conceived in the beginning. They have rather reduced to be white elephants (Bajpai 1992). They do not cover all the unemployed persons, because registering in Employment Exchanges is voluntary. The registration is mainly concentrated in urban areas and many have not registered in the Employment Exchange, as it is not effective according to them. Though vacancies are notified through the Employment Exchange, the employers are not bound to select out of those sent through it. Apart from notifying vacancies in Employment Exchange, they are free to advertise in other Newspapers and Employment News Bulletins. Thus, the very purpose of Employment Exchange has got defeated and there is no benefit from registration in Employment Exchanges. Again, ironically enough, not all the vacancies are notified, rather a few categories of jobs are only notified to Employment Exchange.

In western countries, graduate students register themselves with Employment Department because they get 'unemployed allowance' on maturity, but no such 'benefits' are provided to Indian youth, consequently, only a slight fragment of unemployed get registered with Employment Exchanges. As a matter of fact, about 60.73 percent of the respondents are of the view that at least the government should provide unemployment allowance.

As shown in table 5, about 54.97 percent of the respondents have registered in Employment Exchange, while 45.03 percent of the respondents have not registered. In a separate question, the respondents view is recorded whether it is necessary to get registered in an Employment Exchange in order to get a job. Of which, 52.88 percent are of the view that it is not necessary to get registered to secure employment. It therefore indicates that out of 105 registered respondents, 7.85 percent respondents have registered though they know it is not necessary. They might have registered under the pressure of family members, relatives or under the influence of friends, but have not registered willingly. Thus, in actual term more than one-half of the sample respondents perceive Employment Exchange as not necessary in order to get a job, which clearly depicts its ineffectiveness.

The period of registration of these registered respondents is clearly shown in the same table. And the highest frequency with 23.81 percent for the period of registration is in the category 'more than 5 years'. The validity of every registration is 3 years and has to be renewed after 3 years. Of the registered respondents, the data reveals that 59 respondents (56.19 percent) have at least renewed once. It is therefore quite sure that more than one-half of these respondents have remained unemployed for a long time and the Employment

Exchange failed to help them. Again, those respondents whose period of registration is up to 15 years must have at least renewed their registration 5 times. This long period of registration once again speaks volume of negligence and ineffectiveness of the Employment Exchanges in the state.

Table 5

Distribution of sample by Registration and Period of Registration with the Employment Exchange

Registered	*Not registered*	*Total*
105 (54.97)	*86 (45.03)*	*191*

Period of Registration (total = 105)

Registered Period (in years)	*Number*	*% against the total*
0 – 1	16	15.24
1 – 2	18	17.14
2 – 3	12	11.43
3 – 4	14	13.33
4 – 5	20	19.05
More than 5 years (Up to 15 years)	25	23.81

Mode Period = more than 5 years

IV

Sociologically speaking, family is the heart of social life. It is evident from table 6 that the education and career of the children is always taken care of by the father or the family (94.76 percent). The parents of these respondents spend money not only for acquiring knowledge (59.15 percent) but to get a good job too (35.61 percent). At the same time as already discussed the parents have high expectations from their educated wards; and 26.18 percent of the respondents feel frustrated for they cannot satisfy or fulfill these expectations.

It is also evident from the table that about 55.50 percent are from poor families. And as such their parents could not spend much for their education and job trials. However, 56.54 percent of the respondents are of the view that their parents give or will give freely money for jobs and attending interviews irrespective of family background. Though 60.83 percent of the respondents' parents do not complain about their unemployment, it is not surprising to note that 31.94 percent complains about the unemployment of the respondents. This section of the educated unemployed youth appears to be in 'lost of the trust' of the family by being unemployed. In spite of their unemployment, about 56.02 percent of the family members still sympathize with the educated youth.

About 73.30 percent of the respondents are of the view that unemployment among the educated youth socially taxes the aspirations of parents and relatives. But whatever be the matter, about 58.12 percent of the respondents cannot hope to get a job without the help and support of the family.

Table 6

Educated Unemployed Youth and Family Related Problems

Sl. No.	*Statement*	*Yes*	*No*	*Don't Know/ Can't say*
1.	My father/family has never taken interest in my education and my career matters.	4.19	94.76	1.05
2.	My parents spend money for my education to get a good job more than to acquire knowledge.	35.61	59.15	5.24

(Contd...)

Sl. No.	Statement	Yes	No	Don't Know/ Can't say
3.	Expectations of my parents/ relatives are too high for me to satisfy/fulfill.	26.18	60.73	13.09
4.	As I am from a poor family, my parents cannot spend much on my education and job trials.	55.50	36.65	7.85
5.	My parents gives or will freely give money for jobs or attending interviews.	56.54	29.32	14.14
6.	My family complains of my unemployment.	31.94	60.83	7.33
7.	My family members sympathize with me for being unemployed.	56.02	2.18	17.80
8.	I cannot hope to get a job without my family's help and support.	58.12	31.93	9.95
9.	Unemployment among the educated youth socially taxes the aspirations of parents and relatives.	73.30	5.23	21.47

The social consequences are related to the various problems faced by the unemployed youth. In other words, it is often the outcome of the problem that has been long harboured and suffered. It is essential to discuss the social problems along with its related social consequences. Many of the related consequences have been featured already in the discussion of the problems above. This section of the study discusses some of the more severe consequences of the problem of youth unemployment.

Youth are the human property of the nation; they represent strength, vitality and vigour and are the hope for the future of a nation. But if these youth remains idle, worried and inactive due to unemployment and is forced to do something to become an earning hand, he usually does not care for the social norms and values and becomes subject to many kinds of vices as indulgence into drug addiction etc. True is the Sanskrit idiom; "Bubhukshitah Kim Na Karoti Papam" meaning thereby a hungry man can do any sin (Bajpai 1992).

In the view of 90.05 percent of the respondents, unemployment frustrates the youth's ambitions. The educated unemployed youth are temperamentally frustrated, impatient, and restless (79.06 percent). It is found that the educated unemployed youth feels bored on account of unemployment; dull and the feeling of self-contempt and self-distrust develops. It is difficult even for a strong man to keep his self-respect (77.49 percent) and the unemployed youth will have the feeling that he is not well treated by his people (51.31 percent).

Table 7

Unemployment and Social Consequences

Sl. No.	*Social consequences*	*% Response (Yes)*
1.	Unemployment frustrates youth's ambitions.	90.05
2.	Educated unemployed youth are temperamentally frustrated, impatient, restless, etc.	79.06
3.	Unemployment leads to family disorganization, disunity and discord among the family.	65.44
4.	The problem of unemployment disrupts peace with neighbours.	62.31
5.	Educated unemployment is a serious threat to the society.	97.38
6.	Educated unemployment has contributed to the spread of drugs, alcoholism, smuggling and drug trafficking.	70.70
7.	Educated unemployed youth takes to anti-social activities like bandits, highway robberies, extortionists, etc.	67.54

It is accepted by 65.44 percent that unemployment leads to family disorganization, disunity and discord among the family. About 62.31 percent of the respondents are of the view that the problem of unemployment disrupts peace with neighbours. Educated unemployment is a serious threat not only to the family, or neighbours, but is a serious threat to the society (97.38 percent) today.

As shown in table 7, it is accepted by 70.70 percent of the respondents that the educated unemployment has contributed to the spread of drugs and alcoholism, smuggling and drug trafficking too. The respondents (67.54 percent) believe that due to unemployment, the educated unemployed youth are taking to anti-social activities. These anti-social activities include bandits, highway robbers, extortionists, etc. It can be therefore concluded that the youth has become economically vulnerable; thereby they are increasingly getting into the trap of violence.

The youth of today expects white-collar job and does not like to take risks. He is becoming less adventurous and wants a steady income. He wants to be prosperous and luxurious through a salaried job. There is a general disinclination among the educated youth to look for employment other than the government job (69.63 percent). About 35.08 percent of the educated unemployed look only for government jobs. Self-employment jobs are given a low priority, as against paid government jobs (73.30 percent).

It is accepted only by 6.28 percent of the respondents that the unemployed are not good enough to find jobs, and they seek jobs generally beyond their ability (11.32 percent). It is also accepted by 9.42 percent of the respondents that many educated do not want to take up lower paid jobs and thus, they remain unemployed while they wait for better jobs. Again about 75.92 percent remain unemployed, not only because of waiting for better jobs but preferences for certain place.

To conclude, the problem of unemployment among the educated youth is one of the gravest that the state faces today. Personally, they appear to be in 'lost of the trust' of the family and have lost even respect and sympathy of the people. The educated youth develops a feeling of frustration, self-contempt, and guilt, and looses self-confidence due to long years of unemployment. The educated unemployed youth fails to adjust with his friends, his family and the society. They face financial hardships. And all this has resulted in severe consequences. It has invited the anger of our youth and they are increasingly indulging into illegal, anti-social and other violent and criminal activities too. And this can be read as an expression of their distrust to the system. The deprivations in the matters of recruitment further generate socio-economic problems like corruption, nepotism, favouritism, etc.

Therefore, the problem of unemployment among the educated youth is a serious problem, which needs timely attention and solution. Unemployment should not be viewed as a 'residual' problem to be tackled after the other problems have been solved, but as a 'primary' problem. Determined efforts are needed and appropriate policies, plans and programmes are to be made so that our young men and women can become job creators and not job seekers.

REFERENCES

1. Aggarwal, A.K. (1987). *Economic Problems and Planning in North East India.* New Delhi, Sterling Publishers Pvt. Ltd.
2. Ahuja, Ram. (1997). *Social Problems in India (Second Edition).* New Delhi, Rawat Publications.
3. Bajpai, Pramod Kumar. (1992). *Youth, Education and Unemployment.* New Delhi, Ashish Publishing House.
4. Chadha, G.K. (2000). "Youth Unemployment in India: Past policy Gaps and Future Strategic Options", *The Indian Journal of Labour Economics.* Vol 43, No. 4, Oct – Dec., 2000.

5. Chakrapani, C. (1995). *Unemployment Stress – A Study of Educated Unemployed.* New Delhi, Vikas Publishing House Pvt. Ltd.

6. Colin, Murray Parkes. (1972). *Bereavement.* New York, International University Press.

7. Das, Bhakta. (1992). *Unemployment in Assam, an Account of Human Error.* New Delhi, Cosmo Publications.

8. Douglas, H. Powell and Paul F. Driscoll. (1973). 'Middle Class Professional Face Unemployment'; *Society*; January-February.

9. Kikhi, Kedilezo. (2002). "Educated Unemployment in Nagaland: Trend and Magnitude", in C. Joshua Thomas and Gurudas Das (ed.), *Dimensions of Development in Nagaland.* New Delhi, Regency Publications.

10. Kikhi, Kedilezo. (2006). *Educated Unemployed Youth in Nagaland: A Sociological Study.* New Delhi, Akansha Publishing House.

11. Puttaswamaiah, K. 1977. *Unemployment in India – Policy for Manpower.* New Delhi, Oxford & IBH Publishing Co.

12. Government of Nagaland, Directorate of Economics and Statistics. *Statistical Hand Book of Nagaland.* Kohima.

13. Government of Nagaland, Directorate of Economics and Statistics. *Basic Facts – 2006,* Kohima.

14. Government of Nagaland, Directorate of Employment & Craftsmen Training.

The [illegible] generally [illegible] even [illegible] changes have taken place in the [illegible] between [illegible] and [illegible] of constructing [illegible] has [illegible] and Jakh[illegible] Zakhama [illegible] Jakhama and Kigwema [illegible] Jakhama and [illegible] Chiratlad [illegible] Despite these changes, the Southern [illegible] covered in forests, [illegible] preserved terrace fields.

[illegible] descend[illegible] and Kigwema (Sanyu, 199[illegible]) [illegible] formation and expansion, they formed [illegible] Kigwema, Viswema, Jakhama, [illegible] Phesama, [illegible] Mima and [illegible], these eleven villages emerged [illegible] information on these villages taken from [illegible] Census, D[illegible]

Village	[illegible]	[illegible]	Total	Male	Female
[illegible]	[illegible]	[illegible]	[illegible]	[illegible]	[illegible]
[illegible]	[illegible]	[illegible]	[illegible]	[illegible]	[illegible]
Kezoma	[illegible]	[illegible]	1437	[illegible]	[illegible]
Kezo Town	[illegible]	[illegible]	[illegible]	[illegible]	258
[illegible]	[illegible]	[illegible]	[illegible]	101	[illegible]
[illegible]	[illegible]	[illegible]	120	59	[illegible]
[illegible]	[illegible]	[illegible]	[illegible]	301	[illegible]
Khuzama	[illegible]	[illegible]	2116	1071	1045
Viswema	[illegible]	[illegible]	[illegible]	[illegible]	[illegible]

(Contd.)

Section IV: Issues on Environmental Depredation

9

THE ECOLOGICAL STATUS OF ANGAMI LAND

Thepfulhouvi Solo

Huge rocks that fell from the mountains on 9th October 2007 due to torrential rain the previous night suddenly blocked the National Highway 39 at the Chümukedima gorge. The Border Road Organisation set to clear the road but the rocks were too big to be easily removed, they had to be broken into smaller blocks but the simple labourers of the Border Road Organisation had no modern tools for the job and they were breaking the huge sandy rocks with their pickax and crowbar. It took 2.5 hours to clear the road and vehicles lined up on the road stranded.

For some time I sat in the car but it became hot inside, I therefore got out of the vehicle and went to the roadside under the shed of the trees on the bank of the Chathe River. There, for the better part of one and half hour I stood on the bank in the shed enjoying cool breeze from the river and while trying to while away the monotony of the time I engaged myself in counting the varieties of the various plants and animals I found in my immediate surrounding of about 20 feet by 20 feet. I counted the following varieties:

a.	Grass	9 different varieties
b.	Herb	6 varieties
c.	Climber	9 varieties
d.	Shrub	4 varieties
e.	Tree	17 varieties
f.	Grasshopper	4 varieties
g.	Butterfly	2 varieties
h.	Dragonfly	2 varieties
i.	Fly	2 varieties
j.	Ant	3 varieties

Total = 59 varieties of plants and animals in an area of 20 Ft. Sq.

I did not count the fungi in the decaying organic matter, the insects that could be under the soil or the caterpillars and the beetles that could be hiding under the bark of the tree. The enumeration was not a scholarly one; it was just a cursory ocular count standing in an area of filled-up soil from the cut face of the road. Yet, at this rate of 59 biological species in an area of 40 square feet of land, any hectare of land in the jungle could easily contain a least 214 different kinds of biological species or thousands of biological individuals. Angami area is very rich in biodiversity.

The Angami area ranges in elevation from 200 m [600+ft] at Hotizha [Dimapur Plain] to 9965 ft [322 m] at Japfü Peak and the climatic conditions ranges from hot tropical climate in Hotizha to Alpine condition in the Dzüku tableland. The area receives an average rainfall of some 80 inches annually. The area is not very vast, its total area is only 3114 sq. km. and the distance between the lowest Hotizha Plain and the highest point Japfü Peak is hardly 25 km as the crow flies. But within small area occur one of the richest biological diversity in the world and is part of one of the Biological Hot Spot of the world.

The plants are various and many, in any one of the seasons, while some plants are in flower, others in fruit, and still others are fruitless, deciduous and leafless. In winter most plants shed their older leaves but some plants have evergreen leaves and some even produce young leaves in winter. Thus the area provides food for the animals, birds, and insects every season of the year.

Angami area is one of the richest in wild vegetables; there are some 125 different kinds of edible wild leaves in Angami area. The world is stagnating on the list of vegetable species domesticated thousands of years ago. Modern man has not added much new species in the list of vegetables his ancient forefathers have domesticated and some of the wild vegetables found in our jungle could very well be domesticated to add to the worlds. And as for the varieties of medicinal plants in the wild, the possibilities are perhaps beyond imagination.

The 10 square Km or so Dzüku Valley of the Japfü mountain range contains some 7 different kinds of Rhododendrons including an uncommon yellow one. One, R. Mcabianum was discovered from Japfü mountain first by Mr. McCabe, the first British Political Assistant at Kohima of erstwhile 'Naga Hills' at the beginning of the 19th Century, and Mr. Johnston, one of the early Surveyors of the British East India Company discovered a red Rhododendron and is named after him as Rhododendron Johnstonianum. The virgin jungles of Porba-Phesachadu mountain range is known as Zanibou, a corrupted form of 'Johny' from the name Johnston who established a Survey Station on the peak of the mountain. The tallest Rhododendron in the world [24.59 meters: 79 ft 11 in], the rare Lily and rare Tragopan Bird are native to the Japfü mountain range.

In the early days of the British rule, natives caught a then unknown bird 'Ngou' from the Burail mountain range and sold it to one Mr. Blythe, a Tea Garden Manager in Cachar. That was the first time the rare Tragopan Pheasant became known to the world and it was given the name Tragopan Blythii.

The relationship between plants and animals: ECOLOGY is very delicate, subtle and important. A mysterious Virus caused 'Colony Collapse Disorder' [CCD] syndrome in the Honey Bee population of North America. This resulted in disastrous impact on the 2.5 billion $ [Rs 75 billion] per year Apricot production – 90 % of the world's of North America. The bee, besides producing honey, pollinates the Apricot plant, one of North America's most important agriculture crops and the decline in the bee population has greatly affected the crop and obviously the honey production.

Phoebe Cooperiana / Phoebe Hainasiana / [Hill Bonsum]; one of the finest Naga Log-drum making tree of Nagaland is vanishing because the Hornbill, the Hill Myna and the Red Belied Himalayan Squirrel are no longer available to swallow and disperse the seed of this magnificently huge and beautiful evergreen tree. The endemic plants in Nagaland like – 'Naga Neem' [Spondias Exilaris], 'Khroge' [Zizyphus Recurva] are not increasing in the jungle as the Deer, the Sambhar, the Royal Pigeon, the Great Himalayan Barbet and Bulbuls that swallow the fruit and disperse the seeds, are hunted down from the forests. Without the wildlife these irreplaceable species that characterize the vegetation of Nagaland would vanish in the plant's one life or in one generation of Nagas.

The above are just a few of the infinite examples of the tremendous importance of ecological relationship between plants and animals. It is only now that man slowly understands the delicate ecological web of nature; we do not anywhere near full understand of nature's ecological balance and hence the great need for conservation of forests, wildlife and the environment.

Conservation of Forest, Wildlife and Environment: Nagaland

The great 'necessary evil' of jhum cultivation in Nagaland, from very ancient times, makes it difficult to have vast virgin jungle in the state. The construction of roads under various development schemes, after the birth of the state, enabled the extraction of timber from hitherto unapproachable forest and earns state revenue but this has contributed to the decrease in forest area of Nagaland.

The typical moist evergreen rain forest of the Namsa-Tizit area, Mon district with its incomparable Dipterocarp and Makai trees, soaring hundreds of feet into the sky majestically with their compact Crown creating a permanent twilight on the ground even in the hot tropical sunshine, have vanished forever from mankind due to lack of vision and inability of the state to preserve it.

The primeval virgin forests of Nagaland in Minkong [Mokokchung District], Helipong [Tuensang District], and Mount Tui [Wokha District] have all vanished and those in Satoi [Zunheboto Distirct] and Zanibou [Phek District] are in the process of vanishing. There are now only a few hundred square kilometers of primeval forests left in Saramati and Japfü mountain ranges. These priceless bio-diversity heritages are the only vestiges of the forests 'made with the hand of God' that have escaped destruction due solely to their high elevation and remote location.

One of the most important wealth of the Angami is the biological wealth of its jungle.

10

PROBLEMS OF POLLUTION IN KOHIMA AND DIMAPUR DISTRICTS

Rusovil John

Environmental Pollution means the presence of any solid, liquid or gaseous substance present in such concentration as may be, or tend to be injurious to environment. Environment comprises air, water, and land. Pollute means to destroy the purity or sanctity and pollution means the act of polluting.

Kohima the capital and Dimapur the commercial hub of Nagaland has attracted people from within and outside the state and has been witnessing rapid growth in the recent times. Population is an important resource for development, yet is a major source of environment degradation when it exceeds the threshold limits of the support system. Although technological progress will add to the capabilities for sustaining a larger number of populations, the need for a vigorous drive for population control which has given rise to sanitation problems and water scarcity in Kohima and Dimapur can hardly be overemphasized.

Though pollution as such is much less when compared to many parts of the country, we do have some problems which are:-

Air Pollution

The air quality, particularly in the town of Dimapur has deteriorated to some extent due to human activities such as construction works where the soil is disturbed leading to wind blown dust particles, industrial activities and vehicular pollution. Apart from these, indoor air pollution due to use of wood with poor ventilation is a major air pollution problem.

Air pollution from industries is prevalent in Dimapur where there are a few small-scale industries such as brick kilns, tyre and vulcanizing units, which use coal and wood as their source of energy. These industries emit particulate matter, oxides of sulphur and volatile organic compounds into the air. The location of these industries within the city limits or too close to human habitation is a concern. Besides, brick kilns are also a major factor for land degradation because the top fertile soil is removed for manufacture of bricks. Stone crushers and Sand storage depots along roadside and residential areas in Dimapur are responsible for dust pollution.

Burning of waste so as to reduce the quantity and for aesthetic purpose not only causes air pollution but also emit dioxins; when it contains plastic wastes, and can cause cancer.

Motor vehicles are major sources of air pollution in Kohima and Dimapur. Rapid growth of vehicle population, poor quality of fuel and bad road conditions has resulted in high levels of air pollutants. During the dry weather, buildings near the roads become covered with dust raised by plying vehicles over dusty roads. The number of registered vehicles in 2003 stands at 193,261 in Nagaland. Kohima and Dimapur being the major towns, have the maximum concentration of vehicles.

The NPCB has been monitoring the ambient air quality of Dimapur since 2002. Parameters like the SPM (Suspended Particulate Matter – size 10 microns and above), RSPM (Respirable Suspended Particulate Matter – size less than 10 microns), SOx (Sulphur dioxide) and NOx (oxides of nitrogen) are monitored. The air quality over the years has shown that pollution level increases during the winter months as compared to the monsoon period. This is due to the fact that during the monsoon period, the rain dilutes the pollutants whereas in the winter season due to dry conditions pollution level increases.

Noise Pollution

The sources of noise pollution in Kohima and Dimapur are the use of DG sets to supplement the power shortage. Some DG sets not only cause air pollution but also gives rise to noise pollution. The maximum permissible sound pressure level for new DG sets with rated capacity up to 1000 KVA, manufactured on or after the 1st January 2005 shall be 75 db(A) at 1 meter from the enclosure.

New DG sets nowadays conform to the specifications. However, there are still many old DG sets in use, which neither conform to the noise limits nor are provided with acoustic enclosures thereby creates nuisance in the neighborhood.

Water Pollution

Water is crucial for the survival of all living organisms. In terms of quality, the surface water of the state is unprotected from untreated industrial effluents and wastewater, runoff pollution from chemical fertilizers and pesticides. Water quality also depends on effluent types and discharge quantity from different type of industries, types of agrochemicals used in agriculture, and seasonal water flow and dilution capability of the river system.

Municipal Wastewater

Nagaland has no sewage system as yet. Lack of sanitation facilities in the rural areas and lack of urban sewage system and wastewater treatment facilities, unplanned silting and inadequate latrine system within the town limits and along the roads/ highway also leaves much to be desired. A major program for provision of sewage is needed to arrest the increasing pollution of water bodies.

Another source of concern is the lack of scientific slaughterhouses in Kohima and Dimapur, which not only gives rise to problem of solid waste but also pollutes the water.

Agrochemical

The main sources of agricultural runoff pollution are from the use of fertilizers and agrochemicals. During 2000-2001, 975 tons of Fertilizers and 800 tons of Solid Pesticides, 600 litres of Liquid Pesticides had been consumed in Nagaland. The use of pesticides in our wet paddy fields needs special attention, because of the fact that fishes, snails and small water creatures serve as delicacies and may get into the food chain.

Industrial Effluent

There are no major industries in Kohima and Dimapur. No industrial units have effluent treatment plant, except the mini effluent treatment plant located at the Dairy Plant of DIMUL in Dimapur. All the other industries either discharge their effluents directly into nearby stream / river or into the public drains.

Municipal Waste

The rapid growths of population in Kohima and Dimapur towns with inadequate facilities have given rise to municipal waste littered all over the towns. It is estimated that at present Kohima is generating about 35 tonnes of waste per day out of which only about 10 tonnes is cleared and in Dimapur it is estimated that about 80 tonnes of wastes are generated per day out of which only 40-45% of the wastes are cleared.

Management of waste especially discarded polythene bags leaves much to be desired. Use of polythene carry bags has caused environmental problems, as it is non-biodegradable. These bags are disposed carelessly, thus choking drains and destroying the landscape.

There is no serious effort by the resident to segregate waste at source and also the local bodies responsible for management of solid waste towards systematic recycling of waste, except by the scavengers / rag pickers who extract recyclable material from the waste bins.

Another source of concern is the rearing of domestic animals such as pigs and poultry within the town limits emitting foul smell. The waste from these sources are often directly discharged into the public drains and ultimately polluting our streams and rivers. Discharging of septic tanks directly to the drains is very common in Kohima. Civic sense has to be inculcated in us if we want our villages and towns to be clean.

Biomedical Waste

Medical waste is hazardous. Management of hospital waste has not yet received due attention in our state. No specific guidelines and parameters are followed. There are 465 government healthcare facilities, about 100 private establishments and several military hospitals in Nagaland.

For treating biomedical waste, there are only four incinerators in Nagaland. Two incinerators of 50 kg/hr capacity installed at the Rangapahar and Jakhama Military Hospitals. Two other incinerators of 2.5 kg/hr capacity at the Kohima and Dimapur Civil hospitals. As for the other health-care facilities, they lack proper disposal system and are either burnt or mixed with the domestic waste. The unscientific disposal of biomedical waste creates adverse effect on the ecosystem and the human health. Therefore, the Health Care

Facilities should follow the Bio-Medical Waste Management Rules for effective management of medical waste like storage, segregation, transfer, treatment and disposal.

Conclusion

Land holding system in Nagaland is such that town and city planning or location of industries becomes dependent on landowners. Encroachment into roads and public drains causes traffic congestions, clogging of drains and flash floods.

Our personal habits such as spitting and blowing of nose are done in a very casual manner. In many rural areas open latrines are common even today. Our system of burying the death in the residential areas may affect the ground water sources.

With modernization many of our homes have become comparable to those of the Europeans in terms of luxury and cleanliness. However, as we step out of our homes we are confronted with heaps of unattended waste dumped by us into the streets. This attitude of "Not in my compound is OK" has to change.

The problem of pollution can best be mitigated not by rules but by creating awareness and concern among the people. Nagas are accustomed to organizing cleanliness drives and we often come across communities cleaning their villages and towns; which is rare in other parts of the country. With such good qualities in us we can definitely change our attitude and improve our environment.

Section V: Issues on Health

11

HEALTH STATUS OF THE ANGAMIS

Sedevi Angami

Health is a state of physical, emotional, social and spiritual wellbeing and not just the absence of disease.

This is akin to the definition given to peace – in the Hebrew; it is quoted as Shalom which refers to peace, wholeness, completeness, right relationship. It is therefore not just the absence of war that defines peace.

A healthy society therefore would mean a society that is not only free from disease (which is a human impossibility as long as we exist on earth) but also one that cares for the weak in their midst, the underprivileged and oppressed, and the foreigners in our land who are voiceless and abused. A healthy society is one that is progressive, supportive of new ideas and has high moral values and ethics.

Physical wellbeing does not occur in isolation. Injustice leads to political turmoil which can lead to genocide and famine resulting in diseases like malnutrition, cholera, overcrowding and TB, post traumatic stress disorder etc.

Factional fighting leads to orphans who are predisposed to delinquency, drug abuse and HIV/AIDS or drug resistant TB in the overcrowded jails. When these people are released from jail, they spread the deadly TB around the community and we in the hospitals try to help them with medicines. Prescribing a medicine for a patient is of no use if he cannot afford to buy them because he has no money as a result of his cows dying of disease because they were not vaccinated on time due to ignorance or the lack of communication from the veterinary department to his village because bad roads demotivated the staff from coming there. This pushed him into the money lender's hands and severe debt. Alcoholic liver disease is a direct consequence of a social illness. Medicines are used to treat symptoms of a much deeper problem in society.

An approach to health therefore must take into consideration the wider ramifications of the causes behind the disease and address them in order to meaningfully have an impact on the incidence of the disease.

Angamis are predisposed to most diseases like any other population in the world. Angamis also live in a very heterogeneous society physically, exposed to the same media and political influence. There are a few illnesses which are more common in Angamis due to their lifestyle habits like hypertension due to excess salt intake. However by and large, we have a similar predisposition to disease as the wider Naga family. I will therefore address the medical problems of Nagas (in Nagaland) in general and suggest some practical measures which I feel if taken seriously will certainly make a change in the way disease patterns are impacted in our society.

On a purely technical level, there are many diseases which are peculiar to Nagas.

1. TB hepatitis is a disease seen in Nagas very often and not in the rest of the country.

2. Drug resistant TB has a higher prevalence in Nagaland.
3. Nagas usually do not get symptomatic acute Myocardial infarction or angina. They mostly present with Silent MI, atrial fibrillation and cardiac failure.
4. Hypertension in Nagas is very difficult to control and requires more than one drug in most cases.
5. Renal stones are very common.
6. Stomach cancer in Nagas is possibly related to smoked meat that we eat and they respond very well to chemotherapy.
7. Hypereosinophilia and certain parasitic illnesses are possibly related to the snails and crabs that we eat.

There are a host of other illnesses that are peculiar to Nagas. The list is long. The treatment strategies for these are different from what is mentioned in the text books or currently practiced guidelines and would need to be tailored for the same.

On the other hand, there are problems in the health delivery system which need to be addressed urgently. I will list out the areas and my suggestions as solutions.

Areas to be Considered

1. Research.
2. Vaccination en masse – pulse polio type.
3. PPP – model centers to be tried out.
4. Health in the curriculum.
5. Networking.
6. Planning committee.

7. Churches involvement along with NGOs.
8. Training and development of teams.
9. Medical and nursing council of Nagaland.

Research

We do not have adequate research data into the disease patterns in Nagaland. Therefore we cannot evaluate ourselves about the relevance and success of our health programmes. Without baseline realistic idea of disease patterns and prevalence, we cannot hope to plan out our further activities meaningfully. Neither can we project our health needs in order to get adequate funds to tackle them. There is an urgent need to set up research cells in the state that are run by very highly professional people.

Vaccination

There is very poor vaccination coverage in the state. This is unacceptable considering Nagaland is such a tiny state and the furthest place can easily be reached within a day's time. Epidemics of measles which occur every year in our tiny state is a gross anomaly. This does not occur only in remote places but even well connected villages close by Kohima which are well educated and have good infrastructure and doctors close by. Mass vaccination on a war footing like that of pulse polio if done universally throughout the state can quickly eradicate or control these illnesses. Considering vaccines are so cheap and easily available it should not be difficult to repeat these pulses on a 6 monthly basis.

PPP Model Centres

Today most programmes are run by the government. A large chunk of government doctors do private practice and so earn two salaries. Most doctors in the major cities are full time private practitioners doing a part time government job.

Nurses and other staff of health centres are also often substitutes who fill in for people who have the post but are based elsewhere. Government employees have little support in the peripheries and are frequently transferred and so team building is lacking in most places. We do have some good people in the government who have to do twice the amount of work to fill in for their colleagues. Most of these people are not rewarded for their good work. Negligence and sloth are not punished. There is therefore very little motivation and passion left and a sense of hopelessness wherever you go and talk with people.

Creating more jobs, doing more programmes and spending more money with the same group of people and system is stupidity and can never produce changes that we desire to see. Another definition of madness is to keep doing the same thing and expecting different results.

Diseases like TB and AIDS are not government diseases. Therefore if the state wants to see changes in our health we must have a very robust private – public partnership in the health planning, implementation and evaluation of programmes. This will harness the best of manpower from both areas and will be more effective in carrying out these programmes. To neglect the private sector is to guarantee failure of any programme. Government can lay down rules, provide infrastructure and finance, train and then supervise and ensure that rules are followed by their private partners. We either live and support each other or die together.

One idea could be to hand over a single health centre to a new group consisting of a good NGO, private group, church council, govt. representative and an external expert group. They can run the place autonomously but be provided the required finance by the government based upon a prefixed budget. If this works well, we can try replicating the same model elsewhere. If planned well, there is zero chance of failure and we should see dramatic changes in our health in the next 10 years.

Health in the Curriculum

Health education is the single most cost effective way to bring down disease. Different aspects of disease must be in the curriculum of schools. You cannot import all the information from outside since many diseases are peculiar to our region. We must set up an expert committee of both private and public professionals who can plan and develop a curriculum of the most pressing needs into the school curriculum. This curriculum must be mandatory. If done well, this will greatly reduce a lot of our woes and government spending later in firefighting.

Networking

There must be a comprehensive network of centres both private and public who will work together in fighting disease. This will utilize the best of manpower from both areas. Areas where this can be worked out are in carrying out programmes, sharing of information, resources and manpower, planning and evaluation, research and financial help.

Planning Committee

In order to own a programme of its own, the person or party being inducted must be a part of the planning. Hand me downs are an insult to the professional party involved. Today most committees in the district are headed by the DC. This is foolishness. The health committees in the district should be headed by the most capable person professionally and the DC and other government functionaries should be there to assist in the implementation in whatever capacity they have. If the planning is defective, a programme is doomed to failure. There must be a comprehensive 5 year plan made by representative of all sections of society if we are to see any palpable change soon. This planning must be professionally robust and objective based upon hardcore evidence and evaluation of past performances.

As soon as a chief minister comes into office, the first thing he should do would be to select a panel of highly professional, objective and credible group of experts to help him plan. This would greatly help him in his future political career and change the entire state. A king is only as good as his advisors.

This supreme planning committee consisting of both the public and private partners can decide on the drug policies of the state, appropriate technology, distribution of manpower, pricing etc.

Churches Involvement

Nagaland is considered a Christian state. We have a unique situation where the potential of the church can be utilized. If brought into confidence, most churches are quite willing to be part of change. We need to design a very practical roadmap for the churches involvement in various health programmes of the state.

Training and Development of Teams

Nagaland is a tiny state. There are many health centres in the state which are manned by various personnel. Unfortunately they function in isolation, getting little support from Kohima. Most of the times, they get near expiry drugs of poor quality and inappropriate for the situation. Posting people by mass transfers cannot create motivation. Punishing a person by the rules or vigilantism cannot get health personnel to do better work. Financial incentive cannot do this either. The only answer is to develop teams of people who are committed to each other with a common vision and well supported by the government or a good organization. People who work in the peripheries (defined by the planning committee) voluntarily should be paid double their urban counterparts and their children should have a special privilege in various top schools, stipends or other government jobs. The best cars and accommodation should be given to them instead of giving these to the people in Kohima or Dimapur. Ill motivated people should not be sent to peripheries because anyway they will not stay there properly and is neither going to produce quality work.

Medical and Nursing Council

Today we do not have our own professional councils. Our doctors and nurses have to go to Guwahati to get their respective registrations under much inconvenience and often having to pay bribes to get the job done. If we can get our own council started, we can bypass a lot of these hurdles. The Council can set the rules for the state health personnel – its code of conduct, ethics, and academic standards, help set up health institutions, issue registrations etc. The Medical council can supervise the workings of the health institutions of the state both private and public so that we meet certain standards.

This council must consist of representatives from both the Government and private sectors and be headed by the most qualified professional.

I have put forward certain suggestions which I know are absolutely practical and can make dramatic changes in the health of our state in the next 10 years if we can adopt some of them. I have based these principles on Biblical foundations since these are the most practical of all time tested principles regardless of culture or region. It will require a bold and necessary decision and the willingness to change and try out something new. Continue the way we are and we are guaranteed doom and failure in the health of our state.

Section VI: Old Age and Gender Issues

12

THE PROBLEM OF THE ANGAMI AGED

Ketshukietuo Dzüvichü

[Notwithstanding the differences in the criteria of defining old age, there has been a great transformation in the structure of society and the paper here makes an attempt to examine the socio-economic and health problems of the aged among the Angami Nagas. A study of the social status of the aged involves, among others, an analysis of their age and marital status, educational level, living arrangement and occupation. The study reveals that the Angami aged still enjoy higher status in the society. On the economic status, self sufficiency in terms of food availability which is the top priority in an Angami society is prominent but in terms of income, most of them are in the lower income group.

The study on the health problems of the Angami aged of Nagaland reveals that majority of the aged suffer from one or a combination of ailments but many of them either regard themselves to be in excellent condition or are indifferent to their health or consider it as common in old age. Despite of all ailments and handicaps, the medical facilities available for the aged are inadequate and many aged are compelled to seek help from private practitioners inspite of their poor economic status.]

Human life is divided into different stages such as childhood, adolescence, adulthood, and old age. To age is universal and it is accepted as an inevitable and irreversible process. The process of getting old varies considerably within and between cultures. Getting old is the result of the interplay of biological, social, and psychological factors. In this phase majority of the people face economic, social, psychological, and health problems.

"Old age" and "the elderly" are terms used in both popular usage and academic circles. Despite the frequency with which the terms are used the definition of exactly what is "old age" is problematic because, determination of the old age differs from society to society. We can identify four main approaches to the definition of old age. These are biological age approach, chronological age approach, the political economy approach and old age as a stage in the life cycle.

To elaborate these approaches a little further, biologists refer to aging as "senescence", which is used to describe decreases in the efficient functioning of an organism with age. Strehler (1962) considers aging as the change that occurs in the post-reproductive phase of life, resulting in decrease in the survival capacity of an organism.

Chronological age is first of all mediated by culture. Hence, the age at which old age begins in a person varies from culture to culture. Secondly, the chronological age is intervened by the state, which decides the age at which an individual becomes eligible to receive certain benefits, a pension, or is excluded from participation in the labour market.

Political economy may be defined as a study of the interaction between government, economy, and various socially defined groups. This approach assumes a structural relationship between the elderly and rest of the society, with society constructing the institutions and rules within which the old age is defined. From this perspective, the elderly persons are not seen as a group separate from the wider social context, but as an integral part of society. This approach relates the social and economic status of the elderly to the institutions of society, which are either partly, or entirely, organised around the concept of production. Another approach to the definition of old age is the concept of the life cycle. This is usually conceptualised as an orderly progression from infancy to old age with biological and socio-cultural factors interacting to govern the sequence of progression.

In the Angami society, a person who has become physically dependent or is incapable of doing heavy works due to deteriorating health and age is considered as an old man (*ketsamia*).

Whatever be the definition of old age the term usually implies (implicitly or explicitly) some notion of decline and deterioration in health, vitality, social usefulness and independence (Victor 1987).

Notwithstanding the differences in the criteria of determining old age, there has been a great transformation in the structure of society. Such a shift in the structure of society, which has resulted in the replacement of multi-generation families with two generation units, has also had negative effect on the role of old people many of whom have lost their social security in the family. Gradually most of them have been relegated to the fringes of society where they live in isolation, as unwanted elements, and this is to some extent true in all industrial societies (Kumar 1991).

Social scientists in order to know more about social aging have primarily focused their attention on socio-cultural background of the aged like family, kinship interaction, kinship obligation, mutual love and affection, and the like. Studies on demographic change like family size, fertility, mortality, longevity and late marriage also help to make an analytical framework on social gerontology.

In simple societies, security of members of the family and clan was very important for which the elders assisted by the young were responsible. Thus wisdom of the elders and physical strength of the young combined to guide and continue the family and the clan. The older members in the family were looked after in their old age and also provided nursing and care. This was considered as the moral and social responsibility of the members of the family, an expression of gratitude of the younger generation to their elders for what they had done for them in bearing, rearing, educating, training and protecting them. The care of the aged also arose out of the fact that they had, through their hard work and thrift, created assets, property and other means of production leading to employment and income generation for the younger generation to survive.

Till about half a century ago India had a strong tradition of younger generation respecting their parents, and grandparents. For a variety of factors - social, cultural and economic- the old people were generally respected in society. Old age was considered as one of the stages of human development wherein a person attained wisdom, maturity, social and economic stability, social recognition and emotional fulfillment, leading to the last phase of life which is considered to be of spiritual salvation. In traditional India , society generally showed great respect and consideration for the aged. They were revered as depositories of wisdom and traditions and were not perceived as problems. They occupied positions of prestige, power, and privileges. They also played a significant part in the socialisation of children. The conventional belief, as Pillai (1986) has observed, was that the higher the person's age the greater would be his or her knowledge or wisdom.

But today, this phenomenon is gradually being weakened by forces of urbanisation, industrialisation, modernisation, growing individualism, etc. The present Indian society, its social structure and values are undergoing a transformation. The ultimate responsibility for supporting the aged is gradually shifting from the family to the state. Despite the fact that institutionalization of old people is looked down upon, a slow beginning has been made in recent years by the government which has started old age pension schemes and institutions for the old and the infirm. Inspite of that, the needs of the aged are not met adequately by their families or by the state.

Advances in medical and nutrition sciences have contributed to increased longevity, and we are faced with an increasing aged population. The life expectancy at birth and at different age levels has increased. In India, this is likely to increase further with rapid expansion of the application of medicine and immunisation. This may result in further increase in number of the aged in India. The number of persons aged 60 years and above in India was 24 million in 1961. It has increased to 32.6 million in 1971 and 43.1 million in 1981. As per 1991 Census, aged population in India was 56,681,640 persons, which shows an increase of 5.6% in 1961 to 6.7% in 1991.

The 1991 Census shows that 25.7% of the people in the country live in urban areas. The remaining 74.3% live in the rural areas. About 78.1% of the aged people in India live in villages and 21.9% of the aged live in towns/cities. The resulting problems posed by the increasing number of the aged have to be faced by all, sooner or later.

India's considerably low per capita income testifies to the stark reality of poverty conditions in rural as well as urban areas where poor people are living in hutment or on pavements. Meager income does not permit the young to fulfill minimum requirements of the dependent aged. Apart from this, migration of the young men and women to cities in search of jobs is a loss of social and economic security of the aged in rural areas.

Since the aged population is mostly concentrated in rural areas (Nair 1980) more emphasis is desirable on the study of the problems of the aged in such areas. An increasing number of the aged, in addition to other dependant groups, is likely to give rise, sooner or later, to new social and economic problems arising out of unemployment, poverty, disintegration or economic instability of the family.

Thus the need for understanding the various problems associated with the aged cannot be over-emphasized. These problems are already there and have to be dealt with. There is a great need for initiating studies in this field, as sufficient data are not yet available for a proper understanding and assessment of the problem. The present study on the aged is a humble attempt to fill up this gap.

There is no work known to the present researcher on the gerontology of the Nagas about whom the only mention is made by Hutton (1963) who says that among the Angamis an elderly man is considered to be well informed. All the religious ceremonies are observed according to the direction of an old man. In any kind of disputes, the decision of an old man is regarded as a matter of custom and is more or less final.

Area of Study

The Angami Nagas, one of the major tribes of Nagaland, live in the southern part of Nagaland, i.e., Kohima District. The total area of the district, according to 1991 census, is 4041 square kilometres. The district is bounded by Zunheboto and Phek districts on the east, Assam on the west, Wokha on the north and Manipur on the south. Their territory is administratively divided into four regions:

1) Northern Angami

2) Southern Angami

3) Western Angami

4) Chakhro Angami

According to the 1991 Census, it has a population of 387,581 persons, and an aged population (60+) of 14,138. The present study is concentrated on 4 villages, selecting the nearest villages located in all the four directions from the Kohima Town, the State Capital of Nagaland, which are Kohima village, Phesama village, Jotsoma village and Piphema village.

Methodology

The universe of the present study is the aged population (60+) among the Angami Nagas, living in the Kohima District of Nagaland. The data have been collected from four villages in Kohima District. The aged population in this district is found to be 3.6% of the total population. So the total sample size is 380, which is 3.6% of the total population of the four villages. By using the multi- stage sampling design, first the Angami region has been classified (stratified) into four categories (each region forming a stratum). Then the nearest village from Kohima town in each of the four Angami regions in four directions has been selected. As for the aged population they have been stratified into four strata—Literate Male, Illiterate Male, Literate Female and Illiterate Female. Out of the total sample size 280 respondents are from Kohima village, 44 from Phesama village, 42 from Jotsoma Village and 14 from Piphema Village, making use of such device as stratification and sampling with "probability proportionate to size". The sampling units are then further selected by applying systematic sampling, selecting every k^{th} aged on the list for each village.

Social Problems of the Aged

With the progress of life towards the old age, an individual's mental and physical capacity to perform certain roles gradually gets declined, and when he retires from bread-winning stage he has to experience several socio-economic and psychological problems within the family and society. In an industrialised society, according to Rekha Dutt (1986), the knowledge, experience and skills of the older people do no longer relate to the present. The importance of their functional position thus declines, and consequently their authority and much of the respect and prestige they enjoyed earlier gets faded. This change brings frustration and anxieties to older people.

In our traditional social system, old age was generally considered wisdom personified; the fruit of a well spent life and often commanded unquestionable power, authority and respect. Looking after the old was taken for granted. The aged could disengage themselves from life and yet retain their position of respect. An attitude of reverence towards the aged was considered a virtue and nothing important could take place in the family without the sanction and blessing of the old.

In modern society, old age is no more what it once used to be but a period entered with reluctance and trepidation and crossed with countless hurdles. A multiplicity of factors contributes to the changing status of the aged in society. In a competitive society where usefulness is measured by economic yardstick, the aged is sometimes considered useless. The rapidity in technological advancement and its accompanying social and cultural change bewilders an aged person's attempts to grapple with it. As a result, old people are today faced with a number of social, economic and psychological problems, which need to be understood in order to devise any comprehensive programme for the welfare of the aged.

The study on the Angami aged shows that most aged people enjoy married life and there are more married men than women and more widows than widowers. At the same time, there are more unmarried women than such men. Education is an important determinant of a person's social status. In an Angami society, illiteracy is more pronounced among the aged women than among such men. But among the literate respondents, formal education is more significant among the women than men. None of the aged women has gone for technical education. Most aged respondents have received education from primary to high school level and only a few of them have studied upto graduation or post graduation.

In a nuclear family, birth of a son is a security of the aged people and perhaps because of this most of the Angami aged respondents' stay with their married sons. It is interesting to know that all the aged respondents live in houses owned by themselves. Some of them are staying with their spouses and their children. Of those who are staying with their children in the same household, majority are still the chief bread earners of the families.

About half of the aged people are chief bread earners of their families. One-fifth of the aged respondents are wholly dependent upon others and the rest are partially dependent. Dependency among the women is more pronounced than among the men due to lack of education or employment. Thus, the burden of the aged women in supporting their children is higher than that of aged men.

Some of the aged Angamis are compelled to stay with their in-laws, because they do not have any son or all their daughters are married. Of those who are staying with their in-laws, they are either partially or wholly dependent. But in all other cases, whether the aged are staying alone or with spouses or with children, the aged are by and large the chief bread earners of the family.

Most of the Angami aged respondents are cultivators and they continue with their daily works to maintain their families. Aged respondents doing business is negligible. Only a few of the aged people are retired government servants. Many of them are involved in social and church activities.

Economic position is an important determinant of social status. The study reveals that most of the aged have income of their own. But half of the aged having income of their own fall under the category of lower income group. Thus, though they have income of their own, it is not sufficient to manage their families by that alone. It is significant that about half of the aged draw their income from selling of farm products, and property/house rent and a few from government pensions and old age assistance. Income from salary and wages and interest on saving is very meagre. The study reveals that with increasing age, the earning capacity decreases and the aged people become dependent on their children.

Looking at the economic status of the families in which the aged people in Angami society live, it appears that most of such families are in the lower income group. At the same time, the families in the lower income group have more dependents than in the higher income groups. Thus, as far as income is concerned their economic status is low and also they have more family members to look after.

An analysis of the assets and liabilities of the aged shows that most aged Angamis fail to fulfil their major responsibilities connected with the education and marriage of their children. The aged respondents in the lower income group have in particular more liabilities than the aged people in the middle or upper income groups. In terms of assets, all the aged respondents have a house of their own. 41.57 percent of the aged have two or three houses and most of them fall in the category of middle and upper income groups. The Angami aged are found to be self-sufficient because the study reveals that 72.89 percent of the aged have two or more than two rice bunds, which is enough fcr an average family to survive for one year.

Thus, the aged Angamis in the lower income group have less source income but more liabilities, which make them both poorer and dependent than the Angamis belonging to the other income groups. Though maximum of the aged are in the lower income group, all the aged have enough irrigated or non-irrigated land at their disposal, where they can cultivate rice, vegetables etc. and supplement their income. Self-sufficiency, which is the top priority of the Angamis, is found quite common among of the aged.

Human organs gradually diminish in function over time, although not at the same rate in every individual. By itself, this gradual diminution of function is not a real threat to the health of most old people unless they fall prey to some disease. Diseases are the chief barriers to extended health and longevity. And when they accompany normal changes associated with biological aging, maintaining health and securing appropriate health care becomes especially problematic for older people.

Health in simplest term is defined as the absence of disease or illness. Health is not only a biological or medical concern, but also a significant personal and social concern. In general, with declining health, individuals can lose their independence, lose social roles, become isolated, experience economic hardship, be labeled or stigmatised, change their self-perception, and some of them may even be institutionalised.

According to Phelps and Henderson (1952:217), "old age is a natural and normal condition... Its pathologies are the same as those that occur at any other age period, but they are intensified by illness, family disorganisation, unemployability, reduced income and dependency." Of all the problems of old age, the problem of health is a major problem because it is accentuated by an "increasing number of physical handicaps, more frequent and serious illness, more mental disturbances and a general reaction among the aged that ill health is their major problem."(ibid: 225).

Health status of the aged people varies individually. In this regard De Souza (1982) describes four factors which determine the health status of the aged: (i) the nature and condition of their hard work combined with poor nutrition leads to the state of general disability and most of the aged suffer from what may be called 'deficiency' illness; (ii) environmental conditions such as poor sanitation, lack of basic amenities such as water and proper drainage system tend to make the environment itself a health hazard; (iii) inadequate and unbalanced diet; and (iv) the availability and quality of health services.

In terms of health status, difference between the sexes are clear and women have higher rates of morbidity, though, in fact it has long been observed that 'women are sicker but men die sooner' (Wan 1982).

The aged respondents are normal people. They may also become ill like others. Old age in itself is not a disease. It is normal and natural condition. Every living organism has weaknesses and disabilities. Among human beings too, the pathologies of old age are the same that occur at any other age except that they are intensified with advancement in age. The aged people are likely to suffer a number of physical ailments and handicaps, and more frequent serious illness. Chronic and degenerative diseases and physical immobility are some major causes of dependency among the aged.

The present study has revealed that majority of the aged people suffer from one or a combination of ailments. Many of them either regard themselves to be in excellent condition or are indifferent to their health despite their suffering from illness. When asked about their physical ailments or handicaps common in old age was reported by many but they often considered such problems to be natural. A majority of the aged respondents were found indifferent to their health because their illness had not disturbed them sufficiently or no medical facilities were available nearby or because of lack of money to consult doctors and undergo treatment.

Most of the aged complained about frequent headache, backache and joint pain but they consider it as common in old age and consulting a doctor is not necessary. Only few have consulted doctors for treatment. Because of such notions of the aged, their health problems are likely to be further complicated, although they are also equally likely to develop immunity from many ailments. Women respondents complaining about physical ailments were more in number than the men respondents.

Most of the aged respondents have only some of their natural teeth intact. But this does not seem to bother them much. Since they have become old, falling of teeth is seen as something natural and denture is not considered necessary, which is a misconception among the aged. The aged with complaints of tuberculosis, cancer and blood pressure were very few. All of them consulted doctors and received periodical medical assistance.

Physical disabilities are some of the problems that prevent the aged from attending to their daily chores and put them in isolation. Among the physical disabilities hard of hearing and impaired eyesight are the common complaints among the aged but this do not seem to bother them much since they can continue with their daily chores without using hearing aids or spectacles.

It is encouraging to note that in spite of their physical ailments and disabilities, most aged respondents could move about freely as they liked and did not require any personal attendance. At the same time, they continued with their daily chores.

Though the health status of the aged in general is quite satisfactory, the present medical facilities are far inadequate if the aged people start visiting the government hospitals and dispensaries. Most of the aged people seek medical aid from government hospitals and primary health centres where the facilities are always inadequate. Some of course can afford to seek help from private practitioners.

Thus there are three major health needs of the aged. One, the concept of illness as 'common in old age' should be removed from their mind and for any type of ailment or handicaps, proper medical treatment should be given to them. Secondly, medical facilities in government hospitals and primary health centres should be improved. Thirdly, geriatric units should be set up to let the aged people get easy access to the medical facilities.

REFERENCES

1. Becker, Charles S. (1959). *Towards Better Understanding of the Aging.* Council on Social Work Education, New York.
2. Bhatia, H.S. (1983). *Aging and Societies.* Udaipur: Arya's Book Centre.
3. Birren, J. and V. Clayton. (1975). *History of Gerentology.* New York: D. Van Nostrand Co.
4. Bond, Floyd A., et al. *Our Needy Aged: A California Study of the National Problem.* New York: Henry Holt and Co.
5. Census of India. (1991). *Ageing Population of India.* An analysis of the 1991 census. New Delhi: Registrar General of Census Operation.
6. Channa, S.M. (1992). *Nagaland - A Contemporary Ethnography.* New Delhi: Cosmo Publications.
7. De Souza, Alfred (1982). *The Social Organisation of Aging Among the Urban Poor.* Indian Social Institute, New Delhi.

8. Dutt, R. (1986). *Social Institution in India*. Bombay: Tata Instutute of Social Sciences.

9. Hasan, S.Z. (1960). Report of the Survey of the Incidence of Blindness and Prospects of Employment of the Blind in the City of Lucknow. J.K. Institute Monograph No.8. J.K. Institute of Sociology and Human Relations, Lucknow.

10. Hurlock, J. (1983). *Problems of Aging*. California: Dickenson Publishing Company.

11. Hutton, J.H. (1963). *The Angami Nagas*. Bombay: Oxford University Press.

12. Phelps, Herald A. and D. Henderson (1952). *Contemporary Social Problems*. Prentice Hall Inc., New York.

13. Shanas, E and W. Dorothy, eds. (1968). *Old People in Three Industrial Societies*. Routledge & Kegan Paul, London.

14. Wan, Thomas H.(1982). *Stressful Life Events, Social Support Network and Gerontological Health*. Lexington Books, Lexington.

13

VILLAGE DEVELOPMENT BOARD (VDB) AND THE ROLE OF ANGAMI WOMEN

Visakhonü Hibo

[The concept of 'Village Development Board' is a very unique experience ever introduced throughout the State of Nagaland. In its essence, it means giving power to the people to plan development schemes for themselves, which is commonly called grass-root planning. This is in clear contrast with central planning that the country after Independence has been following initially. After several decades it was found that centralised planning was not really in touch with the grass-root level of society and their reality. In fact, many plans have been responsible only in widening the gap between the rich and the poor. Therefore an experiment was made even in Nagaland called the 'Village Development Board'.]

Origin of VDB

The spirit of socialism had a strong base in the state of Maharashtra and Gujarat in the early days of the post Independent India. It was, therefore, the idea of those idealistic socialist leaders who propagated the need to share the wealth of the state equally between the rich and the poor. In order to achieve this, some fundamental grass-root planning which resembled the existing VDB type of schemes were tried out in other parts of the country. The experiment could not succeed because the recipient villagers were too thinly spread out and not cohesive and compact, as it is in Nagaland. It is for these reasons that this brilliant idea failed to strike root both in Maharashtra and Gujarat too. However, a significant turn was felt in Nagaland when Shri A.M. Gokhale, an I.A.S. Officer, was posted to Phek District as its Deputy Commissioner. Being the son of the famous socialist Leader S.M. Gokhale, he began to toy with the idea of introducing the failed experiment of Maharashtra and Gujarat in Phek District of Nagaland. He was positive that the idea of a village developing its own needs and requirements will surely prove to be effective. He was also encouraged by the close social setting of the people within a compact ecological spread. He also studied as to why the generous funds that were been doled out to the state were not percolating down to the villages in particular. He realised the representatives of the people could only make faint noises in the newspapers, that also rarely, but it was to no effect too. He also noticed that elections come and go but nothing happens much for the good of the people in spite of many rich developmental promises.

In this context, Shri A.M. Gokhale realised the crux of the problem and tried to devise a system in such a way that various funds being allotted will go directly to the people to be planned and utilised according to the local needs. This also disallows the funds meant for the villagers to be exercised by high government officials at their own discretion. This was how V.D.B. took its root in Nagaland. He also formulated a model draft and a model rule which was circulated to a select group of officers to draw useful critical appraisal on the basis of which he could finally distil the idea and after securing the approval of the state cabinet, the VDB took its foundation.

Phek District was the first test pilot area for VDB in action. It actually started at Ketsapomi Village in October, 1976. After a little over one year of implementing the VDB schemes throughout Phek District, it showed phenomenal positive results. VDB scheme became an instant success which prompted the State government to adopt the VDB throughout the State of Nagaland. In gradual progression, according to positive results shown, VDB allocation of fund per household was raised from Rs.100/- to Rs. 200/- to Rs. 750/- to Rs. 800/-, out of which 25% is earmarked for women activities and 20% is earmarked for youth activities. There are 1086 number of VDBs existing in Nagaland. The topic of VDB, of late, is not a very open subject as there have been cases of misappropriation, infiltration of party politics and bureaucratic influence within the VDB and its functionaries. Despite these drawbacks, the VDB concept is still recognised to be the main democratic process of grass-root planning.

There are two main sources of funds for the VDBs: i) Matching grant schemes: the government's contribution to the villagers common fund is equal to the amount of the common fund raised by the villages which are invested for a minimum of 5 years in fixed deposit accounts in the banks followed by continuous re-investments. ii) Grant-in-aid: The department of rural development in Nagaland allots part of the state Government's annual plan fund village-wise instead of sector-wise allotment as is the common practice in other states of India. This ensure recurring source of funds to the villages. iii) The VDBs source of income is also through centrally sponsored funds for Integrated Rural Development Programme (IRDP), State Rural Development Agency (SRDA), also implements IRDP and allied programmes. The VDBs are recognised as its field agencies and subsidy amount is directly released for the same. Consequently rural development department also includes schemes for the weaker sex.

Women's Schemes

In 1984-85, 25% of the grant-in-aid was decided to earmark for women development programmes, and thus far, that same percentage of VDBs incoming funds are reserved for women. Population wise, women are no lesser in numerical strength but the socio-structural pattern with all the age-old practices of the patriarchal system stands in the way of involving women at any decision-making bodies even at the grass-root level.

Field Study

To study the VDB and the role of Angami women, five villages from Southern Angami area were chosen to be the universe of the research. The villages chosen were namely Khuzama, Viswema, Jakhama, Kigwema and Phesama. These highway villages were chosen because they represent villages which are supposed to be on the verge of undergoing the process of social change towards modernisation. Both observation and interview method were employed for the purpose of data collection. Data collection involved both the genders. Some past and present VDB functionaries were interviewed which included both men and women, but more emphasis was given to the female respondents. Other village members were also interviewed using the technique of simple random sampling where the persons met at the place of study, irrespective of gender or qualification, were informally interviewed.

It was found out that all the villages studied had one woman representative to the mainstream VDB but plays no active role in it. At best she is called for attending meetings at times and asked to give her signature for official related papers. If not for that the planning and management of VDB funds are managed separately. The mainstream VDB secretary gets Rs.1000/- as remuneration whereas the women VDB secretary gets no remuneration. She acts, in most villages, as the go-between, between the women society and the mainstream VDB. The study also showed that most of the women VDB funds are planned and managed by the Women Society of the village. The women folks are utilising their 25% funds for managing projects like rice mills, weaving units and building community houses after community houses, with not much idea and scope to invest in other areas. Most of them when asked about their future plans in managing the VDB funds said they will build more buildings. Infact, many of them had already expanded their building projects to towns like Kohima. There are no plans involving the socio-economic upliftment of the individual woman. Infact, all the respondents answered negatively when asked whether any plans are included to lift up the status and welfare of the individual poor woman. Such plans are yet to be included in the horizon of women VDBs at the grass-root level.

The findings of the field- work turn out be quite revealing of the status of Angami women both at the traditional and the modern institutions. The Angamis followed the patriarchal system, from time immemorial, therefore the traditional socio-economic structures firmly followed likewise too. The VDB concept suited the structural and the functional aspect of the clustered villagers. But there was no adequate provision laid to unconditionally include the women folks even in a modern governmental institution such as the VDB. This simple step which has not been included at the initial stages of the VDB is now responsible for creating a huge gap leading to irreparable gender divide at the grass-root levels. The ability to voice out concerns and suggestions at the mainstream VDB by the women is negligible. It was seen only in one instance where an educated woman VDB representative could freely plan and give her suggestions sitting among the other male members. When asked whether developmental works can be done together with the men folks, who will also prevent slicing of the developmental funds into piece-meal manner, most of the women respondents, including the women VDB secretaries were reluctant to the idea. They expressed their view that if they are to be clubbed together with the mainstream VDB in the present situation, they are apprehensive that they may get deleted completely instead of taking part in the planning and development of the village. At the same time, they feel that they are also capable of involving actively in the development processes even at the mainstream VDB. Some even suggested that the men folks are not planning and using the funds wisely and judiciously. This expression was augmented by the fact that the study also revealed that there were more misappropriations of funds and misunderstandings among the mainstream VDB which is operated by men as compared to the women's 25% fund management. The records of the women VDBs were also more meticulously maintained as compared to the mainstream VDB.

Case Study: *Decision-making and the Angami Women*

If VDB is the essence of decentralisation of democracy then decision-making bodies must also exude the principle in its totality. The status of women is directly linked to the level of participation at the bodies that are involved in decision-making. At the grass-root level, the VDBs are also one such important body. But what had been found after going to the field is a contradiction of the very meaning of the origin of VBD: the idea of grass-root planning and execution of developmental works in the villages. There are no villages comprising of only man so it automatically included women too. However, in most of the Angami villages where data collection was done, there was no connection between the mainstream VDB and the general women even though a solitary woman representative was included as one of its members. In the villages studied, a woman representative known as the VDB Secretary functions with other women members separately from the mainstream VDB. They at best get their share of money and operate separately from the main stream VDB. This raises a question as to whether co-existence in decision making is a possibility or not? In this context; a case study of the 'decision-making pattern' of two groups at Viswema village was, thus, conducted to observe as to whether joint decision-making in Angami villages was really an impossible thing or not. Therefore, to reach a comparative gender analysis in this regard, 'Khezü whemi' and 'Zakroho whemi' were compared in relation to the decision-making pattern.

Whemi

'O-whemi' or peer groups are usually found among Angami villages. These peer groups comprises of both the genders and is usually formed among neighbourhood age-groups. The groups are also an important means of socialization. They help each other in times of need; look up to each other for company and entertainment on a platonic level but at times some relationships may lead to marriage. Anybody who does not belong to such a group in the village was looked down upon as something not socially complete and not regarded much. Therefore, some town dwellers even makes special effort to be a part of one or the other whemi. The whemis not only play together but also eats together on many occasions; the essential sociological basis on which the 'we-feeling' concept is built upon in most primary groups. This feeling of oneness encourages the groups to earn together and eat together. It is common practice to earn money through group wage. They work in rich people's fields, carry fire-woods and earn money.

Khezü whemi comprises of the older generations who are almost all illiterate. Many of them are animists with some exceptions. They portray the model of yester years peer groups. When 'Sekrenyi' festival comes, rice is collected from each member's house-hold and 'Zutho' (local rice beer) is brewed together in big wooden drums. They gather in the evenings, jokes together while sipping their Zutho over a flaming bonfire which is also made by collecting fire-wood from all the members' houses. There are no hesitation and no discrimination in any form irrespective of gender but they look forward to these social gatherings. They also have common money which they have accumulated through their earnings. Usually, one or two days are fixed every year to earn money together by working in a rich man's field or by cutting and carrying others fire-wood, manually. The money thus earned is managed by two or more capable persons as their treasurers. What is significant here is that no woman ever has been selected as treasurer or even assigned jobs other than being involved in cooking and making local brews. The decision-making within the peer group is entirely left to the men folks. The women have no complaints and have no awareness or consciousness of being left out at the decision-making processes. When any of their peer group dies or falls sick the male treasurers consult with their male counterparts and some amount of money is given to the affected house-holds. Decisions like how to earn money, how to invest their common fund or where to spend are all decided by the men.

Zakroho whemi in contrast to Khezü whemi, comprises of about 98% first generation educated persons, most of them are graduates and above. Most of them are daughters and sons of members of Khezü whemi. Most of them are also first generation Christians. During their childhood years, their peer-group also followed the pattern of Khezu whemi and many of the decisions were made on the advice of their parents. They also makes Zutho together, drinks together, work together and raised together their common funds too. But as they grew older and became better educated the system of their peer group functions also changed without their notice. Zutho was replaced with tea and the continuous evening gatherings were confined to just one day programme annually due to the constraints of time and distance as most of the members had become town dwellers. They also started changing their leadership patterns both at the structural and functional levels. Both man and woman were chosen as leaders in the form of presidents, general secretaries, and treasurers and so on. There exist no attitude problems even if a woman becomes the president and a man has to be her secretary too. All decisions are openly taken in the presence of both the genders. At present almost all the members of Zakroho whemi are holding jobs and some of their ladies have even got married to members of other whemis, some have even married outside their village too. Another significant point to ponder is that even those married outside the village are still considered as permanent members. They occasionally become treasurers or hold other posts too. A cow or a pig is also butchered every year and equal shares to both men and women are always given. At times, even social services and community developmental works are done by the group concerned. The relationship between the males and females are also typical to that of a very open society with no feelings of inferiority or superiority. This proves that there is no enmity between men and women but there is an unseen barrier which can be broken with another unseen force. This force cannot be that of Christianity alone because churches are also facing the influence of the traditional ethos and practices to some extent. The one factor which has brought a stark contrast between the decision-making process in Khezü and Zakroho whemi is conspicuously and obviously 'education'. An education that empowers is the education that liberates attitudes and thought patterns, a higher education, not just religious literacy which enables one to read the Bible and sing hymns. Nagaland's literacy rate for women is not too less but it should be remembered that literacy rate is counted for all persons above 7 years who can read and write in any language. This gives the impression that education cannot effectively empower women. But comparing Khezü and Zakroho whemi and even other societies, education is undoubtedly seen as one of the most effective tool for bringing about a silent revolution which will also lead to desirable social change. Education leads an individual to an all round development so when each individual changes through quality education, then the society also will obviously change for the better as society is made up of the collection of individuals. Therefore, higher education that is rational and logical should be imputed within the Angami society for progressive development.

Road-Map for involving Women at the VDB Level

The Angami ethnic identity and the patrilineal system of life, be it inheritance of ancestral property or land strictures and so on must be adequately guarded but certain things which can benefit society must adapt with the changing times. Women constitute more than half of the Angami population. And when this sizeable portion of the population is disregarded in the decision-making bodies, the concerned population's needs and requirements will never be seriously known and considered. The concept of VDB is to let people plan for themselves and develop themselves because they know themselves best. Women are a part of that 'people' and when they are excluded the picture is not complete. Majority of the Angami villages still keeps a safe distance from women at the actual practice of VDB related decision-making level. This practice may not really be beneficial at the broader village level. Women without men will be handicapped to a great extent, the same stands for men too.

When the womenfolk receive their shares, money is collected, accumulated and sometimes common buildings exclusively for women are built or some other exclusive programs are made for women only. Many of the respondents when asked of future plans said they have no idea. This brings a gap and questions to VDB system of gender divide. Men and women are different in many ways but they are also complimentary and supplementary to each other, as such when there are too many great divides, it may hamper socio-economic developments. The Hindu caste system has a stratification that always excludes the lower castes like the Sudras and the untouchables/Harijans, and was avoided by the upper castes like the plague. Harijans were not even included in the caste system. After Independence and gradual modernisation, caste system is declining, if not fully. Afghanistan was one country which literally excluded its women folks' in many vital areas. It took the country many years behind others. At the beginning of the 21st Century, if we can think constructively with an open mind, then, not only the status of women will be raised but the Angami society will walk and not limp. Both man and woman must acknowledged that they differ in sexual attributes and so many other differentiations exists but also should recognised that thought patterns and action plans must be contributory from both ends. Man lives within societies comprising of both the sexes, therefore participation of both men and women shall surely win positive rewards.

Angamis from time immemorial had been following the patrilineal/patriarchal system of governance. In this context it is not Angami man who is refusing to admit women at the decision-making bodies but it is the traditional way of life that is still taking time to shift to modern concepts of accommodating women even in a modern and recent construction like the VDB. Many a time, women themselves feel it is inappropriate to be part of the bodies that plans and does the decision-making, especially at the village level, not knowing that they are making their daughters go a few more years backward which in turn will have a very negative impact on the overall societal progress towards positive changes. There are certain concerns in this regard and rays of hope because it involves the government too. A few suggestions can be given:

1. Create VDB bodies where any gender will not have feelings of being left-out or develop feelings of belonging to a minority group. VDB is a decision-making body to develop the village, thus every problem or scope of development must be studied and planned together by both men and women. Reservation of seats leads to discriminations. The Government must not create gender divide by giving reservations to either males or females. It must frame rules and regulations in such a manner that the entire population be adequately represented. No sex should dominate, no clan should dominate, and no individual should dominate. It should be a body that has a sample to represent the whole population.

2. In majority of the Angami villages, one can find a good number of literate women. The practice of not involving women in decision-making bodies' maybe lessened if educated women members at the proper VDB are involved initially, in order to take away the psychological barrier created due to the age-old customs and traditions.

3. The Government should facilitate programmes to accommodate both the sexes together in order to avoid further gender divide and place both negative and positive sanctions to ensure that its directives are carried out effectively. Angami men are sensible and therefore if it is justifiable it will be surely supported.

4. VDB funds can be used judiciously for concrete developmental works and not spent on wrestling

events, hosting of Jubilees etc. It would be a much better idea to invest in higher education.

5. If water systems, proper drainages and other sanitary projects are included from the VDB fund then a lot of health related issues which comes through unhygienic surroundings may be averted. Such suggestions and pressures may come more strongly from the women folks. These issues which require constant developmental approaches for improvements and which are also the domains of women where constructive planning and suggestions may be given by them maybe more practical.

6. Education of the girl child must be given special emphasis because it is the most effective tool to liberate traditional strictures. Even the males must also be encouraged seriously to pursue liberal education because it can make one less conservative. It will help one to recognise quality rather than pre-conceived notions of status based on gender. It is a known fact that families and societies which had the opportunity of being properly educated with quality education are more open to gender related issues and of rectification, if any. So also men who had educated wives and educated daughters have no problems on questions of equity.

7. When it comes to village created common funds, the women folks constitute half of the workforce. No special consideration is used to exempt them from manual works but when fund from various sources comes they are singled out and given 25% share which is a little irrational, if one is to be logical. Therefore, participation and inclusion must be balanced so that any gender does not suffer at the status scale.

8. It will do well for the Angamis in general if the VDBs fully make use of the various funds allotted to the villages for actual developmental works. The future generation's plight of overall societal status and development will depend on how visionary we have been in utilising our village funds. Therefore, long term plans should be adopted to take full advantage of the given opportunity.

REFERENCES

1. Abdul, B. (et. al.) (Ed.). (1979). *Rural Development in South East Asia*. Vikas Publishing House Pvt. Ltd., New Delhi.
2. Ao, L.A. (1993). *Rural Development in Nagaland*, Har-Anand Publications, New Delhi.
3. Bhatnagar, S. and S.S. Chid. (1987). *Rural Development in India: A Strategy for Socio-Economic Change*. Ess Ess Pub., New Delhi.
4. Bordoloi, R.C. and C. Shankarih. (1981). *Extension Education and Rural Development* Vol.-I, International Experience in Communication and Innovation. John Wiley and Sons, R.C. Shankariah, New York. Bruce.
5. Dagar, Rainuka (ed.). (1998). *Manual on Women's Development and Gender Justice*, Institute for Development and Communication (IDC), Chandigarh.
6. Deb, P.C. et al. (1979). *Integrated Rural Development programmes: a case study in Punjab*. Draft sixth five year plan. Government of India.
7. D' Souza, Alphonsus and Kekhrieseno Christina. 2002. *Coping with social change in North-East India: A comparative study of three ethnic groups in North-East India (Aka, Angami and Dimasa)*, St. Joseph's College, Jakhama, Nagaland.
8. ESO-02. 1990. *Women and society*, Indira Gandhi National Open University, New Delhi.
9. Fernandes, Walter and Sanjay Barbora. 2002. *North Eastern Social Research Centre*.

10. Ghanshyam, S and H.R. Chaturvedi. (1983). *Canadia Approach to Rural Development*. Ajanta Pub., Delhi.

11. Gokhale, A.M. (1984). *The Common Fund Programme: A Strategy for Alleviating Rural Poverty in Nagaland.*

12. Hibo, Visakhonu. 1992. Social change and the Angami Nagas, St. Mary's College, Shillong, Meghalaya.

13. Liegise, Buno. 2006. *The Struggle of Rural Women and Winds of Change in Nagaland*, Hudi Dielie, Angami Students Union, Issue No. I.

14. Madam, G.R. 1983. *Village Development in India.* Allied Pub., Delhi.

15. Pillai, Jaya Kothai. 1995. *Women and Empowerment*, Gyan Publishing House, New Delhi.

16. Rao, Digumarti Bhaskara et al. (2000). *Status and Advancement of Women.* A.P.H. Pub., New Delhi.

17. Roy, Aphuno Chase.(2004). *Women in Transition: Angami Naga Women from 1878 to the Present*, Published by the Author.

18. Singh, R.B. (1987). *Planning for Rural Development.* Discovery Pub., New Delhi.

19. State Institute of Rural Development (SIRD) (1999). *Training of the Members of Village Councils & Village Development Boards* (VDBs).

20. Zehol, Lucy. (1998). *Women in Naga Society,* Regency Publications, New Delhi.

14

THE CHALLENGES FACING THE ANGAMI MEN TODAY: A Historical Perspective on the Issues

Niu Whiso Kuotsu

[We have seen in the last fifty years an unprecedented era of progress, development and growth in the history of the Nagas. The progress has been all round: political, educational, economic, social and religious. To the extent the changes have brought progress they are welcome as they will transform us into a modern society. But the journey to modernity will be neither smooth nor promising unless we also learn to solve and handle our own affairs responsibly and competently. And the rapid changes have generated new problems, new demands and new challenges revealing our unpreparedness and inadequacies in coping with the requirements for modern development, management and governance. Some of our major inadequacies are work ethic and dedication, competence and efficiency, integrity and justice – resulting in corruption, nepotism, tribalism and factionalism – and

clarity of vision in formulating polices and plans. These challenges are faced by the whole state and the Angamis also share the challenges with other tribes. But there is yet one more challenge faced by the Angamis as a tribe and that challenge is the decline of their power and influence due to the decline in the quality of their performance in various fields. So although the Angamis had played a leading role in the past in moulding the history of the Nagas, now they are being gradually relegated to a secondary role in almost everything. To these challenges we plan to address ourselves in this paper.]

In the discussion to follow, greater emphasis and also prominence shall be given to the decline of Angami role in Naga affairs. And as this problem is related to our culture which has its roots in the past it may be in order to look into our roots again to see whether our traditional values, which had shaped our culture and to some extent our history, are still intact and strong. This is very essential as it will enable us to acquire a perspective on the problems facing us today.

Traditionally, the Angamis were one of the most influential among the Naga tribes. A factor that enabled them to spread their influence was their comparatively good economy. Their economy was better because they practiced terraced cultivation which is less labour intensive but more yielding. Terraced cultivation is a system of cultivation based on sound scientific principles as cultivation can continue without exhausting the fertility of the land. Because soil nutrients are re-deposited through sedimentation during the rainy season when slushy water flows through the terraced fields. It is excellent even on hill slopes for subsistence farming and a comfortable livelihood can be obtained without much difficulty if supplemented by jhuming. So in the past the Angamis were better fed, better clothed among the tribes and they had more leisure time to think, and in a way this made them a thinking people who had perspective on issues.

Besides, the economy also provided them the means to trade with the neighbouring villages or tribes or even countries, and the traders traveled widely in their known world as they went as far as Burma, Upper Siam (Thailand) and Southern China in the east, and Assam, Dacca in East Bengal (Bangladesh) and Calcutta in the south west. And those days they had to travel on foot. But the experiences gained from these travels were invaluable as the exposures widened their mental horizon.

The Angamis evolved an economic system which powerfully influenced their social and political systems. In an Angami village, everybody owned something - a house, some terraced fields or jhum land or woodland or the right to use the community land and thus had some means to support himself or herself. This was made possible by the merit feast system as it prevented excessive accumulation of wealth in the hands of one or a few individuals, because when a person became wealthy he would aspire to give a merit feast which would enhance his social status. Thus more or less even distribution of property was ensured and maintained by the system. Apart from this, relatives and clan also provided support in case of sickness or misfortunes or calamities. So, as there were some material means and also some measure of economic security for everybody, there were no beggars, no prostitutes, no orphanages or no asylums for the aged in an Angami village.

Regarding political system, in the village polity, democracy in its purest form existed.[1] Because merit alone counted for leadership. The people were governed by no chief or king but by a gerontocracy consisting of elders. The most powerful or influential man in the gerontocracy would be the "peyumia" or "peyuko" (wise, capable leader or leaders). Unlike chieftainship or kingship "peyu" position was not inheritable. One had to distinguish oneself by possessing either talent or prowess and renown in war or wealth. The need to prove oneself in course of time produced a common Angami characteristic ? individualism or independence.

Besides, there are other concepts which form a part of the value system and which underlie the shaping of the Angami character. And these values, to a great extent regulate personal conduct; safeguard the sense of religion, mystery and the transcendent; promote hard work and productivity and instil social concern for public good. The following are some of such values:

1. "Thenga vavi kesi" - being conscious of what is considered shameful or disgraceful socially. This takes care of social conscience.

2. "Kenyü vavi kesi" - being conscious of what is forbidden or sinful. It was believed that violating "kenyü" (taboo or forbidden) would bring swift punishment or chastisement from God. This takes care of religious conscience.

3. "Mhosuo" - competitive spirit. The urge and determination to win and not to accept defeat easily. It helps one to accept hardships and sacrifices with patience and perseverance to carry out one's responsibility or mission faithfully and successfully. It is related to good pride. And a man who has no "mhosuo" is considered spineless and unmanly.

4. "Kethepfü" - bravery. This quality was highly valued as it is an indispensable quality to become a warrior and was vital to the security of the village.

5. "Kedietho" - honesty, integrity or truthfulness. In olden times the Angamis were known for their integrity and their words were proverbially golden. This was essential as all the agreements and even treaties in war were made orally.

6. "Keshurhei" ? diligence or industriousness. As members of an agrarian community, diligence was held in high esteem as it is the key to productivity and prosperity.

7. "Rüsuo Kekhrie" - hospitality. The tradition to welcome and look after friends or even strangers from other villages or tribes. In the absence of hotels in the olden days this tradition served a real humanitarian need for travelers, and it was "kenyü" to refuse food or shelter to strangers who came to one's village.

8. "Mechü Nounyu" - social concern. Social service was those days as important as paying taxes today as there were no paid people and no government to attend to things like roads, bridges, rest houses, etc. So everybody had to contribute labour or cash or kind. Thus, social work was mandatory - it was everybody's responsibility.

9. "Phichümia Kerhu" - respecting parents and elders. It is believed that honouring parents and elders brings blessings from God. So they were treated with respect, dignity and reverence.

10. "Kethezie" - considerateness. It is giving chance or privilege to others especially the old, the infirm and the needy. But this is also an important social lubricant among peers or friends. It is taking the least rather than the biggest share. It is both courtesy and charity. It is the opposite of opportunism. It is promoting others rather than putting them down.

Over and above these, there are also some related ideas which formed a part of the socio-religious thinking of the people. For instance, the concepts of public property and sin. An Angami had a very clear idea about what belonged to him and what belonged to others. So it was easy for him to make a distinction between private property and public property both of which were to be treated as sacrosanct and inviolable. An Angami also had a very clear idea about sin. In Angami "phouma" (sin) literally means "life trapped" - life is no longer free. Moreover, it is also believed to weaken the soul force, the power of which is required to win victories in battle.

The above socio-religious values were useful not only in times of peace but also in war. Because the prevalence of solid values and strong qualities made the Angamis good material for war. This was demonstrated during the Khonoma war with the British, resisting British invasion of the Naga Hills to extend their empire. The villagers were able to put up a strong resistance despite being outnumbered many times by a trained army with superior weapons, because they were good fighters and skillful strategists, well disciplined and well organized, ably led and strongly motivated by love of freedom. The war also demonstrated another quality of the Angami character: the willingness to dare odds for one's beliefs. Because they fought for what they believed was right even if it meant fighting against the greatest power on earth. The same indomitable spirit was demonstrated on a larger scale under Angami leadership at the time of the Naga Revolt of 1956 for independence: they fought for what they believed was right even if it meant fighting against one of the biggest nations on earth.

We could prove our mettle quite well in war. But now let us see how we handle peace. In his book, *Revolution and Counter-Revolution,* [2] Garcia says, "Unless a revolution is consolidated by a counter-revolution the gains are lost." In our situation, the revolution is not yet over, and the gains are only partial gains. But were we able to handle the post-revolution well? In fact we were so busy chasing sovereignty that we couldn't think much of consolidating the gains. And the benefits have gone much more to other major tribes. For instance the bureaucracy has been more or less captured by others, and as they control the financial resources they prosper more economically. Moreover, even in the National Movement, after 1975, other tribes emerged stronger and they have taken the lead for negotiations for settlement. In education, despite the presence of some of the best schools in Nagaland in and around Kohima, the performance of the Angamis is rather unimpressive. Except for some exceptional cases, in general, our students are neither serious nor hard working nor competitive enough to excel in their studies.

Nevertheless, although the power and influence of the Angamis have declined at present due to certain circumstances as well as the decline in the quality of their own performance in various fields, as a major tribe and also as a tribe with considerable experience in leadership, it is incumbent upon the Angamis to continue to play a leading role in Nagaland. Thus the question is not playing a role. That anybody can do. But playing a leading and an effective role with certain class or distinction marked by qualities such as competence and expertise, dedication and sense of service, magnanimity and a tribe-transcending outlook to work for the welfare of all the tribes, and a clear vision for a stronger and better Nagaland. However, to play such a responsible role ? to build as well as to set a standard for others ? is not easy. Responsibility has to be matched by credibility to be fruitful. So we need to prepare ourselves adequately first. And we can begin by doing some soul searching by examining the Angami character which throws light on both our achievements and failures, and by initiating corrective measures in the family which will lead to reforming the society for better performance. Let us take up the Angami character first.

A striking characteristic of the Angami character is its pronounced ambivalence: the capacity to be tough and adventurous and also to be very soft and ease loving. Their toughness was amply demonstrated in their feats in war as well as in peace especially in their enduring power in traveling to foreign lands for trade. Barefooted they would cross plains and rugged terrains, jungles and forests, rivers and ridges, battling hostile elements, facing an uncertain future in a strange land, walking for months without proper food or rest. And this was a part of their life for centuries. Regarding the other aspect of the Angami character, to a great extent we have been influenced by the agricultural cycle. And it has both toughening and softening aspects. In the agricultural cycle people have to work very hard till the transplanting time. But when it is over it is followed by several months of lean season. During the lean season some may work at handicrafts and womenfolk may do weaving, but for the others it is a period of leisure if not of indolence and people develop a very leisurely life style. Then after harvest, festivals begin. Two of them are particularly long: Terhünyü and Sekrenyi each of which lasts for ten days and especially Sekrenyi has elaborate celebrations - eating, drinking, and singing. So though many of us are no longer engaged in agriculture, we are still influenced by the agricultural cycle and the festivals. Because now in towns, the old festivals have been replaced by big Christmas celebrations and big weddings which have become so big that even powerful Churches find difficult to regulate.

Festivals and celebrations are good if they are affordable and meaningful. They make the occasion more enjoyable and memorable. But problems begin when they become excessive and involve too much eating and drinking. They lead to sensuality which weakens the habit of temperance, and indulgence in intemperance harms both body and soul. People who so indulge in it become soft and pleasure loving, lazy and unproductive and make themselves unfit for any serious thing in life.

It is likely that the ambivalence in character is affecting us more adversely than anything else in making our people less successful than we should. Because in general, we have been inclining more towards a soft, ease loving, complacent and indolent life rather than the earlier tough, hard working, energetic, assertive and competitive one with the indomitable spirit. The result is obvious: degeneration into mediocrity. But this is not acceptable. If we want to succeed and prosper as a tribe, we have to reverse the situation. We have to realize that diligence and toughness will lead us to success and prosperity but softness and laziness can lead us only to deterioration and decadence. So to effect changes, we will have to begin with the family, as it is the nucleus from which things can spread to the society at large. It is a miniature church, a miniature school and a miniature society where children are schooled, formed and prepared for life. So the role played by the family can influence and impact the society significantly. And certainly paying due attention to the following issues will effect far-reaching reforms:

Parents as Role Models and Teachers

There is a natural bond between parents and children. And thus parents are closest to their children and they also have the greatest influence on their children. Whatever they do, children imitate them. Moreover, apart from a few hours of school a day, children spend most of their time at home. So parents get enough opportunities to interact with them. And those who do not have any time at all for their children either for business or public affairs or a career, it may help to check again their priorities in life. Because it is the primary duty of every man to see to it that his children are properly brought up. But if he has no time now for this, however successful he may be in his career, he will regret and also suffer the consequences later. Therefore it is very important to invest one's time with the children ? to talk to them, to listen to them, to share their joys and sorrows with them, to do things with them to train them in some trade, or to supervise their studies or to go out with them occasionally. In handling children some skills are required as discipline has to be enforced without causing too much friction. So a few well-known principles may be of help:

(a) To show appreciation when children do something good or well.

(b) To correct them in private but to praise them in private as well as in the presence of others.

(c) To find out their good qualities and talents and nurture them by showing sincere appreciation and encouragement instead of criticizing them or scolding them or condemning and putting them down all the time for their faults. Too much criticism destroys confidence but appreciation builds confidence and self-worth. Appreciation of the good things in children helps them in overcoming their weaknesses as well.

Parents can be very patient and understanding in dealing with children's mistakes, failures or weaknesses. And despite all their problems, children should be loved unconditionally as parents should love their children not because they are good or successful but because they are their children. But when it comes to values, parents will have to be very firm, especially in observing the basic values such as those given in the Ten Commandments as they constitute the core of Christian morality and they shouldn't be compromised. Because they are from God and man has no authority to change them. They are timeless, and still as valid as when they were first proclaimed on Mt. Sinai nearly 4000 years ago, and they shall be valid till the end of the world. So I can neither violate nor give sanction to others to violate them without sinning against God. So I cannot embezzle government money and justify myself saying that others are also doing the same thing. The justification is invalid because others doing it make it neither right nor permissible. It may be a good temptation but a bad justification. Because stealing is an evil act and if I commit it I simply join the company of other evil doers who disobey God. So neither their doing it justifies me nor my doing it justifies them. We simply fall together. The same thing happened to our first parents. Who ate the apple first and who ate it last were non-issues for God. Because sin was the issue. And for sin they fell together and got condemned together.

Another challenge confronting parents today is permissiveness. Permissive influences are coming to Nagaland from the West. Permissiveness is the consequence of Christians loosing their faith in the West. When faith is gone, agnosticism takes over, and prepares the way for relativism and permissiveness. Because when the core values in the faith are gone there is nothing left to hold the value system together and it collapses and disintegrates. Consequently, the distinction between good and evil, the distinction between right and wrong and also the distinction between truth and falsehood get blurred and eventually one becomes as good as the other. In other words, to the permissive people, falsehood becomes as good as truth and vice versa. And thus a perfectly confused and chaotic situation is created. In such a situation, anything goes so long as it serves one's purpose or satisfies one's desire and consequently everything becomes permissible as reason no longer decides what is right but desire takes over and dictates what it wants. Thus good morality and bad morality no longer exists - everything becomes permissible including promiscuity. This is very dangerous teaching. But when influenced by the teaching, our youngsters get the impression that this is what modern people do and they also have to do the same thing to be modern. But this claim is not true. Because, first of all, not all modern people, especially the practicing Christians in the West, are permissive; and only those who have gone astray advocate permissiveness and free love. Second, there is nothing modern about immorality as the desire for it began with the fall of man. Permissiveness is a great threat to the family and society because it destroys families by multiplying promiscuity and infidelity, divorce and broken homes. So it has to be countered by strengthening the Christian faith and also Christian values in the families. The only way to do this is to re-assert very strongly the opposing and related virtues such as temperance, chastity, fidelity, integrity, diligence, prayer and love. Permissiveness is basically selfish and hedonistic but the opposing and related virtues are ascetic and self-sacrificing and thus charitable in nature and so strengthen the family and society. Obviously, in inculcating values, although instructions help, nothing is more powerful than example. We are all impressed by the life of a saint. Because in his or her life we see the *Bible* in action. It is the same thing with the life of a good parent. If he is honest in his public life; faithful, chaste, pure and practices temperance in his private life; and understanding, caring, self-sacrificing, hard working and loving in his family life, children will certainly be impressed and they are bound to be influenced by the good examples of the good model.

Abdication of Parental Authority and Responsibility

We often hear people say, "Children know more than parents these days and we can't teach them anything anymore." To begin with, the statement is at best only a partial truth and at worst an abdication of parental responsibility. Because children may know more about academic subjects but not really about values as, normally, religion is not taught in our schools and colleges except secular, academic subjects. Second, however educated children may become, parents can always teach their children values. Because parents have more experience, greater maturity, more knowledge on values and also more conviction about them. Moreover, in forming children or people, for that matter, it is not so much knowledge but the quality of conviction, the intensity of faith, the firmness of purpose and the authenticity of feeling and love that count more than anything else to make an impact. Third, parents represent God in the family, and thus God has given them authority to discipline, to correct, to advise, and to guide in order to lead them to a righteous life. So exercising this rightful authority judiciously establishes order and harmony in the family and strengthens it, but abdication of parental authority and responsibility invites disorder and chaos and weakens it. Exercising authority is a part of divine plan for order, and respecting rightful authority acknowledges and honours that plan.

Pampering Boys

Traditionally a boy was highly valued not only because he was male but also because he was considered a protector, a warrior on whom the village's security and also the power and the glory of the village or the tribe depended. So he was trained and groomed for fighting. Consequently, most of the mundane domestic chores were left to his sisters. But gone are those days, and there has been a radical shift of roles. Because for defence and security nowadays we have the police, army and even Naga army. Yet we still leave the chores to the girls, and the boys hardly do anything at home as if they were still preparing themselves for war. And many get pampered as a result. Because we are not adapting ourselves to the changing circumstances. But as girls are given more responsibilities at home they become more responsible also elsewhere such as in institutions and they do better in their studies. And girls are surpassing boys both in number and quality and they deserve our congratulations. But it is going to help the boys if work is re-allocated at home. Let the boys and girls share domestic work equally at home such as fetching water and firewood, splitting firewood, working in the garden, cleaning the house, marketing, cooking and so on. We can begin by allowing boys to look after themselves - washing and ironing their own clothes, polishing their own shoes, washing their own plates, sweeping their own rooms and so on. Then, as accepting responsibility makes people responsible, our boys will become more responsible in their studies and also do better in other areas of life as well.

Valuing Education More

Generally the jhum cultivator's value education more than the terraced cultivators because they have to struggle harder for a living and education provides them opportunities for a better life. But why can't the opposite also happen? As terraced cultivators have better economy it should provide them better means for better education. But in general this is not happening to the Angamis. Although they have some of the best schools in Nagaland in their area they are not on the top in education. Because although they want education, they don't value education enough yet to have the needed intensity, passion and care as others. And so they don't have a high degree of motivation to exert themselves enough to put in intensive labour to compete. But this is not wise. Because education is the key to success in any field nowadays and unless you have quality education you get sidelined in the job market. The same thing is going to happen in globalization. Unless our people are prepared with quality education, we will get sidelined and become mere spectators to global prosperity. Because we will find ourselves too ill-equipped mentally either to avail the opportunities globalization offers or to cope with the challenges it poses.

Work Ethic

If we want to make our children achievers, it is important to inculcate in them work ethic. Work ethic is a system of moral principles or rules of conduct relating to work. Some of such principles are the following: punctuality ? by starting and ending work in time; regularity ? by consistently good attendance; dedication ? by working sincerely and wholeheartedly at a job; efficiency ? by achieving with optimal speed what is required to be done without compromising quality; productivity ? by producing the optimal amount within a specified time; love of work ? by considering work as a privilege and a blessing rather than a burden, and also as a source of fulfillment and joy. For us applying work ethic will mean working at least 8 hours in office. It also means working 5 or 6 days a week, 4 weeks a month, and 12 months a year. For farmers and businessmen it means working 8 hours or more in one's field or office or shop or factory daily for 6 days a week. For students work ethic means studying 2-4 hours a day at home doing homework, assignments and preparing for weekly tests during academic session, and studying 8-10 hours a day or more while preparing for final exams or competitive exams.

Family Prayer

It helps the family to grow together. It brings peace, harmony and love. It strengthens the family's bond of unity as it is said, "The family that prays together stays together." (Patrick Peyton).[3] And as during prayer the whole family is brought together, this is also a good opportunity for scripture reading and instruction on the Christian faith. Family prayer brings God's loving presence to the family and thus fills the home with an atmosphere of spiritual vitality. It instills deeply in children the importance of prayer and also the importance of honouring, praising and worshipping God everyday as our creator to whom we owe our existence.

Aim Early for a Profession

Every child should have an aim in life and should be motivated to work steadily towards that goal. Having a goal motivates him to work hard. By class 8, children should have already familiarized themselves with the required subject combinations in class 9 and class 10 to qualify for the stream of their choice in college. And they can begin their preparation for a profession not only by studying the right subjects in class but also discussing it outside class with friends or parents or other relatives or teachers or professionals concerning the intended profession. They also may read and gather information from newspapers, magazines, journals or other literature in the library or may even try the internet. They also may correspond with colleges or institutes or universities concerning courses offered in their institutions or entrance tests to be taken for admission. Choosing the right line for a child is crucial because it can help or hinder his progress in his studies. So while choosing a profession for a child the primary consideration should be his interest, and next is his native ability which should be sufficiently good to cope with the courses. If he has both interest and ability he can do well in that profession. So the role of parents is to find out what the child is good at or, in other words, what nature or God has given to the child in terms of ability and talent so that the gifts may be nurtured through instruction, training and personal guidance in order to develop them into full blossom. The child's interest and ability are usually reflected in his grade card or results. If he is good in a subject he will consistently score higher in that subject and will also invariably spend more time on a subject in which he is interested while studying or reading at leisure. However, it is not advisable to force a child to join a profession in which he has no interest or ability because it is unnatural and it may have unhappy consequences later. First, the choice can become a burden to the child. Second, chances of poor performance or even failure leading to dropping out are high.

Finally, the challenges facing the Angami men today are the problems arising from the need to cope with a new situation. So it involves understanding the past to understand the present. It also involves adapting ourselves to the new without sacrificing the essence of the old especially in the realm of values. But above all it involves accepting the challenge of reincarnating, as it were, in our lives, the traditionally acclaimed qualities of the Angamis such as being hard working and enterprising, conscientious and honest, tough and indomitable, courageous and adventurous, thinkers and visionaries. Then the Angamis will be in a position to play a leading role again once more in the affairs of the Nagas. This role is expected and incumbent upon the Angamis not only because it is a major tribe but also because it happens to be a tribe with considerable experience in leadership in the history of the Nagas. However, leadership does not mean here leadership in the restricted sense of political leadership but leadership in general in any field to uplift the people – socially, culturally, economically, intellectually and spiritually to build a stronger and better Nagaland. Leadership in this sense is giving one's best to serve the people by promoting whatever is good, by solving problems, by fighting for causes to bring about changes and reforms, by initiating new things to update progress and growth to attain global standard or excellence. This kind of leadership benefits both the giver and the recipient and it endures because it is natural. But when leadership is sought for its own sake it neither works nor endures because it is selfish and unnatural and causes its own downfall. Thus, leadership, at its best, has to be the natural outcome of competence and dedication, integrity and justice, magnanimity and nobility, heroism and vision. If we have these qualities and also the indomitable spirit and resoluteness of our forefathers to fight for what is right rather than yield to what is easy or expedient our role in Naga affairs shall not falter but continue to be fruitful.

NOTES

1. This was said by Captain Butler and quoted by Hutton in *The Angami Nagas*, p. 143.

2. The present writer is in the process of tracing the book at the time of writing the talk.

3. Peyton, p. 95.

REFERENCES

1. Hutton, J.H. (1969). *The Angamis Nagas*. Bombay, I B R.
2. Johnstone, Sir James (2002). *Manipur and the Naga Hills*. New Delhi.
3. Ganguli, Milada (1984). *A Pilgrimage to the Nagas*. New Delhi.
4. Elwin, Verrier (1969). *The Nagas in the Nineteenth Century*. London.
5. Mackenzie, Alexander (1999). *The North-East Frontier of India*. New Delhi.
6. Barcley, William (1977). *Ethics in a Permissive Society*. Glasgow.
7. Schaeffer, Francis (1968). *The God Who is There*. London.
8. Garcia (1980). *Revolution and Counter-Revolution*. London.
9. Lewis, C.S. (1985). *Christian Reflections*. Glasgow.
10. Lewis, C.S. (1985). *Mere Christianity*. Glasgow.
11. Lewis, C.S. (1985). *The Abolition of Man*. Glasgow.
12. Peyton, Patrick (1987). *The Family Rosary Crusade*. New York.

Section VII: Social Dynamics and Economic Development

15

UNDERSTANDING ANGAMI TODAY IN THE CONTEXT OF MODERNISATION AND GLOBALISATION

Walter Fernandes

[What does globalisation mean to the Angami tribe? It is difficult to know all of its components for a single tribe. This paper has, therefore chosen the alternative of looking at the main features of both of globalisation and of the Angami tribe and seeing whether and in what way they match. After a look at these main features of both of them the paper will discuss in what manner they can interact with each other. That can give the implications of globalisation for the future. It is thus a search for answers to these questions, not a definitive conclusion.]

The Main Features of Globalisation

The main features of globalisation are a new ethics, a new economy and power relations. Capital gets priority over human beings but the middle class gets its benefits.

Capital and Consumerism

The first feature of globalisation is the ethics of profit alone at any cost as the criterion of judging a person, a society or a nation. Linked to it is consumerism that the producer requires for his profit but it is presented as higher progress. The consumer's humanity is judged according to the amount of money he/she has and the number and type of goods he/she can buy with it. Those who cannot afford them would then be inferior humans who cannot come up to the standard of those who succeed. That is why Corea (1999: 14) describes globalisation "as a fast express train. Countries are urged to get aboard and if they do succeed in getting aboard they will then be carried on to higher and higher levels of prosperity. If they fail to board it, they will be left behind and marginalized. So the message...coming from the North is that globalisation and liberalisation is the best thing that has happened in recent years."

Some think of globalisation as modernisation but they are two different processes. Modernisation is an ongoing social movement from the past to the present with the future in view. It may be economic or may result also from cultural, social and political changes. If directed properly it can be beneficial to the actors involved in it. It is possible for a community to modernise its tradition and thus ensure a smooth transition from the past to the future. It does not always happen because not all social processes are under human control (Huizer and Manheim 1979: 3). It has negative impacts if in the name of modernisation a relatively strong group or social system imposes its values or culture on a weaker community that is unable to cope with them. For example, the individual ownership based formal land laws that are considered modern are often superimposed on many community ownership (CPR) based tribal customary laws of the Northeast. It has often resulted in tribal land alienation or deterioration of women's status (Fernandes, Pereira and Khatso 2007: 25-26).

Though many describe globalisation as modernisation or as a movement towards the "global village" in reality it is an "uneven process, which divides winners and losers. For the most affluent it entails a shrinking world but is very deceptive for the destinies of the deprived majorities" (Dasgupta 2004: 15-16). It is a process imposed deliberately by the powerful to ensure continuation of their domination. It is primarily an economic decision supported by a political system that is geared to its needs. Basic to it is homogenisation of the consumerist culture in order to ensure its acceptance by the masses (Fernandes 1999: 4-5). Its value system is justified in the name of the free market. In reality its freedom is limited to the movement of manufactured goods and capital from the rich to the poor countries. Workers who abound in the latter are not allowed to move in the opposite direction (Kurien 1996: 21-22) unless they are highly qualified of whom there is a shortage in the former. For example, according to a study 60 percent of the doctors from the prestigious All India Institute of Medical Sciences go abroad (Raman 2007). Thus, the country that makes a high investment on them, incurs a heavy loss.

Land, Jobs and Class Formation

Globalisation of labour too exists but not through migration from poor to rich countries. It takes the form of using cheap labour within the poor country to manufacture goods on behalf of foreign investors. These enterprises want no restriction on the use of such labour. So efforts are made to change labour laws to deprive even the salaried workers of their rights to suit the needs of foreign capital. The political system is thus used to ensure the security of capital and to deprive labour of its security (David 1998a: 82-83). In India globalisation also takes the form of special economic zones

(SEZ) in which Indian laws do not apply (Thakur 2007). More than 200 of them are being planned and each of them can use up to 5,000 hectares. Thus, more than one million hectares may be acquired for them during the next three years. Besides, much of the land to be lost for other projects will be tribal. The private sector is eyeing mining land in Jharkhand, Orissa and Chhattisgarh and at least 48 mega-dams are being planned in the Northeast. So there will be more displacement than in the last 60 years, much of it tribal for mining in Middle India and dams in the Northeast (IWGIA: 2004: 314).

Little wonder then, that in the 1994 draft of the national rehabilitation policy the Union Government said: "It is expected that there will be large scale investments, both on account of internal generation of capital and increased inflow of foreign investment, thereby creating an enhanced demand for land to be provided within a shorter time-span in an increasingly competitive market ruled economic structure. Majority of our mineral resources... are located in the remote and backward areas mostly inhabited by tribals" (MRD1994: 1.1-2).

Besides, intrinsic to globalisation is mechanisation based on the IMF conditionality of "rationalisation of labour" which in practice means is reduction in the workforce (David 1998a: 83-84). One sees it happening in the mines, industries and SEZs. For example, in 1989-90 in Andhra Pradesh, 689 large and medium industries employed 444,000 persons, with an investment of Rs 4,100 crores at an average of Rs 92,500 per job. In 1996 1,536 of them employed 644,480 persons at an average of Rs 420,000 per job (Manorama 1997: 569). Similar information is got from coalmines in Jharkhand (BJA & NBJK 1993), copper mines in Orissa (Pattanaik and Panda 1992) and others elsewhere. Preliminary data from the SEZs shows that, with an investment of Rs 100,000 crores, their first 400,000 acres will probably create 500,000 jobs. That works out to an average of Rs 20 lakhs per job. Studies indicate that on an average an acre of land gives work to 2 persons. Thus, some 800,000 persons would have been sustaining themselves on this land on which only 500,000 jobs will be created. As a result, at least 300,000 jobs will be lost. Besides, the peasants who are displaced for it often lack the skills required for the mechanised jobs. So they may be rendered jobless since most jobs will be given to skilled workers from outside (Thakur 2007).

A result of these features is intensification of class formation that had begun with modernisation but it was not intrinsic to it. For example, planned development that was viewed as modernisation was based on the assumption that initially some would have to pay the price of economic growth but that eventually all would get its benefits. As the Second five-year Plan 1956-61 put it the aim of planned development was to take the country towards equality and to ensure that its benefits reached every Indian (Planning Commission 1956: 236). The Third Plan added that this process required modernisation of Indian society and abandoning of superstitions (Planning Commission 1961: Approach Paper No. 7).

Thus, the problem was not with modernisation or planned development per se but with the introduction of modern inputs without preparing the classes that were excluded from it to access its benefits which required formal education, technical training, psychological, cultural and social preparation. But very little attention was paid to these aspects. As a result, those who already had access to education got its benefits. Most of them belonged to the dominant castes and classes. Most tribals and Dalits were illiterate and lacked access to modern technology (Kurien 1997: 135-137). Even among them women were marginalized more than men. Moreover, this form of resource intensive development required acquisition of much land and forests. It is estimated that 25 million hectares of land have been acquired for them and 60 million persons have been deprived of their livelihood in India 1947-2000. Around 40 percent of them are from tribal, 20 percent from Dalit and 20 percent are from other rural poor classes (Fernandes 2007: 204). Thus, class formation and inequalities resulted from modernisation that was introduced in the name of national development not because of deliberate decisions but because steps meant to ensure that its benefits reached all were not taken.

Globalisation, on the contrary, has no such objective of egalitarian development. Its main motive is the investor's profit at any cost. So the producer targets those who can accept the consumerist culture. One does not state that none benefits from it. The middle class that gets much higher salaries and has a better choice of manufactured goods than in the past can afford consumerism. To ensure it, the mass media propagate a culture of individualism and consumerism, through the commercials. Thus homogenisation of cultures, individualism and a selfish middle class go hand in hand (Wallerstein 2004: 91-94). Because the gap between the rich and the poor grows, the middle class that gets its benefits has to be depoliticised in order to ensure that it ignores impoverishment and accepts an ideology of individualism and the TINA (There is No Alternative) factor. Thus, class formation and inequalities are not a distortion of globalisation but are intrinsic to it (Gorostiaga 1999: 79-80).

So are greater gender-based inequalities. Even the present form of modernisation has had many negative impacts on women especially on those from the subaltern classes. Globalisation intensifies them. An example of the negative gender implications of globalisation among the better off sections is the decline in the sex ratio in the 1990s in the 0-4 age group in the prosperous States of Punjab, Haryana and some districts of Maharashtra, Gujarat and Tamil Nadu. It is attributed to higher dowry demands to satisfy the needs of consumerism (Bose 2001: 45-46). To counter this demand prosperous families in these areas resort to sex-specific abortions in order to nip the problem at the source (Srivastava 2001: 184-185).

Also higher land acquisition and mechanisation and the consequent reduction in jobs have serious implications for women. In the past too land loss deprived the woman of the resources through which she catered to the family's food and other needs that are considered her domain. She is expected to continue to play this role even with reduced resources. That results in a lower status of women. Their marginalisation will be intensified with more land acquisition and fewer jobs are created because of mechanisation. One of its impacts is higher female unemployment. Many middle class women may have access to new jobs but even the possibility of work for survival that tribal and other subaltern women had, disappears with mechanisation. For example, the coalmines used to give exploitative unskilled jobs to women. So their proportion in the sector was 30-40 percent in the 1970s. Because of mechanisation it has come down to around 12 percent today (Bhanumathi 2002: 21). There are also indications that over-consumption and use of more natural resources will result in environmental degradation (Chew 2004: 60-64). That too has more negative impacts on women than on men.

The Angami Tribe

The Angami tribe has to be situated in the context of the new value system being introduced by globalisation. In order to do it, based on studies of the present writer and of other researchers this section will attempt to identify their main features. That will help one to understand whether a link exists between the Angamis and globalisation.

Some Features of the Angami Tribe

An outstanding feature of the Angamis, at least those of

the southern Angami area is that they have had better access to modern inputs than most other tribes of the Northeast did. For example, a modern input, religious change, specifically Christianisation made access to another modern input of education possible. One saw it in a 2001 comparative study of 6 tribes i.e. the Aka of Arunachal, the Adivasi, Boro and Dimasa of Assam, the Garo of Meghalaya and the Angami of Nagaland. It showed that literacy was the highest among the Angami and that they had the biggest number of graduates and persons with a salaried job. But all of them continued to own land to grow paddy and other staple food. A substantial number of them were involved in petty business that supplemented their income. As a result, poverty was lower among them than in the other tribes studied (Fernandes and Barbora 2002: 86-93 & 109-111).

In other words, they have dealt with modernisation better than the remaining tribes have done. But other studies make one wonder whether they will be able to deal with globalisation in the same manner. For example, one has mentioned above the demand for more land and forests and has hinted at possible environmental degradation because of excessive use of such resources after globalisation. One finds some ambiguity on this issue among the Angamis. Till the 1980s, they preserved their forests while the neighbouring tribes cut theirs. When many new educational institutions came to their area in the 1970s, they sent their children to school and paid for it by growing potatoes as a commercial crop. Thus, they learnt to a limited extent to combine their tradition of preserving the environment with a response to modern inputs. However, they began to cut their forests in the 1990s when their children reached the college going age and had to find money for it since in the absence of good institutions within the State many had to go outside for it. To earn that money their families cut the forests that they had preserved till then. Thus while getting the benefit of education they also developed skills of dealing with modernisation but after a certain point it led them towards the process of environmental degradation (D'Souza 2001a: 28-29).

This ambiguity in their approach to the preservation of their natural resources is one of many instances of a clash between their tradition and modernity. To be exact while they try to modernise their value system, their tradition seems to stand in their way. Another example is the contract the Jakhama village signed with the Kohima municipality to ensure regular supply of water to the town. The youth protested against it and prevented the elders from implementing the contract because they viewed water as basic to the food security that their generation required in their terrace-cultivation based economy (D'Souza 2001b: 109). But the elders seem to have viewed water also as a commodity for sale to Kohima and in the process they paid inadequate attention to the food security of the next generation. Thus the clash is in reality between two sets of values, those of their tradition in which the natural resources are their sustenance and renewable and the modern system to which they are commodities.

One notices a similar clash between modernisation and women's status which is better than that of the non-tribal communities even of the Northeast. Their somewhat high sex ratio and level of education are among the indications of this status. The 2001 study showed a sex ratio of 956 among the 189 families studied (Fernandes and Barbora 2002: 75) against the national average of 933. A second study of 2004 showed a sex ratio of 1,074 (Fernandes, Pereira and Khatso 2007: 56) in the 100 families studied. Thus there are minor differences but both of them show that Angami women enjoy a high social status than those in the caste communities do but they are not equal to men. Their social status is somewhat high because they as well as most other tribes keep a clear separation between the family and social spheres. The woman is in charge of the family and of its decisions and production systems. It is true in particular of shifting cultivation societies (Menon 1995: 101-102).

Political Processes and Gender Relations

However, this status does not go beyond the social to the political level and it does not make the woman equal to men because the man controls the social sphere. The high sex ratio is a sign that this terrace-cultivation tribe does not consider the woman an economic liability as settled cultivation based dowry-giving communities do. But men continue to control their society. Inheritance of land and other clan property is exclusively through the male line. Only what the parents buy can be gifted to the daughter (Fernandes, Pereira and Khatso 2008: 40-41). However, some modern inputs such as the opening of schools in the Southern Angami area in the 1970s and 1980s have helped women to take a few steps towards gender equality. Their customary law limited education to boys but their Christianisation made it possible for girls to enter schools in the sense that the Church did not forbid their education.

Whether they really gained access to schools or not depended on other processes. One such input, the political process of the Naga Nationalist struggle made it possible for southern Angami girls to avail of this possibility in the 1970s. Their tribe was in the forefront of resistance to the British colonialist. A. Z. Phizo who brought most Naga tribes together against the common Japanese enemy was an Angami (Sanyu 1996: 97-98). This involvement continued after 1947 with Phizo as the leader of the Naga nationalist struggle with the Angami in the forefront. As a result, in the 1970s many young men were in hiding or were with the militant group. That put the woman who was already in charge in the family in charge also of their society. The entry of high schools in their area at this stage made it possible for girls to enter them and they did it in fairly big numbers. Many of them continued their studies at the college level too. As a result, 41 out of 68 graduates among the members of the 189 families studied in 2001 were women. Their number was probably higher because more women than men had migrated away from their region in search of jobs. Some others had left their village after marriage (Fernandes and Barbora 2002: 87). The 2004 sample had 48 women against 33 men among the graduates and post-graduates, 65 girls and 50 boys were at school and 36 and 33 respectively at college. However, of the 124 persons who had done professional studies 81 (65.32%) were men and 43 were women (Fernandes, Pereira and Khatso 2007: 72-73). Thus, after the ceasefire and when men returned to the village the gender gap in education was closing.

The access that girls thus gained to education should have laid the foundation of women's equality but it has not happened because their customary law and tradition continue to be patriarchal. For example, one found somewhat positive gender attitudes among men in their 40s and 50s who had passed through the political process of the nationalist struggle but not among younger men. One of its signs is the number of women who have remained single mainly because their tradition demands that the husband be at least as educated as the wife and there are not enough men with such educational qualifications. The State too seems to view the man alone as the breadwinner. While women were 60 percent of the graduates in the 189 families studied in 2001, they were only 38 (22.49%) of the 169 family members having salaried jobs (Fernandes and Barbora 2002: 110). That jobs in the administration were the main cause of this cause of this contradiction became clear in the 2004 sample of 100 families that had 161 members with salaried jobs, 104 of them men and 57 women. But out of 137 persons with government jobs, 97 (70.8%) were men and 40 were women. Out of 24 persons with jobs in the private sector 17 were women and 7 were men (Fernandes, Pereira and Khatso 2007: 73). Also the fact that more men than women had done professional studies indicated that better jobs that required higher professional qualifications were going to men.

The tilt towards men in employment despite the higher level of education among women highlights the fact that social power remains with men and it is being strengthened as a result of the effort to return to the customary law. Very few men are ready to let women own land and other clan property. Some changes are taking place in this tribe because of the higher education of women. For example, a few villages have admitted the president of the women's association into the village council but all the members stated clearly that they will not become presidents of the village council or village chiefs. They justified this stand in the name of their customary law. Thus these changes remain marginal and one does not see a major shift in male-female power relations occurring in the near future. Efforts made to introduce changes meet with resistance. For example, apart from Ms Rano Shaiza, a Rajya Sabha MP in the 1970s, Nagaland has not had a single member of Parliament (MP) or of the legislative assembly (MLA) since its formation in 1963. A woman who contested the 2003 Assembly elections lost badly so did the three women who contested in 2008. Some who wanted to contest the 2004 Lok Sabha elections had to abandon their effort because of opposition.

Money is another component having an impact on gender relations. Unlike in many other tribes, Angami women have not lost their financial power completely but one notices a shift in relations on this issue too. As stated above, there has been a changeover to commercial crops in order to earn money for children's education. With it many decisions on the type of crops to grow have shifted to men but the shift is not strong as in many other tribes studied. The woman retains control over the sale of the agricultural produce that are considered part of the family sphere. But much power over the rest of the market seems to have shifted to men (Fernandes, Pereira and Khatso 2007: 79).

Thus, as in the political arena so also in the economic sphere the movement towards equality exists but it is minimal. It is mainly because their tradition has not changed with the times in this as well as other spheres. For example, 36 family members in the 2001 sample declared petty business as their occupation but their involvement in commerce is limited to the sale of agricultural produce and handicrafts. Very few Angami men or women are involved in the economy beyond these traditional items. The market in Kohima and other towns continues to be in the hands of outsiders. However, modernisation has resulted in the growth of individualism and class formation in the Angami and other tribes of Nagaland. A sign of it is internal land alienation within the tribe that has given birth to a form of absentee landlordism (Barbora 2002).[1]

Thus there is a contradiction in their response to modernisation. On one side, they have resisted changes that can introduce gender equality. On the other, they have accepted changes such as individualism that can result in class formation and can go against the community as a whole. That creates a dichotomy between modernity and tradition. They remain two parallel systems without adequate interaction with each other.

Implications for Globalisation

The above section shows that, the Angami have had very little experience with globalisation till now but have interacted with modernisation. This experience is inadequate to draw any conclusion. So one has opted for the alternative of analysing the main features of the Angamis and of globalisation in order to look at possible impacts of this interaction.

The Main Features

The above discussion shows that the Angami have got more benefits of modernisation than the remaining tribes studied have done. They have thus, laid a foundation for dealing with the processes of globalisation. Religious change, the first step of modernisation combined with the political process of their nationalist struggle has made it possible for them to retain their autonomy while interacting with the forces of modernisation. These inputs have also made it possible for women to gain access to education and retain some of their autonomy. On the other side is the growth of individualism symbolised by aspects such as internal land alienation and the consequent class formation in their traditionally democratic and egalitarian society. It also indicates that the elite emerging among them is becoming selfish and is losing the community spirit that is basic to tribal sustainable living. One does not claim that the community or clan were absolutes among them. Unlike others like the Aka who till recently lacked even the concept of individual ownership (Fernandes, Bharali and Khezo 2008: 24-25) the Angami had a healthy combination of village, clan and individual ownership (D'Souza 2001a: 56-57).

What is new is not individual ownership but individualism. In their tradition even individual ownership had a community dimension. Individuals or families owned land in the name of the community, which accorded it sanction and recognition. The phenomenon of internal land alienation results from their interaction with modernity and lacks community sanction. The formal law and administrative systems follow an individual-based approach even while dealing with community-controlled resources (Fernandes and Pereira 2005: 173-174). Education imparts mainly individual values, so does Christian ethics. The elite seem to have internalised this value but have not allowed their community to be modernised in other aspects.

This contradiction is clearly visible in gender relations. Like individualism that has its origin in modern inputs like formal education, religion, administrative and legal systems, also gender equality has its base in modernisation. Religious conversion made it possible for girls to attend schools. Education gave women a sense of social worth because of which aspirations of equality grew in them. However, the Angami tradition has overtaken this search. But for some minor concessions such as including a few women in the village council, male control over their society remains strong. Even the State continues to view the man as the breadwinner despite women's high level of education and bigger contribution than in the past to the family economy.

In that sense their tradition of separation between the family and social spheres remains intact and has been modernised. To some extent the man-woman cleavage has got intensified and has been extended to modern areas such as salaried jobs. They seem to have transferred many traditional values to modern systems without allowing them to interact with each other and build on the positive points of both. In practice, the elite have adopted the value of individualism that can go against the community but has resisted the value of gender equality. To ensure continuation of male control they have fallen back on the customary law without adapting it to the present.

Thus, in their interaction with modernity, the Angami (and other Naga tribes) seem to have made a choice between the modern and the traditional and have not allowed the two to benefit from each other. To a great extent their tradition and modern inputs have remained parallel. An example is commerce. They are involved in petty business but have failed to go beyond it to macro-commerce and have for all practical purposes allowed trade in items beyond handicrafts and agricultural produce to remain in the hands of outsiders. Their dealings with the market and the school have not entered their homes and their tradition has not entered the formal sphere as one can see in the polarisation on the issue of gender relations. In that sense they have modernised the traditional separation between the family and social spheres and have not allowed women to enter the political sphere though they are educated and are capable of getting involved in their administrative systems.

Implications for Globalisation

The above discussion makes it possible for one to compare the main features of globalisation with those of the Angami society as they have evolved through inputs such as education, religion and commerce. An understanding of how their society has interacted with modern inputs can give one an inkling of how their society will deal with globalisation. One may add that most changes noticed among the Angami are unconscious social processes and are not based on conscious decisions. But they have laid the foundation of their interaction with globalisation. For example, from the fact that they have got many benefits of modernisation, one can hazard a guess that they will also be able to get some benefits of globalisation. The level of education, the political processes they have passed through and the identity they have developed while dealing with the external forces can restrict the negative impact of globalisation. The aspirations of equality that women have developed through education can counter its negative gender impacts. Also their tradition of protecting the environment can be of use.

Apart from these positive influences one has also seen other processes can strengthen the negative forces of globalisation among them. The new ethics of profit at any cost and consumerism to suit this need that are basic to it, requires individualism and a de-politicised middle class that does not pay attention to growing poverty or views it mainly as the fault of the poor who cannot come up to the standards of their own class (David 1998b: 20-21). This attitude is basic to growing social and economic inequalities emanating from globalisation. The Angami elite seem to have absorbed this value from modernisation and are trying to monopolise some resources as seen in internal land alienation. Globalisation can strengthen selfishness and growth of individualism that goes hand in hand and can thus intensify class formation and weaken their community more than at present. Thus, the processes initiated by modernisation may be strengthened at the cost of the community.

Another area of concern is jobs in the globalised world. They need technical skills. Though the level of education is good among the Angami, one is not certain that they have their education has imparted to them the skills that the new jobs require. Much of the education is in the arts and humanities and is geared to jobs in the administration, not to the productive sector. Those who have done professional studies seem to have restricted themselves to service or tertiary sector oriented techniques such as the information technology or medicine. Very few have taken to production-oriented engineering and related techniques. This disjunction between their education and jobs should be seen together with the fact that investment in the secondary sector is low in the region. Nagaland has very few industries and that increases pressure on land.

Also preparation for dealing with commerce seems to be weak. Not a negligible number of Angamis, men as well as women are involved in petty business in family oriented items. Commerce beyond them does not seem to have entered the Angami culture. In that sense, a dichotomy seems to have developed between their tradition and modernity. The two systems seem to grow side by side. The domestic sphere is modernised through petty business but the bigger social sphere remains outside their control. It can be destructive while dealing with globalisation that is geared to the homogenisation of culture, as such does not have the tolerance required for modernising their tradition. It can weaken their egalitarian culture and take them towards greater inequalities and class formation.

Moreover, because their tradition and modernity remain parallel, when the pressure of globalisation begins to build on them, their tradition may be too weak to resist its negative impacts especially on the gender issue. On one side the Angami elite has yielded to the individualistic trend of modernisation. On the other it has pulled back from gender equality despite education and the political processes that could have facilitated it. Angami men, especially the elite among them, seem to be trying to strengthen patriarchy. As stated above, gender differential grows with globalisation. By pulling back from the aspirations of gender equality, the Angami society may be laying the foundations stronger patriarchy in their tribe.

Conclusion

An effort has been made in this paper to look at the main features of globalisation and of the Angami society and understand their interaction. It is a tentative step towards an understanding of the possible impacts of globalisation on the Angami. In order to understand it their interaction with modernity has been analysed. It can give one an idea of how they may deal with globalisation that is presented as advanced modernisation but is different from it. Modernity has some positive as well as negative values. It is a social process within each society. Its response to them depends on the forces it sets in motion. The Angami have benefited from some modern inputs and have felt the negative impacts of others.

Globalisation, on the contrary, depends less than modernisation does on the social processes of a society. Through tools such as mass communications it ensures that culture is homogenised and strengthens individualism and selfishness in the middle class. Economic and social inequalities are intrinsic to it. Since the Angami society has developed some traditions of dealing with modernity, some of its members may be able to get the benefits of globalisation. However, not much effort has gone into the modernisation of their egalitarian tradition. This failure can play into the combination of growing individualism and strengthening of patriarchy and can result in greater gender and class equality.

As a result, the benefits of globalisation may reach a few and the majority may feel mainly its negative impacts. To counter this division and growth of inequalities in their society it is important for their leaders to take cognisance of factors that go counter to their society. Education in which investment has been high needs to be given a direction towards technical aspects. Through a political process their tribe has developed a new identity but it has taken a strong patriarchal and individualistic form. Their tradition of environment protection seems to be getting somewhat weak. In order to interact with globalisation, the Angami society needs to study these processes and direct them towards an identity based on gender and class equality.

REFERENCES

1. Barbora, Sanjay (2002). "Ethnic Politics and Land Use: Genesis of Conflicts in India's North-East," *Economic and Political Weekly,* 37 (n. 13, March 30-April 5), pp. 1285-1292.

2. Bhanumathi, K. "The Status of Women Affected by Mining in India," in Anon (ed). *Women and Mining: A Resource Kit.* New Delhi: Delhi Forum, pp. 20-24.

3. BJA & NBJK (1993). *Social Impact: Piparwar and the North Karanpura Coal Fields.* Hunterganj: Bharat Jan Andolan and Champaran: Nav Bharat Jagruti Kendra.

4. Bose, Ashish (2001). "Black Holes in India's Demographic Transition: Collapse of a Civilisation," *Health for the Millions,* 23 (n. 3, May), pp. 45-48.

5. Chew, Sing C. (2004). "Globalization, Ecological Crisis and Dark Ages," in Samir Dasgupta (ed). *The Changing Face of Globalization*. New Delhi: Sage Publications, pp. 48-77.

6. Corea, Gamani (1999). "The Challenge of Globalisation," in Walter Fernandes and Anupama Dutta (ed). *Colonialism to Globalisation: Five Centuries after Vasco da Gama. Volume 1: Main Issues around Colonialism and Globalisation*. New Delhi: Indian Social Institute, pp. 14-21.

7. Dasgupta, Samir (2004). "Introduction," in Samir Dasgupta (ed). Op. cit. pp. 15-47.

8. David, James (1998a). "The Challenge before Trade Unions," in James David and John Desrochers (eds). *Dimensions of Globalisation*. Bangalore: Centre for Social Action, pp. 81-96.

9. David, James (1998b). "Globalisation: Past, Present and Future," in James David and John Desrochers (ed). Op. cit. pp. 17-27.

10. D'Souza, Alphonsus (2001a). *Traditional Systems of Forest Conservation in North East India: The Angami Tribe of Nagaland*. Guwahati; North Eastern Social Research Centre.

11. D'Souza, Alphonsus (2001b). "The Traditional Angami Naga Forest and Water Management: Implications for Climate Change and Sustainable Tribal Living," in Walter Fernandes and Nafisa Goga D'Souza (eds). *Climate Change and Sustainable Tribal Living: Responses from the Northeast*. Guwahati: North Eastern Social Research Centre and Vishakapatnam: Indian Network on Ethnics and Climate Change, pp. 88-113.

12. Fernandes, Walter (1999). "Globalisation, Liberalisation and the Victims of Colonialism," in Michael Amaladoss (ed). *Globalization and Its Victims as Seen by Its Victims*. Delhi: Vidyajyoti Education and Welfare Society and ISPCK, pp. 2-25.

13. Fernandes, Walter (2007). "Singur and the Displacement Scenario," *Economic and Political Weekly*, 42 (n. 3, Jan. 20-26, pp. 203-206.

14. Fernandes, Walter and Sanjay Barbora (2002). *Modernisation and Women's Status in North*

Eastern India: A Comparative Study of Six Tribes. Guwahati: North Eastern Social Research Centre.

15. Fernandes, Walter and Melville Pereira (2005). *Land Relations and Ethnic Conflicts: The Case of North Eastern India*. Guwahati: North Eastern Social Research Centre.

16. Fernandes, Walter, Melville Pereira and Vizalenu Khatso. (2008). *Customary Laws in North East India: Impact on Women*. New Delhi: National Commission for Women.

17. Fernandes, Walter, Gita Bharali and Vemedo Kezo. 2008. *The UN Indigenous Decade in Northeast India*. Guwahati: North Eastern Social Research Centre.

18. Gorostiaga, Xavier (1999). "Is the Answer in the South?: A Latin American View," in Michael Amaladoss (ed). Op. cit. pp. 26-64.

19. Huizer, Gerrit and Bruce Mannheim (1979). *The Politics of Anthropology: From Colonialism and Sexism Toward a View from Below*. The Hague and Paris. Mouton Publishers.

20. IWGIA (2004). *The Indigenous World (2004)*. Copenhagen: International Work Group for Indigenous Affairs.

21. Kurien, C. T. (1996). *Global Capitalism and the Indian Economy*. New Delhi: Orient Longman.

22. Kurien, C.T. (1997). "Globalisation: What Is It About?" *Integral Liberation*, 1 (n. 3, September), pp. 133-140.

23. Manorama (1997). *Manorama Yearbook 1997*. Kottayam. Malayala Manorama.

24. Menon, Geeta (1995). "The Impact of Migration on the Work and Tribal Women's Status," in Loes Schenken-Sandbergen (ed). *Women and Seasonal Labour Migration*. New Delhi: Sage, pp. 79-154.

25. MRD (1994). *The Draft National Policy for Rehabilitation of Persons Displaced as a Consequence of Acquisition of Land*.

New Delhi: Ministry of Rural Development, Government of India (Seond Draft).

26. Pattanaik, Gopabandu and Damodar Panda (1992). "The New Economic Policy and the Poor," *Social Action*, 42 (n.2, Apr-June), pp. 201-212.

27. Planning Commission (1956). *The Second Five-Year Plan*. New Delhi: Planning Commission, Government of India.

28. Planning Commission (1961). *Towards A Self-Reliant Economy: India's Third Five-Year Plan 1961-66*. New Delhi: Publications Division, Government of India.

29. Raman, Anuradha (2007). "Rein on Their Parade," *Outlook*, March 19, pp. 22-24.

30. Sanyu, Visier (1996). A History of Nagas and Nagaland: Dynamics of Tradition Village Formation. New Delhi: Commonwealth Publishers.

31. Srivastava, Alka (2001). "Declining Sex Ratio: The Indian Girl Child," *Integral Liberation* 5 (n. 3, September-December), pp. 183-190.

32. Thakur, Debdulal (2007). "Budget and Policy tracking of the Union Government," *Budget Track* 4 (n. 2, Feb), pp. 3-5.

33. Wallerstein, Immanuel (2004). "Cultures in Conflict: Who are We? Who are the Others?" in Samir Dasgupta (ed). *Op. cit.* pp. 79 - 97.

16

CHANGING LAND RELATIONS AND ANGAMI SOCIETY

Kekhrieseno Christina

[This paper deals with the changing land relations in a tribal society, namely the Angami society of Nagaland. In general, the term 'land relations' refers to the relationship of people to land in an agrarian society and by agrarian society is meant a society that depends primarily on agriculture as the principal economic activity.]

In an agrarian society, the term 'land' itself is comprehensive because it includes all types of land, agricultural and non-agricultural, as also forests and water resources. While agricultural land is used for cultivation, non-agricultural land includes house sites, grazing grounds, and land set aside for other non-agricultural activities. Forests of all type have a direct bearing on agriculture because they are not merely a source of fuel, fodder and manure, but also because they are essential for an ecological balanced use of land. Water resources may be in the form of rivers and streams, springs and wells, canals and drains.

Land relations in an agrarian society are in the form of ownership, control and access to the use of land. Basically, ownership means the right to control, use and dispose of the thing owned. Ownership implies exclusiveness because it limits access to the owners and denies it to others. There are different types of ownership. They are ownership by individuals, by households, by groups such as clans, and even by a community such as a village. The nature of ownership and the rights implied by it are usually recognised by law, whether such law is only traditional and unwritten, or enacted and codified.

The different types of land relations are closely related to the type of agriculture. There are different types of agriculture in different societies in the world. B.H. Farmer (1968) classifies the types or systems of agriculture into four board categories. They are: i) shifting cultivation; ii) simple sedentary cultivation with hand tools; iii) simple plough cultivation; iv) cultivation dominated by the use of more advanced mechanical tools.

Shifting cultivation is the system under which temporary clearings of land, usually forest land, are done and cultivated for short periods and left fallow for some years so that it regains its natural vegetation and fertility. In North East India it is known as *jhum* cultivation. It is widely practised in the hilly areas of North East India, including Nagaland. The main objective of shifting cultivation is to grow food crops, particularly rice and maize, though various types of vegetables are also grown.

Simple sedentary cultivation represents the fixation of shifting cultivation. In Southeast Asia, the most ancient and surviving type of cultivation is the use of permanent gardens to grow banana, yam, and tree crops like coconut. In parts of Africa there are "women's gardens" in the village. The gardens are kept fertile with the manure of the goats, chicken, household refuse and ashes. Such a type of cultivation of vegetables is usually done close to the residential site of the village, and is often found along with shifting cultivation.

In the system of terrace cultivation food crops are grown in permanent terrace fields with an assured supply of water for irrigation. A basic feature of terrace cultivation is that all the work is done by hand. The main purpose of terrace cultivation is to grow paddy or rice and other food grains, while shifting cultivation provides important cash crops like potatoes, cabbage, beans and other vegetables. Simple plough cultivation refers to the use of plough in cultivation, especially to improve the fertility of the soil.

The fourth type of agriculture is dominated by the use of modern technology. Extensive use of machines and artificial fertilisers, along with assured irrigation through canals and pumps has turned this form of agriculture almost into an industry. It was this type of agriculture that led to the so called Green Revolution. In India this type of agriculture is found in Punjab, Haryana and some parts of Uttar Pradesh.

There is a close relationship between the type of agriculture and land relations. Where shifting cultivation and simple sedentary cultivation predominate, communal ownership tends to be the norm. Land is owned by the community and an individual household is either allotted a plot or selects a plot for cultivation according to their needs. In such a situation, there is no question of tenancy and therefore no significant economic inequalities. But with plough cultivation, individual ownership becomes significant. Some form of tenancy can also emerge. This, in turn, leads to significant economic and social inequalities and results in class formation. As the importance of plough cultivation increases, land relations become more complex leading to greater inequalities and the emergence of other classes like that of agricultural labourers. Thus differences in types of agriculture give rise to different types of land relations, which in turn result in the formation of different agricultural classes and different forms of agrarian structures.

Land Relations among the Angami

The Angamis are one of the major Naga tribes living in Nagaland. On the basis of information available from the Census of India, the Angami is the fourth largest Naga tribe. In 1991, there were 97,433 persons in Nagaland who stated that Angami language was their mother tongue (Census of India, 1991:66). In 1991 the Angami constituted 8.06% of the total population of Nagaland.

The Angami Naga tribe is made up of different groups. Hutton (1921:15) identifies four distinct groups among the Angami. They are the Khonoma group, Kohima group, Viswema group and the Chakroma group. At present, it is common to identify these groups on the basis of their geographic distribution. Those living in Kohima and the surrounding villages are known as the Northern Angami, those living to its west are the Western Angami, and those to the south of Kohima are the Southern Angami, while those living on the slopes along the National Highway from Kohima to Dimapur are the Chakroma Angami. This paper will emphasise on the Southern Angami group, who now usually call themselves the *Japfüphiki*, that is, people living under the *Japfü* peak.

The Southern Angamis identify themselves as the *Zuonuo-Keyhonuo* and demand that this name be granted recognition as distinct from the Western Angamis called *Tengima* (Das 1987:133-134). In fact, the Southern Angamis can claim for a distinct identity for several reasons. They have a clearly identifiable territory. They also have distinctive features in their social structure, and cultural practices. Their spoken language differs from other forms of Angami. Thus the Southern Angamis are a distinct group of the larger Angami tribe. At present they prefer to call themselves *Japfuphiki* meaning those living in the shadow or vicinity of Mount *Japfü*, the highest peak on the Japfü range of mountains. In any case, the *Zounuo-Keyhonuo* group continues to remain part of the Angami, though it forms structurally and culturally, a distinct socio-territorial group (Bareh 2001:159).

The Southern Angami or the Japfuphiki area is a compact geographical unit covering 403.8 sq.km. The National Highway 39, passing through Kohima and going towards Imphal in Manipur, cuts across the higher slopes of the Japfu range and traverses the entire Southern Angami area roughly in a north-south direction. It links the most important villages of Phesama, Kigwema, Jakhama, Viswema and Khuzama. It also provides an access to the other villages situated away from the National Highway. A road from Mao traversing along the ridge of the Kedima-Kezo-Chazuo range links Kedima, Kezoma and Kezobasa to Chakhabama (D'Souza 2001:36-37).

A general description of the Southern Angami area was given by L. W. Shakespear in 1914 in the following words.

To a stranger suddenly arriving in the Angami country nothing strikes him with greater surprise and admiration than the beautiful terraced cultivation which meets the eye everywhere, on gentle hill slopes, sides and bottoms of valleys, in fact, wherever the land can be utilised in this way. In preparation, upkeep, and irrigation, the greatest care is taken, far in excess of anything seen in the north-west Himalayas. The appearance of the countryside for miles south of Kohima, for instance, is such as to suggest the handiwork of labour of a far higher order of people than these wild Nagas. These terraced fields are often bordered with dwarf alder bushes, are carefully irrigated by an elaborate system of channels bringing water down from mountain streams, and luxuriant crops of rice are grown on them (Shakespear 1914: 206-207).

The description given by Shakespear is generally valid even today, though in recent times changes have taken place in the Southern Angami area, particularly between Kohima and Viswema. A considerable amount of construction activity has taken place along the Highway especially in Kigwema and Jakhama. This is because of the establishment of Zakhama Military Station which straddles Jakhama and Kigwema villages, St Josephs' College in Jakhama and Japfü Christian College in Kigwema. Despite these changes, the Southern Angami area has a considerable area covered by forests, perennial streams, and well preserved terrace fields.

According to tradition, the Southern Angamis are the descendants of two brothers named Zuonuo and Keyhonuo (Sanyu1996:28). In the process of migration and expansion, they formed ten villages. They are Kigwema, Viswema, Jakhama, Khuzama, Kedima, Kezoma, Phesama, Pfuchama, Mima and Mitelephe. Later Kezobasa, the eleventh village, emerged from Kezoma. General information on these villages, taken from the Census of 1991, is given in the table Source: D'Souza, (2001:37).

Village	*Area in Hectares*	*Number of households*	*Population*		
			Total	*Male*	*Female*
Kedima	1230	380	2618	1273	1345
Kezocha	850	43	272	137	135
Kezoma	690	199	1437	720	717
Kezo Town	110	106	524	266	258
Kezobasa	280	42	218	101	117
Mitelephe	1800	36	120	59	61
Chakhabama	420	99	599	301	298
Khuzama	3100	395	2116	1071	1045
Viswema	4600	829	5466	2683	2783

(Contd...)

Village	*Area in Hectares*	*Number of households*	*Population*		
			Total	*Male*	*Female*
Sweba	4100	54	215	122	93
Jakhama	4500	803	4576	2436	2140
Jakha Town	4300	211	1035	634	401
Kigwe Town	1700	97	402	198	204
Kigwebasa	3700	8	24	13	10
Kigwema	1800	617	3346	1665	1681
Mima	1900	238	1716	848	868
Phesama	3700	335	1884	930	954
Pfuchama	1600	103	701	368	333
Total	40380	4596	27269	13826	13443

Some of the older villages are very large both in area and population. As there has been no systematic land survey, information on the area of the villages is based on estimates accepted by the Census of India. Some of the larger villages have off-shoots, which are not recognised as autonomous, though they are recognised as distinct human settlements by the Census of India. All the villages have their own legends or myths of origin, always indicating that the original settlers came from some other village or area. Some legends link two or more villages as founded by brothers. Some of the original villages are definitely old, perhaps more than a thousand years. All the off-shoots are of recent origin as people from the original villages moved closer to their fields or towards the National Highway and set up independent households.

Land and other types of Property

In order to understand the nature of land relations among the Angamis, it is important to consider the nature of land as a form of property. According to Carruthers and Ariovich, the concept of property concerns the relationship between people and things. (The Sociology of Property Rights 2004:24). This relationship implies rights on the part of the people over things. It involves a bundle of rights, including the exclusive right to use and alienate things. The one who holds these things is the owner and the object owned is the property. Property rights vary over time and between societies with regard to the following dimensions: i) who can be an owner; ii) what may be owned; iii) what constitute a legitimate use; iv) how it is transferred or alienated and v) the nature of exclusiveness.

With regard to what can be owned, the Angami accept different types of property, namely, immovable and movable. The chief forms of immovable property are the house, the residential site, and all types of lands. Chief items of movable property includes agriculture implements and tools, weapons, personal objects like clothing, ornaments, livestock, stores of food grains, and any other items that is considered valuable. As we are more interested in land and other immovable forms of property, we shall examine their nature in some detail a little later.

With regard to the use of property, the Angami recognize the right of the individual to use his personal property as he or she pleases. But in the case of communal property and resources like forests, there are restrictions on the use of such resources. For instance, an individual may cut as many trees as he needs for his personal use or for his household. Any form of wasteful use of common resources is forbidden.

Among the Angami, there are clear norms regarding the transfer and alienation of property. All forms of property, including land, may be sold or exchanged. However, in the case of communal property, all those who have a right to its use must agree to the sale or transfer.

There are also definite norms regarding the transfer of property from one generation to the next through inheritance.

In general, only males can inherit ancestral immovable property like the house and land. However, personally females can inherit acquired immovable property, including the house and land. Among the Zuonuo-Keyhonuo, usually eldest daughter also inherit mother's fieild known as 'pozuopu' land at marriage. Pozuopu land is not evenly distributed among all the daughters; elder daughter being entitled to a larger share of land. Other daughters are also given a part of father's own agnatically inherited land (Das 1984: 87). Only males can inherit items that are used exclusively by males like weapons. They can inherit all items that are considered proper to the use of females.

With regard to exclusiveness, the Angami tradition recognizes absolute ownership in the case of individual property, both ancestral and acquired by the individual. It is thus "private property" in the strict sense. But there is no such absolute exclusiveness in the case of communal property. For instance, all the member households have access to a patch of forest that is owned by a clan. What is more interesting is that any member of the village has access to such communal property for certain purposes. For instance, any member of the village can collect from forests such items as dry branches of trees, edible fruits and roots, medicinal plants and similar things.

Land as Property

Land is the most valued form of property in an agrarian society. In the Angami society land has a fundamental significance because it confers membership of the village to an individual. This is because, every patrilineage *(serra)* and each of its component segment is anchored to a subdivision of the territory within the khel or clan territory. For this reason, an Angami without land is an anomaly. Hence, the oft-repeated saying that there is "no Naga without land" is true in the case of the Angami because every household *(misokeswe)* owns some land. Hence, there can be no Angami household without owning land.

The term 'land' is broad because it includes not merely all types of land but also forests and water sources like streams and rivulets. It is common to distinguish between agricultural and non-agricultural land.

Among the Angami, the only strictly non-agricultural land is the residential site called *pheba*. It is reserved for the purpose of constructions like residential houses, *kichüki* (bachelors' dormitory), *mechüki* (community hall, churches and other structures meant for common use within the residential site of the village.

Agricultural land can be of two basic types: one that is actually used for cultivation and the other that is potentially available for cultivation. Actually cultivated land is in the form of fields. Potentially cultivable land includes forests. The forests themselves can be of different types.

The predominant mode of agriculture among the *Japfuphiki* Angami is terrace cultivation. Therefore, terrace fields are the most valuable type of land. There are three types of terrace fields. They are: *i) Dzutse, ii) Vakhra, and iii) Khutso* (Das 1984: 90). *Dzutse* are terrace fields located near a natural stream and have a completely assured supply of water. Maintenance of these fields is easy as it does not require much labour. *Vakhra* fields are a little away from the stream and are irrigated through water channels, which carry water from the stream. If the stream does not have enough water due to scanty rains, the *vakhra* fields cannot be irrigated. Therefore, they do not have an assured supply of water. *Khutso* are terrace fields that cannot be irrigated by means of water channels from a stream because they are on higher levels. Therefore, they depend entirely on rain. Shifting cultivation plays on a secondary role. The Angami practices shifting cultivation mainly to raise vegetables and various cash crops. Fields used for shifting cultivation are called *melu*. These fields are located on higher levels, between the terrace fields and the forests. They depend entirely on the rains for irrigation.

Forests are important forms of property. There are different types of forests. *Sokha* is the forest that is close to the terrace fields. It can also be a grove of trees. It is carefully preserved and dry branches are regularly trimmed. This type of forest is of critical importance for maintaining a desirable level of moisture in the terrace fields during the dry season. Another type of forest is *ketsalie*. It is close to the fields used for shifting cultivation. In fact, it is often used for the cultivation of vegetables and other cash crops that grow in the shade of trees. Beyond *ketsalie* forest and at higher slopes of the mountains is the *ketsa* forest. It is forest in the strict sense and is the source of timber, firewood and other forest produce. In general, the Angami have preserved their forests with great care. The reason for this is the close link between Angami practice of terrace cultivation and forests. A system of religious beliefs and traditional norms are used for an effective conservation of the forests (D'Souza 2001). It is well known that religious ideas reinforce people's sense of veneration towards the forest and this plays a significant role in the preservation of forest" (Qinghua 2001: 2848).

At present two opposing forces are operative with regard to forests. The first is the tendency towards commercial exploitation of forests for timber and firewood. The second is the growing awareness that forests must be preserved and used as a community resource base for timber, firewood, medicinal plants, various edible fruits, green fodder for the cattle, and so on.

Rivulets and streams are also important forms of property because they are the primary source of water for the fields.

Similarly, water channels that carry water to the fields are also important forms of property. Water channels or *dzüyie* are carefully constructed and maintained.

Two aspects of immovable property, particularly of land, must be noted. The first is that every field, plot of land, or at least an area of the village, has a name. Usually the name indicates the type of field or plot and its use. But much more importantly, the name of a field or plot indicates that it has an owner because the very fact of naming implies the establishment of ownership. The Angami used this argument in 2003 to establish their traditional ownership of *Dzukuo valley*. When some persons from Manipur advanced a claim to the valley, the Angami Public Organisation, the apex body of the Angami, declared that the valley belonged to them by virtue of the fact that the name of the valley was derived from an Angami word.

The second aspect is that every field or plot or area, and even the village itself, has a clearly demarcated boundary. The traditional demarcation of boundary is very simple and convenient and it is still followed. Rivulets, streams, stones, trees, ridges and any other identifiable features are used for boundary demarcation. These objects may be movable or stationary but it is an offence to remove them. The owner of a field or patch forest regularly visits his property to see that boundary markers are intact. Whenever possible, on these visits he takes his young sons and points out the boundary markers to them. Hence, a tampering with boundary markers is a serious offence and open invitation for penalty.

Ownership and Related Questions

Ownership of land in agrarian societies can be individual or communal because land can be owned by an individual or a group or community. Individual ownership implies that the land exclusively belongs to an individual and others have no access to it. Common ownership implies that individuals have access to the land owned in common.

In Nagaland there is no land without an owner. The meaning of the expression "no land without an owner" implies that ownership of land is private and is vested with individuals, households, clans, khels and the village as a whole. There is no concept of the Government being the ultimate owner of the land. In fact, if the Government needs land, it must acquire it through purchase from the private owner. All ownership rights are recognized customary law, which in turn, is protected by Article 371A of the Constitution of India.

Land owned by an individual can be of two types, namely, ancestral land and personally acquired land. Ancestral land is inherited from one's ancestors, while personally acquired land is acquired through purchase or exchange or received as a gift. Such individually owned land, whether ancestral or acquired, can be of any type. It can consist of terrace fields, *jhum* fields and even a patch of forest. In practice, individuals own all the terrace fields, while fields used for shifting cultivation and forests are mostly communally owned. Communal ownership of land is vested with the lineage, clan or village. Such land can be fields used for shifting cultivation, forests, water channels, streams and rivulets. Such land is known as *kayie* (inherited) land. In order to have ownership rights to *kayie* land, an individual must be a member of the unit or group, which owns it. Outsiders can be granted such rights only if they are adopted or assimilated into a patrilineage or clan through a recognized process. However, such communal ownership is not absolute because even those who do not have ownership rights have some access to it provided they are members of the village. We have already noted that any member of the village can collect dead branches, edible fruits and medicinal plants from anywhere in the village land. Such general rights imply that in former times communal ownership was the norm and that individual ownership or the institution of private property evolved later on.

Angami traditional law gives absolute rights to the individual owner of land so that he or she can do with it as he or she wishes. He or she may alienate it by sale or gift. He or she may mortgage or rent it to others. He or she may bequeath it to his or her children in the manner he or she wishes. However, there are some restrictions on bequeathing ancestral land to daughters, According to customary law only sons can inherit the ancestral house and ancestral land, though such restrictions are now sometimes overlooked. On the other hand, there are no restrictions on gifting or bequeathing to daughters any personally acquired land. If a daughter receives land as a gift from the parents, she may deal with it as she wishes. In most cases, however, she gifts that land to her daughters giving rise to a situation in which some land is passed on along the female line.

Traditional Angami law permitted all types of transactions in land. Almost all property is alienable in some measure, and so shifts between different owners. As for land, already in 1892, Davis noted: "Amongst the Angami land, particularly terraced permanent cultivation, is freely sold and bought, there being no more difficulty in selling a terraced field than in selling a pig or cow" (Davis 1892: 250). This does not mean that an individual could sell his or her land to anyone. In former times, there were various restrictions as to whom land could be sold or transferred. Members of the same lineage or clan had the first right to buy. If there was no buyer within this unit, the owner could sell it to someone within the *khel*. Only when there was no buyer within the *khel*, the owner could sell it to someone within the village. In former times, selling land to someone belonging to another village was practically out of the question because of rivalry and even enmity between villages. However, one could sell it to a buyer from a friendly village. But, land was never sold to a non-Angami and certainly not to a non-Naga. At present the law forbids the sale of land to non-tribals (D'Souza 2001:44-46).

It is not known when the institution of private property came into existence among the Angami. E.R. Grange, one of the British officers who toured the Naga Hills in 1840, noted that landed property among the Angami was hereditary (quoted in Elwin 1969: 224). This indicates that the institution of private property was not merely a usufructuary right found in most tribal societies as noted by Pathy (1988: 84-85). It is possible that the institution of private property came into existence among the Angami due to their practice of terrace cultivation. Unlike shifting cultivation, terrace cultivation is labour intensive and requires constant care of the field throughout the year. Probably, this nature of terrace cultivation favoured the emergence of private property among the Angami.

As already mentioned, the concept of private property, whether individually or communally owned, implies a certain amount of exclusiveness. Private property excludes others from access and use of that property. It has also been mentioned above that there are clear demarcation of boundaries between fields. Nevertheless, disputes over land occur among the Angami as in any other tribal society.

Among the Angami, there are different types of land disputes. There may be a dispute about a boundary between two fields or plots of land or patch of forest. There may also be a dispute about ownership and usufructuary rights over a field or piece of land or forest. When there is a dispute between two individuals, clans, *khels,* the *khel* or village council settles the dispute. If the parties involved fail to compromise, the council may asks the claimant to take an oath. On failure to do so, the disputed land goes to the aggrieved person. On the other hand, if the council of elders is satisfied through the statement of facts that both the parties have equal rights, then the disputed land may be divided among the contending parties. Disputes between two villages are settled through negotiations and arbitration, and now through an intervention of a higher organization like the Angami Public Organization.

There are three basic types of land in an Angami village, namely, i) terrace fields, ii) *jhum* fields, and iii) forest. A household can individually own all the three types. In any case, it must own some terrace fields, because the ownership of terrace fields goes with the membership of the village. A household that does not own some terrace fields in an anomaly. In addition to the terrace fields, a household may or may not individually hold *jhum* fields and forest. If it does not individually hold *jhum* fields and forest, it still has access to such land owned by their lineage, clan or *khel*. There are four possibilities with regard to the ownership of land by a household. These possibilities are the following.

1. A household may own only terrace fields.
2. A household may own terrace fields and *jhum* fields.
3. A household may own terrace fields and forest.
4. A household may own terrace fields, *jhum* fields and forest.

The general belief among the people is that at the time of the first settlement of the village, land was distributed among the different lineages in the sense that different lineages occupied and began to cultivate land in places in the village. Within a lineage there were the original households which later developed into clans. At this point community ownership by the lineage was the norm. A household cultivated as much land as it could, or as much land it needed to produce sufficient food. It is probable that terrace cultivation came into vogue from the time of the establishment of the village. As terrace fields require more attention, it can be presumed that individual ownership by a household in the terrace fields it cultivated came to be recognised. As the original household developed into a lineage, terrace fields were constructed for each new household. In fact, the traditional practice was to construct some terrace fields for every newly born male child, the potential head of a household. Thus, practice of individual ownership of terrace fields is probably as old as the village itself.

Even when individual ownership in terrace fields came to be recognised, forest was owned by the lineage as a whole. In course of time, some of the forest area lying close to the terrace fields was converted into fields for *jhum* or shifting cultivation in order to grow additional food grains and vegetables for human and animal consumption. It is likely that each year a household was either allotted or selected a portion of the forest for shifting cultivation. However, ownership of forest, including the portion converted into *jhum* fields, continued to be communal. Thus the normal situation would be for each household to own some terrace fields, and to have access to the *jhum* fields and forest owned by the lineage. However, this normal situation has changed over time and at present private ownership in *jhum* fields and forest is recognised. As a result, at present a household can own all the three types of land. These inequalities are due to the acquisition and loss of land. It is not easy to know the exact extent of land owned by a household. This is because in the hills of Nagaland no systematic survey of land has been conducted. It is only in recent times the practice of surveying land has come into vogue, and that too only when the Government or some public organisation wants to acquire land.

Land Transactions

Various types of transactions in land or transfer of rights in land have been taking place even in the past. In fact, transactions in land are more frequent than one would expect in a tribal village. Transfer of rights in land or land transactions take different forms. These are: i) inheritance;

ii) giving and receiving land as a gift; iii) renting out and renting in land for cultivation; iv) selling and buying land.

Inheritance

Possession of ancestral land is important for a household and an individual because it confers membership of clan, khel and the village with all the rights and privileges that such a membership implies. Thus possession of ancestral provides a basis for identity. Possession of some ancestral land is so important that even when a person is forced to sell his land for some reason or other, he will always retain some portion of the ancestral inherited land. In any case, it is essential for a male to inherit at least a small portion of ancestral land.

It is important to note here that in the patriarchal and patrilineal system of the Angami, ancestral land can be inherited only by the males. In the absence of a male child, ancestral property goes to the male members of the lineage. There is, however, a special case when a daughter can inherit ancestral property. This can happen if the father has no male issue, and the married daughter comes along with her husband and children to live with her father. At his death she acquires the ancestral property. But the patrilineal principle is still observed because she has to make a symbolic transfer of a small piece of ancestral land and household articles to the father's male kin.

Land as Gift

If females cannot inherit ancestral land, they can inherit land that is acquired by her parents. A daughter can inherit the personally acquired land of her parents in the sense that she can receive it as a gift from her parents, both the father and the mother. In the Southern Angami area, land received as a gift from the mother is usually transmitted from mother to daughter. Thus the practice of giving and receiving land as gift is embedded in the Angami tradition and continues even at present. This implies that land has an intrinsic value in itself.

Renting Land

The practice of renting land for cultivation has been in vogue among the Angami even in former times. A basic feature of renting in all these cases is that it is done between members of the same lineage or between persons who are closely related. But this can easily change and even those who do not belong to the same lineage may rent out and rent in land. The practice of renting is not new among the Angamis. Even in former times a close relative or the member of the lineage cultivated fields belonging to others and gave a share of the produce. But now it is becoming more common. In recent times many Angami men have received education and are employed in towns like Kohima and Dimapur and have shifted their residence to these towns. What is significant is that a new category of absentee land owners together with the category of those who cultivate fields for rent is emerging. This indicates the emergence of a form of tenancy unique to the Angamis in which land is considered as a factor of production and not merely a form of wealth.

A more interesting type of tenancy is now emerging among the Angamis. Such land is cultivated with the help of outsiders, chiefly non-Naga labourers. The owners have a house on the land and occasionally supervise the work of the labourers, and after the harvest they sell the produce in the market and bring part of the produce to the village for their household consumption. Such cultivators may be described as landlords or even as absentee landlords. For them agricultural land is a form of capital.

Buying and Selling Land

Buying and selling land, including terrace fields has been

practised by the Angamis even in former times. In fact, the transaction of buying and selling of terrace fields seems to be more common than would be expected in a tribal community where land is the basic source of livelihood. There are several aspects in the selling and buying land which need to be examined. First of all, there are several restrictions on buying and selling land in an Angami village. An outsider, in particular a non-Naga, cannot buy land in the village. This norm is now enforced also by the Indian law which forbids a non-tribal from buying tribal land. However, in the Angami tradition, normally land is not sold to an outsider because that would give an outsider the rights and privileges of membership in the village. On the other hand, when someone wants to sell land, he usually sells to his lineage or clan members if they are willing and when there is no buyer within the lineage, he can sell to someone else. The second aspect that needs to be seen is the reasons for selling land. Two most common reasons are: i) to raise money for the education of children, and, ii) to raise money in a crisis situation like medical treatment. A third reason is when the government or some public body wants the land for some specific purpose. The next question is the value of the land and the mode of payment. In former times when the barter system was prevalent, the value of a field was measured in terms of cattle. There are instances when a field was sold for a cow in return. After the introduction of money as the medium of exchange, the value of land is measured in terms of money.

Land Acquisition for Public Purposes

Another form of land transaction is in the form of land alienation for public purposes. All government offices in the villages in Japfuphiki are private or communal property acquired by the government which is given or contributed by the villagers for common purpose.

Other land transactions

There are other cases of loss of land through gambling. In former times gambling was done while playing some games with sticks and stones. But after the arrival of playing cards were used. What is significant is that in all such cases land is gambled away as any other piece of property or item of commodity.

Changes in Land Relations

Thus ownership of terrace fields by individual households was well established probably centuries ago. But ownership of forest and *jhum* fields was communal because it was vested in the lineage, clan and *khel*. Thus the traditional form of land relations was that of individual ownership of terrace fields and communal ownership of all other types of land, including water sources. This type of land relations has undergone changes. Following are the changes noticed:

Emergence of absolute ownership by individuals

Ownership of terrace fields by the household is now accepted as ownership by the head of the household. It is true that even in the past individual members could own a terrace field. Thus a man could buy terrace field and give it as a gift to his daughter. What is new is the concept of absolute ownership by the individual without any reference to his household.

Transition from communal ownership to individual ownership in jhum land and forest

In former times, ownership of *jhum* land and forest was communal. The lineage or clan or the *khel* were considered as the owners. This began to change with the construction of permanent *jhum* fields. Individual households continued to cultivate the same *jhum* plot and even plant alder trees on the plot. Thus, through continued use over several years by one household, the plot came to be seen as the property of that household. The next step was that such a household acquired absolute ownership rights over the particular plot. This is an indication that there has been a transition from communal ownership to individual ownership leading to recognition of the absolute right of ownership. A similar process has taken place with regard to ownership of forest.

Emergence of tenancy

Land has always been an economic asset. In former times, land was also a social asset. Buying and selling of land, and giving and receiving it as gift, was practised even before the British came on the scene. Thus land was perceived as a form of wealth. As long as the size of population was small and land was abundant, this did not create any problem because a person could always bring new land under cultivation and even construct new terrace fields. But with the growing population, when land became scarce, particularly in modern times, there came into existence a class of people who began to cultivate the *jhum* land for commercial crops. In addition, they also began to cultivate for rent the land of others, especially of their kinsmen. It must be stressed that such tenants always owned and cultivated some land of their own; they were, therefore, tenants only in a broad sense. Nevertheless this development implied that land was considered as a form of capital which could bring income to the owner in the form of rent and that land could be rented for cultivation. This was the new perception of land as an exploitable asset and as a form of capital. The next step was the commercialisation of land, beginning with the *jhum* fields, many of which were converted into construction sites for houses and hostels. Selling and buying of land became common.

Thus the major change is that, in addition to the traditional forms of ownership, a type of tenancy has emerged.

In this process land which was formerly seen as a source of livelihood and gradually came to be seen as a form of capital and now as a mere commodity that can be sold and bought.

Factors of Change

Several factors have been at work to give rise to the present situation in *Japfuphiki* with regard to changes in the agrarian structure and in land relations.

Demographic Factors

Steep rise in the number of households and population has been a fundamental factor in these changes. The increase in population means, among other things, more mouths to feed, more persons to be educated and more persons to be clothed and housed. This requires more food grains to feed the additional mouths, and money to provide education and other basic necessities.

As more terrace fields cannot be constructed, some households have brought in more land under *jhum* cultivation. Secondly, some have taken fields on rent from others in order to grow more food grains and cash crops. Thirdly, many have begun to raise cash crops in the *jhum* fields. Fourthly, some have sold their *jhum* fields, and occasionally even terrace fields to raise money for the education of children, particularly higher education outside Nagaland. All these trends have contributed to the change in land relations. They have stimulated the process of converting communal ownership into individual ownership, and the practice of renting land for cultivation.

Political Factors

Various political events and factors have also contributed to the changes. It is beyond the scope of this paper to study the political factors but it is sufficient for us to know that the so called "16 point Agreement: in 1960, the creation of

Nagaland as a State in 1963, the Shillong Accord of 1975 and the present Cease-fire Agreement are the major political events that have deeply affected Nagaland and the Nagas, including the Angamis. Moreover, there has been relative peace. Secondly, new political institutions like the elected village council, elections on party lines to the new legislatures and the Indian Parliament have affected the life of the people. Thirdly, due to new administrative structures and developmental activities, there has been a significant rise in government employment. In the fourth place, there has been a regular flow of government funds as salaries of government servants and for developmental activities.

Among the various consequences of these developments the most basic one is that of a significant change in the occupational structure with a shift from agriculture as the main source of income to non-agricultural occupations. All the categories of cultivators have been affected by this.

Cultural factors

Conversion to Christianity and the spread of modern education are the two important cultural factors. At present, most of the people of the region have accepted Christianity, though they belong to three denominations or churches, namely, Baptist, Revivalist and Roman Catholic Church. The acceptance of Christianity has meant the rejection of traditional animist beliefs. A fundamental animist belief is that the forests are abodes of the spirits and that there are spirits associated with every geographical feature. This invested fields and forests with a sort of sacredness. With the acceptance of Christianity such beliefs have weakened and fields and forest are seen as nothing more than material things. This change of perspective has made it possible to think of fields and all types of land as a form of commodities.

Modern education came to the region with the establishment of Government schools. In the first place, modern education, as a channel of scientific and liberal ideas which influence the world view of the people, also affected the manner in which land and agriculture are seen. Secondly, the spread of education has meant an increase in the number of educated persons, including the educated unemployed, leading to change in the occupational structure of the population, which has experienced a shift from agricultural occupations.

Economic factors

While other factors are of relatively recent origin, economic factors have a longer history because they made their entry with the coming of the British into the area. The British came into this area of Nagaland in 1832. Though their immediate objective was to open a road from Manipur to Assam, they also had economic interests. These colonial economic interests were to identify exploitable natural resources. As British involvement in the area developed, they introduced the money economy into this area. This was institutionalised when they imposed house taxes to be paid in cash. This was the beginning of the incorporation of the area into the colonial economic system. The colonial economic system had different aspects. In addition to the introduction of cash transactions, they also brought in machine made consumer goods never seen in the Naga Hills till then. The integration of the Naga Hills into the Indian colonial economic system intensified after Independence. In spite of the Naga movement the process of economic integration with the rest of the country has continued. In recent times because of economic liberalisation and globalisation, the entire State of Nagaland has been affected.

Due to these general economic processes, the life of the people has been irreversibly affected. The traditional self-sufficient subsistence economy of the village has been incorporated into the national and even global economy.

Along with other factors, these processes have led to various changes in the economy, agrarian structure and land relations. The most fundamental change is the decreasing importance of agriculture as the mainstay of the village economy. Traditional agriculture meant primarily to produce food grains for domestic consumption is becoming market oriented with the introduction of cash crops. *Jhum* fields are easily converted into construction sites for commercial purposes. Plots of forest are being planted with commercially valuable tress. Such changes in the use of land imply that land is seen no more as a form of property but as a commodity that can be sold and bought or leased out for a rent in cash.

The commodification of land indicates a new pattern of land relations. The concept and practice of absolute ownership by individuals has begun to spread. There has been a transition from communal ownership to individual ownership. Further, the practice of tenancy has emerged. Thus, changes in land relations have been accompanied by a change in the agrarian structure.

Although this paper deals with the unique nature of agrarian changes in Angami society, such changes may be found in other Naga tribal societies as well. This is because the same forces of changes are at work also in other tribal societies in Nagaland.

REFERENCES

1. Bareh, H. M. (2001). *Encyclopaedia of North-East India: Vol VI, Nagaland*. New Delhi: Mittal Publications.
2. Carruthers, Bruce.G. and Laura Ariovich (2004). "The Sociology of Property Rights", *Annual Review of Sociology*. 2004. 30:23-46.
3. Census of India (1991). *Nagaland State: District Profile 1991*. New Delhi: Census Publications.

4. Das, N. K. (1984). "Land Management, Dual Inheritance and Redistribution among the Zonuo-Keyhonuo Naga" in S. S. Chakravarti, B. K. Ghosh and Ajit K. Danda (eds.): *Agrarian Situation in India, Vol II.* Calcutta: Anthropological Survey of India, Ministry of Education and Culture, Government of India.

5. ——————(1987). *Ethnic Identity, Ethnicity and Social Stratification in North-East India.* New Delhi: Inter-India Publication.

6. Davis, A. W. (1891). *Census of India, 1891, Assam, Vol 1.* p.250. Quoted in Verrier Elwin, 1969. *The Nagas in the Nineteenth Century*. Bombay: Oxford University.

7. D'Souza, Alphonsus (2001). *Traditional Systems of Forest Conservation in North East India: The Angami Tribe of Nagaland.* Guwahati: North Eastern Social Research Centre.

8. Elwin, Verrier, (1969). *The Nagas in the Nineteenth Century.* Bombay: Oxford University

9. Farmer, B. H. (1968). "Comparative Technology" in David L. Shills (ed) *International Encyclopaedia of the Social Sciences, Vol 7&8.* New York: The MacMillan Company and The Free Press.

10. Hutton, J. H. (1921). *The Angami Nagas*. London: Macmillan & Co. Reprinted 1969. Bombay: Oxford University Press.

11. Pathy, Jagnath (1988). *Ethnic Minorities in the Process of Development*. Jaipur. Rawat Publication.

12. Qinghua, Wang (2001). "Forest Management and Terraced Agriculture: Case Study of Hani of Ailao Mountains, Yunnan", in *Economic and Political Weekly* (No.30 July 28): 2848.

13. Sanyu, Visier (1996). *A History of Nagas and Nagaland: Dynamics of Tradition - Village Formation.* New Delhi: Commonwealth Publishers.

14. Shakespear, L. W. (1914). *History of Upper Assam, Upper Burma and North Eastern Frontier*. London.

17

DEVELOPMENT A COLLECTIVE JOURNEY - WELL-BEING ITS DESTINATION: Some Reflections in the Context of Naga Society

Chandan Debnath & G. Singaiah

> *["Lose not the hard working spirit for we are not beggars, nature provides you everything to feed your stomach and to have a shelter if you hold your dao and hoe".*

Previous studies and research findings have brought home the realization that cultural beliefs, values and institutions play a vital role in managing transitions along with determining the direction and rate of development. Economic development is a product of individual initiative and institutional support, working in tandem upon the resources of nature. The strength of a culture lies in inducing aspirations among individuals to excel. Institutional backup in this context connotes a general consensus in supporting individual initiatives through reward and recognition, respect for diversity and dignity of labour. The efficiency with which individuals and organizations work upon on the bounties of nature marks the process and progress of development. Individuals as social entities bank on its collective knowledge base. Cultural beliefs and values set the parameters of action by ascribing values such as most desirable, desirable, neutral, undesirable and most undesirable. Beliefs and values set the standards of what is desirable and undesirable in respect of human endeavor in general and life in particular.

Cultural factors affecting programmes of economic development can be divided into two classes: individual motivation and societal support. The motivational aspects involve factors such as: attitudes and approach to life, time, wealth, competition, work, innovation, risk orientation etc. It also involves a minimal consensus on social goals such as higher standards of living, education, health, managing conflicts etc. Secondly societal support consists of status and recognition, patterns of authority, leadership, reference groups, space for sharing ideas etc. Thus culture is essentially an adaptive mechanism and not conflicting to human need and desire to grow, progress and excel.

The paper is a modest attempt to understand the cultural dimensions of the Naga society and how beliefs orient approach towards work in particular and life in general. Further the study reflects on the esteemed opinions and understanding of distinguished academicians, policy makers and public leaders of the state and agrees that developmental process in Nagaland can be best achieved by evolving social partnerships. This paper reiterates that development is a participative exercise which involves common strength, combined resources, collective wisdom to make it effective. Anything which calls for common strength, resources and wisdom has its source in the culture of the people.]

Contemporary society illustrates many paradoxes and complex problems. However man with higher faculties is consciously and subconsciously aware that, being pulled down by these insurmountable paradoxes and problems is a sign of immaturity unbecoming of men placed in the higher strata of life. Transition is always a difficult affair and strength of a society/community lies in managing transitions. Experience and research findings have brought home the realization that traditional values and institutions play a vital role in managing transitions and in determining the direction and rate of human development. Taking note of this all important factor, the contemporary trend is towards comprehensive planning that takes note of entire complex of ideological, motivational and institutional factors that significantly condition and govern the process of economic development.

Development a Collective Journey

To begin with, it is safe to assume that no cultures shall be openly receptive to the entire gamut of change offered through development initiatives. It is natural to question change process rather than blindly fall in its bandwagon. However wisdom warns us of the danger of making conclusions such as: culture and tradition come in the way of change and innovation. In this context (Dube: 1994) states that cultural frontiers perceived to be resistant to change if any is symbolic rather than real. From a prehistoric existence as hunters, food gathers, we humans have journeyed to the 21st century wherein the vastness of the physical world has been reduced to a miniature village. Thus it shall be whimsical to identify any society as primitive as, all of us knowingly or unknowingly have experienced significant changes in our individual and collectively life. The reason for differences across societies in terms of growth and development can be attributed to the few early and quicker steps of some societies while others remaining a bit slow in catching up. Probably in a very simplistic way this explains the reason for the gap between the advanced societies and others who rank slightly lower to them in terms of material and economic wellbeing.

This reiterates the proposition that no society is stagnant, change is immanent and managing the pace of change as per the needs and resources of specific communities can be termed as effective development. Thus, change devoid of planning and direction makes the journey in search of value circuitous and long. Planned steps make change natural refreshing and accommodative in all respects.

In this context it shall be pertinent to understand the meaning of economic development. Economic development is a product of individual initiative and institutional support working in tandem upon the resources of nature. Individual initiatives are guided by needs, need for achievement, orientation towards wealth, merit, incentives and rewards etc. Propensity of the need for realizing wellbeing acts as a catalyst for generating value and surplus, which in turn can satisfy his/her, needs and at the same sustain a passion for excellence. Needs are expressions of aspirations and the simple relation being, higher the aspiration/expectation higher the need for value and well-being. The strength of a culture lies in inducing aspirations among individuals to excel. Organizational support in this context connotes a general consensus on supporting individual initiatives through leadership, reward and recognition, respect for diversity and dignity of labour. The efficiency with which individuals and organizations work upon on the bounties of nature, it marks the process and progress of development. Individuals as social entities bank on its collective knowledge base. A society's knowledge bases are its beliefs, values, symbols, material artifacts, customs, rituals, practices etc. Cultural beliefs and values set the parameters of action by ascribing values such as most desirable, desirable, neutral, undesirable and most undesirable. Beliefs and values set the standards of what is desirable and undesirable in respect of human endeavor in general and life in particular.

Culture – Tradition and Development

Beliefs and values as part of the culture set standards that guide behaviour towards work and realizing well being. They represent desirable, neutral and undesirable facets of life and work behavior. As each culture hold neutral beliefs and values it shall be wrong to blame culture-tradition standing in the path of development. This necessitates evaluation of the various elements in the schema of development individually and severally. First a close examination is required from the point of view of culturally perceived need and than from the point of view of compatibility to the beliefs and dominant values that culture holds and supports. Cultural factors affecting programmes of economic development can be divided into two classes: individual motivation and societal support. The motivational aspects involve factors such as: attitudes and approach to life, time, wealth, competition, work, innovation, risk orientation etc. It also involves a minimum consensus on social goals such as higher standards of living, education, health managing conflicts etc. Secondly societal support consists of status and recognition, patterns of authority, leadership, reference groups, space for sharing ideas etc. Thus the above understanding brings forth that culture and traditions are supporting knowledge systems and it gets refined/adjusted to accommodate the change demanded by uniqueness of time and situations. A culture is essentially an adaptive mechanism and not conflicting to human need and desire to grow progress and excel. No culture is static. It can be believed at any point of time it has elements of change and continuity. Since culture represents communities knowledge and experience it can be fairly assumed that, culture believes in community well-being and means for it lies in enlisting community participation in development and change. At this juncture it is pertinent to evaluate the meaning and effectiveness of community charted development initiatives.

Community Development

The Panchayat Raj institution, Village Council and Village Development Board as in the case of Nagaland is a milestone achieved towards involvement of community in economic development. These institutions were built on noble grounds focused on the principle objective to generate consensus on major issues concerning geographical need and spread of development. In this respect collectively society needs to question on the following: Are grassroots level organizations performing effectively in shaping peoples aspirations. Do they appreciate participation? Are they empowered to act as pressure groups? Do they believe in equity and democratic principles of functioning? Are they bounded by narrow boundaries of political selfishness etc? Taking note of all the above questions Prof. Dube states, "*the experiment of community development in India has been comprehensive and imaginative. Experimental and flexible in nature it has refused to adopt the doctrine approach*". No doubt in terms of input-output relationships it achieved major quantitative growths. But in achieving true ideals of community development it has experienced difficulties almost at every step. Dominant reasons for the underperformance in the national context are:

1. There is a relative absence of community consciousness in the Indian villages. The rural India even on this date is fractured by its own internal contradictions of class caste loyalties, religious segmentations and economic differentiations. Thus evolving a consensus amidst multiplicity of narrow segmented loyalties is a task of immense magnitude.

2. Internal differences as stated above bring to forefront the negativities associated with lack of focus. Beyond the realm of catering to subsistence needs there is hardly a consensus on long term perspectives.

Dominance on the present appears to be the principle reason for stagnation.

3. The caste system though disintegrating still appears to have a profound impact on equality of wok opportunity and consequent mobility. Why do we still have to think that the cobblers come from the *Chamar* community, sweepers from the scavenger's community etc. On the other side when a person of high caste begs for alms it is considered religious duty, a part of his ascetic life. Does it not amount to patronizing parasites who otherwise also shoulder equal responsibility to contribute to social wealth and well-being? Contrary when a person from the so called lowly man made strata achieves a certain position by virtue of merit; his/her ability is doubted. The basic issue of this discrimination is questioning dignity of labour. In such a scenario can one think of community participation when deliberately people are differentiated on certain criteria or flimsy grounds? Ones at the receiving end of these discriminatory policies, over the years have loads of pent up frustrations. It limits mobility due to taboos, injunctions and opportunities in terms of education, skill and knowledge up gradation etc. In such a scenario marginalized communities lack space and freedom to equip themselves for vertical and horizontal growth, so as keep pace with the needs of time and situation.

4. Our society guided by collectivist norm is another reason for relative backwardness. The reason being, in collectivist society figurehead and reference group plays a dominant role in developing consensus. It is imperative that the figure head and reference group working in the capacity of change agent must ensure

a consensus rather than force or manipulate consensus. However this reference group by virtue of better education and higher exposure are tacitly guided by their self interest rather than collective interest. This disarrays collective effort as reference group directs work/activity in areas that fits their interest and understanding. Such negativities of the reference group, community leadership discourages divergent thinking, innovation, rational participation and risk taking abilities. Absence of rational participation perpetuates dependency. It does not widen the base for enhanced earnings and wealth in relation to efforts put in. There is a pressure to confirm to group norms and constructive differences are perceived as challenging leadership without seriously evaluating their ability to add on to community well being. The end result is cosmetic or symbolic participation in place of objective and unconditional participation which is a prerequisite for community development.

5. The practice of vesting authority on men and placing women in subordination on areas of strategic and development initiatives is also laying its toll towards community participation. Men are granted the greater say because; he shoulders the responsibility of providing, sustaining, protecting and supporting the family. Can we justify the discrimination of women on this ground overlooking the valuable contributions women make in building families and societies? The traditional role of women is stated to be bearing children, caring and management of household affairs. I believe that managing families is similar to managing modern corporate entity. In her role as a manger she has to prioritize on demands of family members but the same times ensure that at the end

of the day everyone is satisfied. It allows no scope for errors as slight fumbling shall dent the goal and objectives of the family (organization) that she heads as the ex-officio manager. The question that needs to be pondered is: Can men be justified in overlooking the managerial effectiveness of women that they personify. Will it not be beneficial to accord them due recognition. On a whole these factors seem too responsible in negating community participation in our society.

Naga Culture – Influence on Economic Development

The socio-cultural differences between the developed and underdeveloped societies have been explained by Hofstead (1980) in his land mark study *Motivations leadership and organization: Do American theories apply abroad?* The four dimensions suggested by him to mark the differences between developed and developing countries in an organizational context are: uncertainty avoidance, power distance, individualism-collectivism and masculinity versus femininity. Using these dimensions Kanungo and Jaeger (1990) have characterized socio-cultural environment of developing countries as high on uncertainty avoidance and power distance and relatively low on individualism. On the additional dimension, abstractive versus associative thinking suggested by Bhagat and Kedia (1988) developing countries are low on abstractive thinking and high on associative thinking. Each of the five cultural dimensions is assumed to orient our behavior and approach towards work, having an influence on productivity and the consequent development process. Taking note of the above cultural variables the paper desires to understand their implications on development efforts in the Naga society.

Collectivism: a Way of Naga Life

India is categorized as a developing society and Nagaland

as a part of India reflects the features of a developing society. From the Naga cultural beliefs and values it can be assumed that Nagas' are a collective society as since time immemorial the emphasis always has been on achieving and promoting collective well-being. Some cultural practices, traditions and beliefs which is felt to support the above argument are: i) community celebrations cum feasting, ii) group hunting and sharing the game with kith and clan, iii) existence of clan/ village land and forest resources, iv) clan members assisting one other in agricultural operations and the near absence oh hired labour, v) having places of worship belonging to distinct community/ tribe, vi) low preference for migration outside respective tribal domain or beyond the state, vii) practice of forming numerous organizations, unions to protect village, clan, range or tribal interest etc, viii) villages established and inhabited on clan lines, ix) the tradition of sovereign village states and the collective responsibility of defending it, x) Practice of community learning enabled through the institution of *Morung*, xi) Last but not the least the importance accorded to social recognition by the Nagas. Therefore from the above citations one can assume that Nagas are a collective society and their collectivism has strengths which can be roped in for effective social and economic transformation of the state.

Power Distance

In the Naga society age and seniority is respected both in the present and in the past. For receiving social recognition and to be accepted as a leader, one had to prove their worth and merit to his/her clan/tribe. In the past the title of chief were bestowed on those who excelled themselves in different walks of life. Further the title was not hereditary to a single family or clan especially in the case of Angamis (Some Naga tribes had the concept of hereditary chiefs). Rationality guided them in according and accepting power and position.

Merit was sole criteria of according social importance and equal opportunity was extended to one and all to earn recognition vide ones individual merit. Thus analysis of cultural practices vis-à-vis power distance brings forth a conclusion that Naga's believed in respecting merit objectively. They also gave credence to seniority. To them age was equated with experience and experience coupled with wisdom called for due respect. The existence of Low power distance in the society is evident from the fact that all issues concerning common interest were democratically addressed. Naga's basically are a classless society and all the cultural believes and practices cited above indicate existence of low power distance in their society.

Uncertainty Avoidance

This basically is a measurement that indicates cultural preference for risk or its avoidance. In the context of Naga's their cultural beliefs and practices point towards low uncertainty avoidance. This belief can be authenticated by the following cultural beliefs and practices. All Naga tribes are essentially head hunting tribes and head hunting expedition's involved colossal personal risk. There is a particular type of game played by the children which consciously and sub-consciously has been instrumental in building risk management capacity in them. In the game children divide themselves in two groups, each carrying some toy guns or for that matter anything that resembles like a gun or which can be symbolized as a gun. Hiding themselves they stealthily approach the enemy group and take on each other in a mock do or die fight. The rule is – the moment an enemy is sighted and is believed to be within range for a direct hit, one shouts in ecstasy fire... fire... and the opponent so targeted in the mock drill must fall down in order to be presumed as dead or marginalized. Thus through such innovative games children learn to master the art of guerilla warfare which in the process can be believed to condition their mind to accept and confront challenges latter on as a youth and responsible citizenry. From the above analysis one can believe that Naga's are not averse to risk and uncertainty when challenged or when their common interest stands jeopardized.

Masculinity - Femininity

Nagas as patriarchal society indicates the existence of dominant masculinity in their personality. For a Naga loss of face is a major issue and identity is crucial to them. Till today an average Naga believes his/her Naga identity is far more precious than the larger Indian identity. The common sentiment among all tribes is, first they are Nagas and the Indian identity is secondary to them. The desire to compete and excel can be seen in many of their cultural practices. To seek the hand of a beautiful dame an eligible bachelor had to prove himself through his work. This was needed to convince the brides' family of his capability and eligibility as the most natural choice in comparison to his compatriots or similar age groups. An eligible bachelor has to own a house before seeking a bride so that the couple can live independently. Their culture appears to induce in them a sense of independence befitting the image of complete man. Though in Naga society women enjoy better status but they do not enjoy property rights. Share in the parental property is the sole right of male siblings in the family. In case of agricultural land women enjoy cultivable rights over the property but do not posses the property. Man are expected to be aggressive and the *Nagamese* phrase '*maikinisena na koribi*' (don't act like a woman) is indicative of the same. Nagas as warrior tribe is known for their uncompromising nature especially while dealing with foes or with individuals who have willfully sullied their image or challenged them on something which seriously impacts their life. Conflict arising from any of the above is always carried to its logical end i.e., fight to the finish and if required go on till victory is achieved. From the above one can believe that Naga personality reflects masculinity features and it guides their approach and attitude towards life in general.

Locus of Control

It refers to the degree of control that people perceive to have on their own lives. When people perceive that they are masters of their own lives, the locus of control is inward or internal and vice versa. It reflects a choice between fatalism and self assurance in shaping ones existence to the best of an individual's capacity. In the context of Naga tribes, though they practice certain rituals or customs which normally can be termed as superstitious, yet their day-to-day activities directed at adding economic value to their life, reflects their internal locus of control. To substantiate the aforesaid view, we are aware that bulk of Naga villages is either placed at mountain tops or on ridges. Definitely finding means for daily existence was challenging. Further their economic belief of building and sustaining a self – reliant village amidst the rugged mountains was an arduous community task. The fact that Naga villages in the past were self-sustaining sovereign states proves that they truly achieved what they aspired by dint of hard work, ingenuity and commitment. From salt making to producing other necessities of life along with meeting safety and security needs, they mastered different skills and passed the same to successive generations to add on. All this testifies their internal locus of control and of their being guided by their self conviction. Their practice of observing a host *gennas* and *pennas* can be interpreted as, showing respect to the forces of nature and seeking their benevolence and support. More it was understood as a means to forge partnership between nature and man so that nature vide her power and bounties could support men in a totality of purpose.

Fig. - Sociocultural Milieu of Nagas

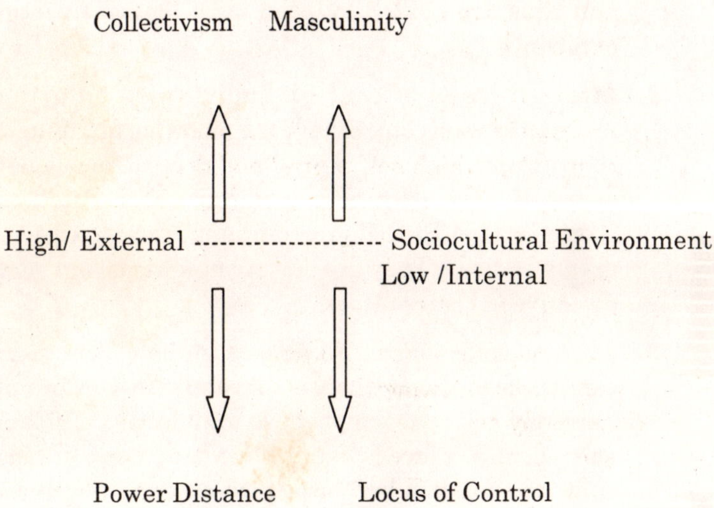

Cultural Dimensions and Influence on Work Approaches

One key aspect of development process is society's orientation towards work and value generation. The end result of work is value generation. Efficiency of a community in value generation accelerates the process of development. From the beliefs and practices of Naga tribes the following can be inferred to have a strong impact in influencing a positive work behavior:

1. *Low power distance*: A society with low power distance can indicate the following: existence of a classless society, belief in democratic traditions, low acceptance

of dominance or insubordination, absence of inferiority complex, believe in just, equity, fairness and transparency and communication is a two way process. Individual accord high importance to merit and thus are guided by need for achievement and excellence.

2. *Internal locus of control*: Individuals enjoying internal locus of control have the following attributes: they exhibit high self control and dependency is not approved. They are rationalistic in approach. Fatalism is discouraged. Straight forwardness is preferred over manipulations. They are open to new ideas and very objective in their outlook.

3. *High on collectivism*: Societies high on collectivism exhibit the following: there is a greater stress on formal harmony and cohesion, believe in collective problem solving, loss of face is major issue here, large groups split into small subgroups based on certain criteria such as clan, or ethnic and other affiliations. Generally people are warm and responsive to the weak and the feeble.

4. *High Masculinity*: In masculine societies people are motivated by competition, ambition and challenges. Emphasis is placed on winning and winners take all. Believe offensive strategy is better than being defensive. People are guided by materialistic attitude rather than on being contended with what one owns or possesses.

5. *Weak uncertainty avoidance*: Society that score low on uncertainty find existence of challenges as stimulating. People feel comfortable in unstructured situations rather than highly structured work situations. Showing emotions is considered a weakness. Societies having this trait believe in plain

taking rather than appeasing. Intellectual disagreement is encouraged and people do not feel threatened by differences or disagreements.

Cultural Strengths of Nagas - A Profile

From the above discussion a profile of the cultural strengths of the Naga community can be built. Further they can also be considered as strengths that induce work motivation, social cohesion to facilitate community participation in development in the broadest of meaning, purpose and utility.

1. High need for achievement to materialize self reliance.
2. Concept of egalitarian society visible in their high democratic traditions.
3. Strong community identity.
4. Guided by rational beliefs – open society.
5. Emphasis on merit.
6. Concept of according social recognition.
7. High concern for individual freedom.
8. Community practice and participation.
9. Material orientation visible in their need for status.
10. Collective problem solving approach.
11. Low acceptance of dependency.
12. Belief in pioneering innovation.
13. Existence of social groups.
14. Straight forward and non manipulative by nature.
15. Guided by the present.
16. High self efficacy and self esteem.

17. Respect for age, seniority and reference groups.

18. Warm and hospitable.

19. Believe in open communication.

20. Adopt situational approach in managing affairs and conflicts.

The above cultural beliefs and values can be said to influence behavior and approach towards work. In this context it shall be appropriate to understand the meaning of work, development and means towards development as envisaged by host of luminaries of contemporary Nagaland.

Menon (1995) highlights that division of work in the work in the Naga society was gender friendly. The man controlled the community resources and the social system and the women were in charge of the family, the domestic economy and production. As long as the community owned the resources women exercised some control in running the family economy. However modernization process integral to which is individual land holdings have seriously affected the status of women as they lost control over resources where they could earlier contribute productively.

Lohe (1997) highlights the change visible in Naga work culture from ancient to modern and points out the reasons that led to the loss of work culture. In the past the need for self reliance motivated people towards hard work. People were competitive in nature as society as a whole accorded status to individuals and groups based on merit. Of late modern education instead making people socially responsible is rather making the society self-centered. He believes that Nagas can regain their past glory if all sections of the society work towards common betterment rather than chasing only individual benefits. As a first step he advocated the need to create awareness of Naga work culture among the youths in the society.

Lotha (1997) states that Naga society just four decades back was vibrant and buoyant. It was a well knit society characterized by simplicity, honesty, truthfulness, loyalty, hardworking and fearless in all aspects of its social life. Nagas in their beautiful mountainous country lived, worked, laughed and suffered together. Defining work culture as an attitude of the mind to be productive in all fronts called upon the youths to imbibe the pristine work values of their ancestors along with the advantage of modern education and thus contribute towards building a new Nagaland and this shall be a fitting tribute to the ancestors for the sacrifices rendered.

Thepfulhouvi (1997) reasoned out that the development or well-being of any society largely depends upon its work culture. The way people think or do forms the rock bottom of our culture. He suggested that in order to develop work culture the importance of profit motive, dignity of labour, search for excellence, hard work, proper use of time etc., should be inculcated in the mind of our people.

Pesye (1997) in his deliberations argued that developmental initiatives will fail if people lack in dignity of labour and work-ethic. He points out somewhere in the course of development process, Nagas in general have fallen prey to the temptations of making a living without work. The lure of easy life has eroded age-old Naga character of being good, simple, honest and hardworking. To revive the lost Naga pride the focus should be in spreading quality education, stressing on moral values and qualities such as fearlessness, steadfastness, forbearance, purity in personal life and truthfulness. Lastly he states that Nagas being Christians, religion should motivate a change of heart.

Manen (1997: 49-57) states the importance of work culture by quoting from the genesis, "by the sweat of thy brow, you will eat your food until you return to the ground", essentially meaning work is central to man. Stressed that

Nagas should appreciate and imbibe the Puritan work ethic of the 17th century, which led them to regard the accumulation of material wealth through labour (work) as a sign of God's favor and religious progress. The paper concludes by stating that Nagas in the past attributed work as a divine duty i.e. to work is to pray, in addition to fulfilling the need for survival and the new generation must attempt to revive the work spirit of the past in order to benefit from the opportunities of the 21st century industrial economics.

Vedayi (1997: 1-5) emphasized on the need to protect the Naga identity, as self-contended people, self-confident people and self-reliant people. This is possible when Nagas reaffirm themselves with the work values of forefathers, "Lose not the hard working spirit for we are not beggars, nature provides you everything to feed your stomach and to have a shelter if you hold your dao (knife) and hoe (spade)".

Alemtemshi (2002) highlights that to bridge the infrastructural gap, Nagaland requires Rs. 11000 crores. He states that providing this massive fund within a determined time span is difficult and hence there is the need to look beyond the plan funding and evolve indigenous economic models of development that requires the participation of all- both the government and the people. Further states that one effective mechanism to work for development will be through the communitisation route.

Kaka (2002) in his submission titled, "*Is under-development the cause of Insurgency in Nagaland*", provides valued insights about the Naga economic and cultural scenario, past and present. He states that "*Naga economy was tightly knit in the social customs, traditions and culture of the Nagas. The prosperity of the economy resulted in the social prosperity of the individual, clan, khel, and even neighboring villages*". In conclusion he states, underdevelopment is not the cause of insurgency in Nagaland but is connected to lack of sensitivity to address the issues that created insurgency in the state. He states that true economic development can only take place in an environment that is free of political conflict and hostilities.

Kilangla (2002) adopts a different approach and calls for a structural change in the economy of Nagaland. In order to make development constructive and meaningful she emphasizes the need for change in attitude. To quote her (p - 76) "keeping in mind the present scenario, Nagaland needs the creation of a new man, the citizen of a new state, the man in the era of science, the industrial man", probably meaning that communities should shred their tribalistic differences and find a unity of purpose to contribute and gain from the profits of a new industrial Naga economy.

Kikhi (2002) understands that under development and unemployment are interrelated that is one giving rise to the other. According to him there cannot be socio- political stability if its youths (human assets) remain idle or lack opportunities to contribute vide fruitful employment.

Tiarenla (2002) echoes on the various inequities visible in the Naga society which development should attempt to overcome. She cautions that, development must not be assessed solely in terms of incomes, industrialization or reaching the level of material wellbeing of the advanced western countries. True development should mean absence of poverty, ignorance, diseases or injustice, where every man can enjoy and exercise basic rights, and live with a sense of security and dignity.

Kiewhuo (2002) points out those societies cannot progress under the turmoil of political conflict. Further no proactive incentives can succeed till a constructive political agreement is arrived at.

Shimray (2006) in his study highlights that land alienation in North-East is principally due to rising individualism often enthused by state machinery. He cites that in the past the concept of landless did not exist in the Naga society as land apart from individual holdings there was the practice of collective land holdings in the form of morung land, clan land and village land. However of late state by issuing land pattas is encouraging individual holdings more in the form of an asset to wield power and influence contrary to the traditional belief where land was considered as a source for community sustenance and existence. It has strengthened class formation in the society along with giving rise to male dominance and patriarchy.

Thenucho (2007) voicing his thoughts in the seminar on 'Modernization without Westernization" called for 'indigenization of modernization.' Gracing the occasion in his capacity as hon'ble Home Minister, he emphasized on the need to develop 'our own model' of modernization, according to culture. According to him westernization is not necessarily modernization. "We can be modern without imitating the liberal west", he told the seminar, adding, that modernization and westernization are entirely two different concepts. In this context he stated, "We must also influence others with our culture, and to do that we must master our culture".

From the discussions and presentations made by the distinguished personalities the following observations can be made:

1. Community in the past had a strong work culture, vibrant institutions and which because of certain reasons are loosing value. Thus there is an urgent need to revive the strengths of the past for a meaningful development and existence.
2. There is a need to build indigenous model of development and the means to build the same is the communitization process.

3. Development goals should be guided by the belief of promoting wider and collective well-being and not guided by individual well-being.

4. Development to be meaningful in contemporary Nagaland requires change in attitudes and rationalistic work beliefs. It needs scientific and industrial orientation i.e. a shift from subsistence to being progressive.

5. Development should facilitate expansion of work opportunities for youths to engage.

6. Meaning of development in specific Naga context means freedom from poverty, ignorance, diseases, injustice and exploitation so that every man can enjoy and exercise basic rights, and lives with a sense of security and dignity.

7. Naga personality is vibrant and buoyant. The society well knit characterized by simplicity, honesty, truthfulness, loyalty, hardworking and fearless in all aspects of its social life. Nagas in their beautiful mountainous country lived, worked, laughed and suffered together.

8. Naga work culture in the past emphasized the importance of profit motive, dignity of labour, search for excellence. The concept of living without work was absent.

9. Work culture stressed on the need for independence rather being dependence. The work belief was, "by the sweat of thy brow, you will eat your food until you return to the ground", as laid in the Genesis.

The work belief as embodied in their work culture can be summed as "Lose not the hard working spirit for we are not beggars; nature provides you everything to feed your stomach and to have a shelter if you hold your dao (knife) and hoe (Vedayi Nyeka).

Underdevelopment – A Product of Human or Cultural Constraint

At the outset it may appear to be a very open ended proposition. Often individuals attribute underdevelopment to factors such as cultural rigidity, traditional outlook so on so forth. However this line of argument carries lot of inherent dangers. Culture of a community defined as repositories of human knowledge is conditioned by the dominant expectations of people, time and situations. This essentially means no culture is static, values and beliefs change to accommodate newer expectations and need. In the light of the above understanding, how culture as such be considered to be a constraint in the path of development? Therefore the alternative being, underdevelopment is more an effect that can be attributed to human inefficiencies. It is similar in nature to a journey which lacks direction and priorities. When a society lacks confidence in its own cultural and economic strengths there is a tendency to replicate the approaches and means of others. The basic assumption is if they are successful with it, well it works here too. Such form of development lack collective appreciation and often the means used to carry out the same is a top down approach. The problems get compounded in a society which has very low power distance, believes in equity and participation, and group problem solving. Will such an approach work? The obvious answer shall be no. Collective societies place great importance to consensus and participation. Thus development to be meaningful has to be rooted in people's strength and participation. In the absence of the above strength development remains an alien concept. The recent fiasco with North Eastern Council (NEC) vision 2020 document reflects this weakness. When the document was released to the press for expression of public interest it met with a cold shoulder from grass root organizations and civil societies. The ground for dissent was the programme and goals envisaged to be achieved was directed rather than evolving plans, programmes based on consensus. Development in Nagaland can be effective when it is charted and empowered by social agreement. Devoid of social agreement it shall continue to be an underdog in its meaning, objectivity and purpose.

Conclusion

The need for development is never static but is always progressive. It expands with the increasing need of the people. In fact there is no limit to developmental process in any society. The question that automatically follows from the above understanding is: How do we make development meaningful in spite of varied odds and constrains. In this analysis one thing is certain that is, government alone cannot be expected to make development matter. The reason being, development does not resemble one-way traffic to flow utilities from one end to the other. Development is a participative exercise which involves common strength, combined resources, collective wisdom to make it effective. Anything which calls for common strength, resources and wisdom has its source in the culture of the people. Culture in the broad anthropological sense connotes 'design for living' and development in this context can be understood as community policies and practices in planning and implementing that design for living. Therefore one can establish that development is a community approach, where in peoples participation holds the key for its effectiveness. Alemtemshi (2002: 2) quoting Sukla Commission report cites that, for infrastructure alone Nagaland needs a hopping 11000 crores. The question is, wherefrom will such enormous amount come. Govt. alone cannot provide the funds but at the same time the need for infrastructural growth cannot be overlooked. The answer lies in evolving a mechanism that supports people's participation at all levels. The roots for community development as a mean for collective well-being can be traced to the early hunting expeditions of prehistoric men. However its importance as an alternative approach to development can be linked to the first Mechanics' Institute set up in 1823 by Lord Brougham an aristocratic turned philanthropist (Mayo 2000: 85-90). Community development in the current context cannot be understood simply as some basic programmes in literacy, health, vocational training etc. It does not mean only digging of wells, roads, occasional social works; it is more properly the development of stable, self-reliant communities with an assured sense of social, political and economic responsibility among people. In the truest sense communitisation means democratization aimed at generating a sense of equity. Nagas as collectivist society can make community development process very meaningful and the reasons are same as cited earlier. Their culture supports and accommodates participation and hence community development based on people's participation can place the state higher in the developmental plane of the region. What is required for its success is commitment and dedication to the cause, open communication, transparency and respects for partnership - its core strength. The advantages of community participation in development especially in the context of ethnic society like the Nagas can be manifold:

1. Community participation can evolve a community perspective in building broader understanding on diverse issues that confront the society. Side by side it shall pull the society out of narrow segmented loyalties which often is believed to be the potent cause for lopsided development.

2. It can be instrumental in developing a consensus on long term and short term economic and social goals.

3. Community participation can harness the patterns of influence of kin and clan towards development and

modernization. In doing so it shall rebuild the integrated structure and solidarity that traditional order contained. Community participation by synthesizing the old and the new, tradition and modernity can stimulate economic growth by cutting down on dependency. Dependency can never be a facilitator for meaningful development.

4. Lastly participation shall minimize the stress and strain any society undergoes in the transitional phase as it brings change as per requirement of the people and not on whims and fancies of those in authority or power. Development understood in the above perspective shall make the journey in search of wealth, utility and well-being a meaningful endeavor.

REFERENCES

1. Bag, G.N. (2001). *Rural Transformation in Tribal Areas*, New Delhi: Akansha Publishing House.
2. Dube, S. C. (1990). *Social and Cultural Factors in Development*, New-Delhi: Vikas Publishing House. pp.1-16.
3. Hofsted, G. (1980). *Cultures Consequences: International Differences in Work Related Values*, C.A: Sage Publications.
4. Huib, Wursten. *Mental Images: The Influence of Culture on Economic Policy*.
5. Hutton, J. H. (1969). *The Angami Nagas*, Oxford University Press.
6. Iralu, Kaka D. (2002). "Is Underdevelopment the Cause of Insurgency in Nagaland" in C. Joshua Thomas and Gurudas Das (ed.), *Dimensions of Development in Nagaland*, New Delhi, Regency Publications.
7. Jamir, Alemtemshi. (2002). "Keynote Address" in C. Joshua Thomas and Gurudas Das (ed.), *Dimensions of Development in Nagaland*, New Delhi, Regency Publications.

8. Jamir, Kilangla. (2002). "Structural Change in the Economy of Nagaland" in C. Joshua Thomas and Gurudas Das (ed.), *Dimensions of Development in Nagaland,* New Delhi, Regency Publications.

9. Kanungo, R.N. and Jager, A.M. (1990)."The Need for Indigenous Management in Developing Countries" in A.M. Jager and Kanungo, R.N. (eds.), *Management in Developing Countries*, London: Routledge.

10. Kikhi, Kedilezo. (2002). "Educated Unemployment in Nagaland: Trend and Magnitude" in C. Joshua Thomas and Gurudas Das (ed.), *Dimensions of Development in Nagaland,* New Delhi, Regency Publications.

11. Lohe, Z. (1997). *The Naga Work Culture,* Kohima: Naga Cultural Society.

12. Lotha, T.C.K. (1997) *The Naga Work Culture,* Kohima: Naga Cultural Society.

13. Mali, D. D. (1990). *Development of Tribal Entrepreneurship in North East India,* Guwahati: Tribal Research Institute.

14. Mannen, T. N. & T. C. K. Lotha. (1997). *The Naga Work Culture,* Kohima: Naga Cultural Society.

15. Mayo, Marjorie. (2000). *Cultures Communities, Identities: Cultural Strategies for Participation and Empowerment,* New York: Palgrave, pp.85-90.

16. Nyekha, Vedayi. (1994). *The Naga Work Culture,* Kohima: Naga Cultural Society.

17. Pattnaik, K. M. (1986). *Rural Industrialization*, Cuttack: Kitab Mahal, pp.9-10.

18. Sanjay, T Menon. (1994). "Designing Work in Developing Countries" in Rabindra N Kanungo and Manuel Mendonca (eds.) *Work Motivation Models for Developing Countries*, New Delhi: Sage Publication. p. 95-96.

19. Saraswati, Baidyanath. (1998). *The Use of Cultural Heritage as a Tool For Development*, New Delhi: Indira Gandhi National Centre for the Arts.

20. Sen, Amartya. (2004). *Argumentative Indian,* London: Penguin.

21. Shimray, U. A. (2006). *Tribal Land Alienation in North East India,* Guwahati: North East Social Research Centre.

22. *Statistical Hand Book,* (2003). Govt. of Nagaland, Kohima.

23. Solo, Thepfulhouvi. (1997). *The Naga Work Culture,* Kohima: Naga Cultural Society.

24. Thomas, C. Joshua and Gurudas Das (ed.), (2002). *Dimensions of Development in Nagaland.* New Delhi, Regency Publications.

25. Yadav, R. P. (1980). *Peoples Participation: Focus on Mobilisation, Local Level Planning and Rural Development,* Bangkok.

18

CODIFICATION: A SWANSONG FOR CUSTOMARY LAW?

Melville Pereira

[Customary law has been criticized for being outdated, rigid, gender-biased, and gerontocratic, and thus a hurdle in the process of the development of tribal communities. Pressure has been brought to bear upon tribal communities all over the world to modernize their customary law. One of the preferred ways of modernizing it has been through a process of codification. Proponents of codification argue that codification of customary law leads to certainty and uniformity in its application, equality of the sexes and elimination of restrictive and archaic rules. This paper, while affirming the need for modernization of customary law, argues that codification, instead of reforming the customary law, may sound a death-knell to its very existence. A better alternative could be documentation of these age-old laws by a representative body of the tribal community, which includes men and women across age-groups. The documentation process could be widely discussed and debated in the tribal community, paying attention to issues of gender justice, common property resources and strengthening of self-

governing institutions. The final step could be seeking governmental recognition as has been done in Article 371A of the Indian Constitution in the case of Nagaland.]

Introduction

Ever since the second half of 19th century, with the intrusion of colonial forces into the Naga political and social fabric, unprecedented changes have been taking place in Nagaland in the educational, cultural, religious and political arenas. These changes, while ushering in an era of modernity and change, have in some instances threatened to wipe out the rich cultural and social heritage of Naga communities. The charm and attraction of the new and the novel has been so striking that some cultural values and practices have been trampled underfoot to make place for the new. One such area that has been adversely affected by the tremors of modernity is the customary law of Naga community.

Change is an inevitable phenomenon and customary law is not an exception to this. Change occurs as a response to an encounter with external forces as well as internally triggered developments. In the context of customary law, change occurs due to the continual dialectic between tradition, a concept containing the ancestral wisdom and knowledge of a particular community, and modern life conditions (Svensson 2002: 2). Those aspects of tradition that are appropriate for current usage undergo reform, adapting to the demands of changing times. Conversely those elements in customary law which are inappropriate and obsolete get purged, making way for new norms. Thus customary law has been 'subject to constant revival and reinvention by indigenous people' since its inception (*ibid*).

The changes and adaptations in customary law were engineered by the affected society in response to requirements and demands of a particular period of history. The formulation, adoption and reinvention of customary law were associated with the *Geist* of each particular people and never a top-to-bottom movement. This paper argues that the idea of codification of customary law in order to modernize it is an effort initiated by the state and, as such, does not arise from people. The consequences of codification of customary law, if taken to its logical end, will be disastrous and may sound its death-knell. Instead, statutory recognition of customary law after a process of documentation initiated by the people themselves is a better alternative to modernization of customary law.

Preliminary Remark

An observation, which deserves to be mentioned at the outset, is that customary law is not just a matter of jurisprudence, but a part of culture (Fernandes et al. 2005: 18). Often times, customary law has been treated exclusively as a conflict resolution mechanism and hence just a part of an indigenous legal system. This amounts to limiting the overarching reach and dynamic influence of customary law in tribal societies. Customary law is the visible expression of the values, ideals and principles a particular culture upholds. Hence it is a vital part of a culture and this is one reason why tribal communities all over the world are falling back on their customary laws in an effort to preserve their culture and identity (Svensson 2002: 4-5).

Further, this narrow perception of customary law, as an adjunct to the statutory legal system in a nation-state, leads to an easy but erroneous conclusion that customary law can be conveniently replaced by a statutory legal system. In this thinking, the role of the customary law as an instrument in the maintenance of tribal solidarity and identity takes a back seat. This paper takes issue with such thinking and argues for a much wider conception of customary law, not merely as normative and traditional rules of governing people but also as a unifying factor of keeping the tribe together.

Relevance of Customary Law

The idea of codification of customary law presumes its relevance to tribal communities. It may be pertinent to pose some questions to examine the significance of customary law to its practitioners. Can customary law be relevant and suitable in an increasingly modern and globalized world? Is customary law flexible enough to meet modern norms on human rights, particularly gender equality? As a part of conflict resolution system in a society, is it able to meet the legal requirements of its adherents? An attempt at answering these questions may highlight its value and importance to present times. Although an elaborate discussion of these questions is beyond the scope of this section, a brief discussion could prepare the ground for the main theme of this section: what direction modernization of Naga customary law should take?

There is a divergence of views regarding the meaning and significance of customary law among jurists and legal experts. This difference of opinion is due to the varied conception of the term 'law'. For the Austinian or the analytical school of jurisprudence, the essence of law is that it is imposed by a sovereign will. On the contrary, for the Savignian or the historical school, the essence of law is that it develops within a society of its own vitality (Allen 1961: 1-2). In the former, the approach to law is top-to-bottom but in the latter it is bottom-up. While the Analytical school treats customs as just 'rules of morality' which have no binding effect, the Historical School treats these large mass of unwritten rules as legal and binding (Roy 1910:10).

Both schools do not dispute that these customs are moral rules and norms guiding society. The intrinsic goodness of these age-old laws is not contested by the schools. Their point of departure is regarding its legal and binding effect, and this difference of opinion among them is irreconcilable.

Despite this irreconcilable difference, it is clear that both schools agree that in many societies, before the inception of any system of law-making and law-dispensing, the conduct of human beings was governed by customary rules and norms.

While their intrinsic goodness cannot be doubted, there are certain aspects of customary law, which critics assail as failing to promote life and resulting in the violation of human rights. An appraisal of these disagreeable aspects of customary law will be addressed in the next section on the need of modernization of these laws.

Some have questioned the relevance of customary law in a globalized world. For them these laws seem to be out-dated, ancient, out of touch with reality and gerontocratic[2]. At the same time, there have been demands from tribal communities all over the world to find suitable accommodation for these laws within the nation-state system. For instance one of the office bearers of Angami Public Organization stoutly defended customary laws.

> The customary laws of the Nagas are quite different from the state laws. The entire approach of customary law is not to punish the guilty but rather to bring back the accused to community. The approach is reconciliation and claiming back the one who has gone astray. For those who are educated and accustomed to state laws, this may not sound just and fair but it has a rich background. Once an offence is proved, the person is given a chance to reform and rejoin the community. I feel that these laws are fair and are relevant to our times and we need to make efforts to preserve this alternative system of justice.[3]

As the interviewee points out, the conflict resolution process in customary law system is holistic in its remedies. The focus in this system is reconciliation and rehabilitation of the affected parties. The approach in finding a solution is not to condemn the guilty. The effort is to set right the disturbed equilibrium in the community by trying to reconcile the warring parties. "In the case of dispute resolution, since the parties from rural indigenous communities must face each other in their small community after the dispute is settled, efforts are almost always made to produce two winners instead of a winner and a loser."[4] Thus customary law system seems to emphasize harmonious communal living over any other considerations. It foregrounds community dimension and not merely utilitarian concerns because community has to be sustained first which would create an atmosphere for individuals to live in harmony.

However, in an increasingly competitive environment in which customary law has to compete with other prevalent legal systems, utilitarian calculations cannot be ignored. They can be strong defense against the encroacher. According to Human Development Report 2004 (HDR 2004), justice is swift and cheap in a customary legal system, as the courts are run with minimal formalities in venues close to the disputants' homes. The local language is used in the court and the practices of the court allow the community to cross-question the witnesses and testimonies (Human Development Report 2004: 59). These advantages of the customary law system observed by HDR 2004 are echoed in the African Conference on Local Courts and Customary Law, which was held at Dar-Es-Salaam, Tanganyika in 1963. On the advantages of customary law system the participants concluded:

> (a) Their proceedings were understood and consequently accepted by majority of the people; (b) They brought justice to the people, rather than making people travel far in order to obtain justice; (c) Most of the cases that they dealt with were concerned with facts or usages of the area of which these courts had special understanding; (d) They enabled participation in the

administration of justice by laymen of standing; (e) They did not impose a heavy burden on the budget of the state, and they were inexpensive for the litigants."[5]

There are many other benefits that enhance the relevance of customary law system. The culture birthed and nourished by customary law is founded on the pillars of cooperation, collaboration and community values. It is a worthy alternative to the capitalist society based on individualism, competition and consumerism (Haksar 1998: 172). Others have found customary laws playing a significant role in achieving the goal of sustainable resource management (D'Souza 2001; Orebech et al 2005). Most important of all, customary law is the repository and storehouse of tribal culture. The rich heritage of tribal culture is preserved and developed in its customary law.

Despite its many benefits that bolster its relevance, there are certain rusty areas in customary law system that need touching up so as to make them meaningful and acceptable. These areas of concern, which we shall discuss in the next section, need to be critically examined so as to bring about the required changes in order to reform the customary law.

Need for Modernization of Customary Law

In the previous section, the many advantages of customary law system were briefly enumerated, its continued relevance was taken note of, and an observation was made that there are some rough edges which need to be smoothed. These rough edges could be many but this paper will focus on certain areas that need urgent attention. The process of reflection and deliberation a community undergoes in order to bring about the required reforms in customary law to make them updated and sensitive to human rights is what is meant by their modernization in this paper.

As already mentioned, the areas that need reform in customary law could be many and an exhaustive list of these aspects could be a topic for another paper. It is prudent to choose those areas that need immediate and urgent focus for change and call for modernization. Some such areas are gender rights, presence of some antique rules, decay in traditional institutions and loopholes in conflict resolution process.

Gender Rights

Women in tribal societies have enjoyed a higher status compared to non-tribal societies though usually without being equal to men (Menon 1995: 101; Nongbri 1998: 223). In the system of communal ownership of property and resources, women played an important role in the agricultural operations of the family (Fernandes & Menon 1987: 72-76). They had a say in the economic issues affecting the family (Thong 1997:93; Fernandes et al 2005: 89). Yet there was subtle discrimination against them which continues even today thus denying them participation in the social and political arena of society (Kelhou 1998: 56).

Customary law of some tribal groups seems to contradict many United Nations Conventions on Human Rights, especially rights of women and children (Roy 2005:23). If certain questions are raised in the area of gender rights, one is bound to bump into gaping holes that point out that much remains to be done in bringing about gender parity. How many women are judges in the customary law courts? What about the representation of women in corridors of power, especially in village councils and in state politics? Are women discriminated against in inheritance rights? These are uncomfortable questions but they need to be openly debated[6]

Angami women are fiercely attached to customary law.[7] But their staunch attachment to these laws does not stop them from assessing customary law in a critical way. One of the interviewees had this to say about Naga customary laws:

> All Nagas are attached to their roots, to the village where they were born no matter how urbanized a person might be. When it comes to certain aspects of life, we always fall back on our roots and customs that we practiced in the village. While we are closely attached to the tradition and customs, we also are aware that there are certain aspects of this tradition that need to be amended and I see gender rights have to be somehow inserted into this body of laws.[8]

While asked to substantiate on how to bring about gender parity, the interviewee said that women should have voice in decision-making institutions of the village, they should have inheritance rights and they should be given maintenance in case of divorce. She went on to mention that though one third of the seats of Village Development Board are reserved for women, it is seldom that one finds women members in the said board.[9] She stressed the need for the implementation of strong legal provisions for the empowerment of women.

Recent studies on the customary law of various tribal communities in Northeast India point out to weakening of the rights of women in the context of globalization (Pathak 1991; Fernandes & Barbora 2002; Fernandes et al 2005). Even Garo women, who enjoyed higher status due to matrilineal system, are experiencing discrimination against them. According to a Garo scholar, these days Garo men wield more social and political power than in the past (Marak 1997: 60-69).

Thus customary law would need reform in granting rights of women to inherit property, to claim maintenance in case of divorce and allow participation of women in policy making bodies of the village.

Presence of Antique and Cruel Rules

One of the complaints against the application of customary law is that it contains outdated, obsolete and inhuman laws which need to be wiped out. But there is no unanimous opinion regarding the archaic and callous nature of customary law among the interviewees. According to some, certain laws are harsh, inhuman and anachronistic. For instance, according to a Naga youth leader, there are

> ...guidelines in our customary laws to handle murder, killing and suicide. But some of them need change. According to its provisions when deliberate killing takes place the person can be mercilessly killed. This is inhuman way of handling a situation.[10]

But this view of the youth leader is contested by an elder[11] who finds the penalty for deliberate murder is in keeping with human standards. The culprit needs to be either killed or permanently banished from the village. The elderly among the respondents and interviewees seem to uphold the relevance and applicability of customary laws while the youth seem to push for their reforms and updating by eliminating the cruel and inhuman elements of punitive measures.

While some found the punishment harsh, others found the quantum of penalty insufficient. Some interviewees felt the penalties imposed are inadequate and that is one of the reasons why people go to police. A Garo woman in Tura, Meghalaya, had this to say about the inadequate penalty imposed on the culprit.

> The highest penalty that a *Nokma* or *Laskar* can impose is Rs 50. This is silly. The police are tougher in their punishments. They can beat up the culprits and put them in jail. This has made police more attractive compared to the *Nokmas* in dealing with disputes. The powers of police are far superior compared to that of *Nokmas*.[12]

A Naga teacher speaks in similar vein in the context of punitive measures imposed by customary law courts and its inadequate infrastructure to deal with the perpetrators of crime.

> If we are talking in terms of compensation and punitive measures like imprisonment and so on, customary law courts will lose out on these aspects. The punitive measures of the customary law courts are definitely inadequate. Due to this insufficiency in customary law courts, many have started approaching the police and other statutory courts directly, thus bypassing the customary law courts.[13]

The out dated nature of customary law, along with its harsh penalties, as well as the insufficiency of quantum of penalty has been pointed out both by Garo as well Angami participants in the interview. These aspects of punitive measures of customary law system would need a re-look and revision in order to make the system updated and human.

Decay in Traditional Institutions

In the past, most of the training in customary law took place in *morungs* or bachelor dormitories. The *Morung* was a place where the new members of the community underwent the socialization process. They were trained to fight in wars and in the traditional practices of the community. These *morungs* have declined or even disappeared from the villages due to the introduction of modern education. The current education system gives scant attention to local history and to traditional law and the lacuna left by the *morungs* has not been filled by contemporary education system.

This has an adverse effect on the functioning of customary law courts which has slowly led to its deterioration. There are complaints that some *gaonburas (GBs)* and *dobashis (DBs)* are not sure of the intricacies of customary law. At times some cases are judged according to the whims and fancies of GBs and DBs. Some of them are too young and have little experience in interpreting these age-old laws. People are skeptical about their grasp and knowledge of customary law. One of the interviewees expressed this genuine concern in no uncertain terms.[14] This has led some people to have recourse to statutory law courts in search of justice.

To overcome this limitation, the All Angami Gaonbura Association (AAGBA) compiled and published the Angami customary laws in 1980s so that there was a legitimate source of information made available for customary law courts personnel to consult in case of doubt. No doubt that this is a step in the right direction, but it has not completely tackled the limitations faced by the customary law personnel leading to the decay of self-governing institutions. While there are a swarm of native lawyers and advocates specialized in the modern legal system decorating the portals of statutory courts, steps have not been taken to train personnel to shoulder the customary law system of tribal communities.

Inadequate Investigation Procedure

Another allegation against the customary law system is that the procedure of conflict resolution in customary law courts is inadequate and the rules of evidence are not adhered to. The Naga lawyers point out that cross examination of the witnesses by the opponent is not practiced in the conflict resolution procedure[15]. To the extent the cross examination is missing, the verdict of court does not stand scrutiny of reason. Since the rules of evidence are not applied by customary law court personnel, the verdict of the customary law court becomes biased.

But the proponents of customary law system argue that the approach of customary law is reconciliatory and this approach does not stress on nailing down the culprit. Certain times the culprit may even go scot-free. The ultimate aim of customary law court is to harmonize the imbalance in society caused by the act of the offender. But some others argue that this results in unfair verdict to one party. Sometimes the verdict is thrust on a party against its wish. For the sake of peace and harmony in the village, compromises are brought about between the parties and the justice is not delivered.[16]

This is an area of tension among the adherents of customary law. While some would uphold an individual's right for just and fair verdict, others would stress on the priority of group rights. On the one hand, harmony and peace in society should not be made to suffer because of the demands of justice of an individual. On the other hand, community should not impinge on the freedom of an individual's claim to justice. The reform process will have a difficult responsibility of balancing the rights of the individual as against that of the community.

The above discussion drew attention to some grey areas in customary laws which need to be re-looked and reformed by the concerned tribal communities. It pointed out that measures favouring gender equity need to be introduced, anachronistic and harsh penalties need to be purged, decay in traditional institutions should be halted and procedural aspects of conflict resolutions process tightened. What would be the mode of reform? What would be effect of various modes of reform? Who initiates the reform process? These questions would be dealt in the next part of this section.

Modes of Modernization of Customary Law

In an effort to give boost to the integration of Naga-inhabited areas, the Government of Nagaland had mooted the idea of a single Naga customary law a couple of years ago (Our Correspondent 2005). The then minister for art and culture, Mr. K Therie, had said that such a step would 'further the integration process'. He had also mentioned that no final decision had been made. What would be the mode of unifying the Naga customary law was not mentioned, but what was presumed is that these laws have to undergo a process of codification.

Codification seems to be the preferred way of modernizing customary law. This issue is of great importance in Northeast India, because many tribes want to go back to their customary law in their search for a new identity amid what they feel are attacks on their culture and economy. Many women associations in the Northeast, too, have supported codification since this process gives an opportunity to remedy the historical injustice meted out to them[17]. The Chakmas in Mizoram have codified their traditional laws. In Meghalaya, the Garo Hills District Autonomous Council (GHDAC) has initiated this process in 2005 and the codification committee set up by it has submitted its report. Though it is nearly two years since the report has been submitted, the GHDAC is yet to deliberate upon the report.

There are roughly three approaches or modes of modernizing customary law. They are:

- Documentation of Customary Law
- Recognition of Customary Law
- Codification of Customary Law

In this section an attempt is made to bring out some implications of these alternatives. Since codification is hot on the agenda of politicians and others, the discussion that follows will focus mostly on codification. This paper is of the view that though codification is at times presented as the best way forward, it will raise more questions than answers. The better option may be for each tribe to first document its customary law and then get the state to recognize them.

Documentation of Customary Law

Documentation refers to a comprehensive collection of the customs and practices that a tribe has revered and practiced for centuries. It can be done either by the tribe concerned or by an external agency. For example the Law Research

Institute, Guwahati, has been documenting the customary laws of many tribes since 1980s while the Mizo customary law was documented by their own community.

Consideration has to be given to two crucial factors in the process of documentation, namely, the composition of the documentation committee and the geographical limit of documentation. The composition of the documentation committee is vital because it can decide on the particular slant a specific customary law takes. For instance, if the committee is comprised only of elders, they may endorse stringent measures on youth. Therefore it is important that while forming a documentation committee effort be made to give representation to men and women of all age-groups.

Each village has a unique set of customary laws which is specific to them. Though there are a lot of similarities in them, they vary from village to village. Therefore the question arises about the geographical limit of documentation. Should the documentation be limited to the village as a unit? Or should it be at the larger level of traditionally recognized group of villages? Or should it be at the level of tribe as a whole? If each village documents its customary law, its uniqueness is preserved and the variety is upheld but at the cost of uniformity. The documentation process can take place at the level of range or region since each range has lots of similarities that lead to a unique set of customary law. And finally, documentation can take place at the highest level of tribe, which leads to uniformity but at the cost of leveling down the differences and variety at village and region level. Therefore each tribe has to decide the geographical unit of documentation, being aware of the repercussions of its option.

A key benefit of documentation is that customary law is recorded for posterity. Because the elders, who are the transmitters and keepers of the ancestral laws, are passing away, it is necessary that steps are taken to record these laws. This record then becomes a ready digest to customary law officials to refer in case of doubt.

On the flip side, experience shows that documentation alone is a futile exercise. For instance, the laws of the Hmar and Paitei of Manipur who are threatened with displacement by the Tipaimukh dam can be documented. But if the State does not recognize them, their fate will be that of the Rongmei who lost their land to the Loktak project without being counted among the displaced or compensated (Fernandes and Bharali 2002: 23; Barooah 2002: 103-104).

Recognition of Customary Law

Recognition of customary law refers to the government accepting it as legal, as was done in Nagaland and Mizoram. The Union Parliament amended the Constitution in 1963 to introduce Article 371A to allow the civil affairs in Nagaland to be run according to their customary laws. The same was done in the Mizo accord of 1986 to introduce Article 371G for Mizoram (Haksar 1998: 170-171).

Recognition has the best of advantages for the preservation of customary law as can be noted from the experience of Nagaland and Mizoram, though much needs to be done to purge the unwanted elements in the customary law of these two states. Typical to the spirit of customary law, recognition gives scope to these laws to remain as people's laws to be moulded and shaped by them as and when required. Far from being rigid, they remain pliant, fluid and flexible, to be interpreted according to the specificity of each case. Further, there is minimum intervention from state in the case of this approach, giving it autonomy to do its work of administration of justice.

There are certain limitations in this approach since there is less intervention from the state. One such limitation is a tendency to remain isolated, which may lead to a conservative interpretation of customary law. Reforms and modifications may be slow since elders who are slow to change officiate in the customary law courts.

Codification of Customary Law

Codification includes documentation of customary law at the behest of state, making them undergo a process of standardization and finally ratifying them in the state legislature (Vijayakumar 2006: 11). Once they are ratified in the state legislature, they can be amended only by the legislators thus bringing about an element of rigidity. The customary laws become statutes and no longer customary laws. What follows in the next section is a rather elaborate critique of the codification approach to customary law, pinpointing its limitations and its numbing effect on the very existence of these age-old laws.

Critique of Codification

To grasp the implications of a codification project in all its complexity, it will be beneficial to examine the codification of Hindu personal law that took place in the 1950s. Since many countries on the African continent went through codification debates after becoming sovereign states, the lessons learnt from their experience can also shed some light in assessing the pros and cons of the codification of customary law.

In the years 1955-56, four acts[18] were passed in the Indian parliament, which are now referred as the codification of Hindu law (Hooker 1975: 70). The desire for unity and certainty of the law, equality of the sexes, and the elimination of restrictive and antique rules seem to have been the objectives that guided this legal reform.[19]

One of the main objectives of codification was the unity of the law. The drafters of code argued that this had to be realized first among the Hindus and it was thought that this would have a multiplier effect on other religious communities, namely the Muslims and Christians. According to codifiers, this would eventually lead to the Uniform Civil Code as envisaged by the Indian Constitution in Art. 44 (Derrett 1968: 330). They further argued that the rules being enforced in the courts were not certain and hence reform was needed to make them rigorous.

> Not only are we in great difficulties in attempting to give expression to our conception of the law in any given jurisdiction, but we are really in doubt as to whether the law itself exists in an expressible form. Whatever is known about the law is a hotchpotch of rules, often inconsistent with one another, ill assorted, mutually incompatible, intellectually lacking in uniformity, unsatisfying... Encumbered with rules which do not govern, principles which do not guide, maxims which are ambiguous, sources which may be followed or not at choice and rules of interpretation which are as flexible as the sources upon which they are supposed to throw light, the system – if it deserves the name – is unlike any other now in force.[20]

The primary objective of the codifiers was to bring about uniformity in Hindu Personal Law across various Hindus sects and regions. The second important argument in favour of codification was the demand for equality of the sexes. The drafters were keen on doing away with a tradition that restricted the role of women in family and in larger society. The code was aimed at giving them inheritance and maintenance rights. "The influence of Western standards and the expansion of opportunities for Indian women was nowhere more violent than in contexts where tradition obliged the female to remain subservient to the male."[21]

Elimination of restrictive and antique rules was another aim that led the drafters to push for codification. This was an effort to abolish the caste system from Indian society. They pointed out the dichotomy that existed between the Constitution of India and Hindu Law. "It is said that caste, which has been condemned in the constitution, and which is no longer to be regarded in any secular matter, is perpetuated by the current Hindu Law...All this is quite unnecessary and out of accord with modern needs, except in the view of the "orthodox", to whom the caste-system still stands for a natural phenomenon of spiritual significance."[22] The drafters argued that in order to abolish differential treatment in private law on the ground of caste, Hindu law had to undergo codification.

Of course there was a rebuttal of these arguments by orthodox Hindus that the Hindu law was divine in origin and hence beyond change. Orthodox Hindus pointed out that the code adversely affected the religious doctrines of Hinduism and that parliament was not the right forum to bring about changes in Hindu Laws. It was the prerogative of the *pundits*. Interestingly they also mentioned that in case of codification litigation will increase and the laws will become rigid.[23]

One of the damning criticisms of codification was that it would result in rigidifying the flexible nature of customary laws (White 1965: 89). In fact, Maine had pointed out this in his works.

> At the touch of the Judges of the Supreme Court, who had been trained in the English school of special pleading, and had probably come to the East in the maturity of life, the rule of native law dissolved and, with or without his intention, was to a great extent replaced by rules having their origin in English laws books. Under the hand of the judges of the Sudder courts, [the chief court of appeal from the *Mofussil* or District Courts in Calcutta till 1862] who had lived since their boyhood among the people of the country, the native rules hardened and contracted a rigidity, which they never had in real native practice.[24]

Maine assumes that native law was flexible and codification 'fixed' its meaning and application and thus made it rigid. The aim of native law was to settle disputes in such a way that it resulted in the harmonizing of relationship between two quarrelling parties. The application, analysis and interpretation of the rules are not of primary value in the context of dispute resolution. Through compromises and negotiations the conflict is resolved (Bennett & Vermeulen 1980:213; Gluckman 1973: 21; Buxbaum1967: 4). This flexibility will be lost, according to Maine, when codes come into existence.

For instance, in Indian villages, dispute resolution was the function of the village *panchayat*. The guiding spirit in a *panchayat* in dealing with clashes and conflicts was that the conflicting parties later on had to live together in the village and therefore, not strict adherence to rules but negotiated settlement through compromises had to be worked out. "The effort in a *panchayat* was to find a solution which would not sever ties but maintain them; this was done through long talks and informal pressures on the concerning parties."[25]

However, Bhattacharya finds this argument of native laws getting ossified and rigid due to codification problematic.

> The common argument that customs are frozen through codification is premised on a simple contrast between the oral and the textual. The oral tradition is seen as fluid, open to a variety of interpretations and meanings, a range of appropriations according to the contests. When the oral tradition is textualized the fluidity disappears, meanings are fixed: put into writing, they become frozen into codes. We now recognize that this opposition is problematic. Texts too can convey a variety of meanings; and new meanings are continuously inscribed onto texts in the process of interpretation and elaboration. Codes, like all texts, are open to multiple reading, and the same code can produce different

> judgments. Codification may seek to fix the meanings of practices, but the original intentions do not always materialize in the same ways. Judicial records reveal how codes were read in conflicting ways, questioned and rewritten. The search for certainty and fixity remained elusive.[26]

A similar tenor of argumentation can be noted among those who drafted the Hindu personal law in 1955. Pointing out the experience of continental countries, they argue that this accusation is ill-based. "In most continental countries, where the vitality of the civil law cannot be doubted, codification has been tolerated sufficiently well, and reform of the civil codes is a process which quietly incubates, readily springing into action at infrequent intervals, and bringing the provision of the relevant articles up-to-date, whenever they cease to find effective champions."[27] That codes give sufficient space for interpretation and re-interpretation seems to be the argument put forward by the drafters of codification.

The proponents of codification assert that uniformity and certainty of law was one of the major objectives of codification of customary law. They argue that it eliminates issues of conflict between different species of customary law. In their view, this is required for smooth administration and for just settlement of disputes. It is true that uniformity will lead to efficiency in administration – but at a considerable cost. Allott (1981: 66) points out that the moment a customary law or usage is codified; its bonding with people is cut. It no longer remains a custom, which is shaped and moulded by the community. In truth it becomes a statutory law.

Another accusation hurled at codification was that it would unleash a flood of litigation (Derrett 1957: 39). Such an accusation has an in-built presumption that the very existence of a court system and judicial organization will result in endless litigation and mushrooming of lawyers. This will make the legal field specialized, and this in turn will make the dispute resolution process expensive. In fact, there seemed to have been a massive increase in the volume of litigation before the courts after the civil and criminal codes came into existence in 1860s (Hooker 1975: 64).

The proponents of codification project are not blind to this limitation. They agree that there would be a sudden increase in litigation, but that this would be just a transitional feature (Derrett 1957: 50). There has been no strong rebuttal of this accusation by the supporters of codification because in this case they are on weaker ground. There are cases where people who are economically better off would drag their opponents to the court in order to win the case (Hooker 1975: 65).

Another drawback of codification, according to its detractors, is that the codified law would tend to see the suit as between individuals alone. This is at the risk of neglecting the community dimension of a case and it would result in jeopardising the peace and unity of a village (Hooker 1975: 64; Durie: 2006; Vijaykumar 2006: 93-96). While the customary law system looked at the cases from the point of view of the community, the codes tended to stress on the individual dimension.

According to the customary law system, a conflict disturbed the equilibrium of the community and this should be set right by reconciliation. As Driberg, an administrator and anthropologist, found out "...the aim of the law was the maintenance of equilibrium, and it was based on 'collective organisation' and not, like western law, on 'an individualistic assumption'. Because the law sought to restore the balance, judgements were 'constructive and palliative' and not penal."[28] Gluckman's work among the Lozi tribe of Barotse in Zambia, too, echoed this dimension. He elaborately describes the dispute settlement process in a Lozi *kuta* (court) and how the members of the jury find ways of setting right the broken bonds.

> The *Lozi* disapprove of any irremediable breaking of relationships. For them it is a supreme value that villagers should remain united, kinsfolk and families and kinship groups should not separate, lord and underling should remain associated. Throughout a court hearing of this kind the judges try to prevent the breaking of relationships, to make it possible for the parties to live together amicably in the future. Obviously this does not apply in every case, but it is true of a large number, and it is present in some degree in almost all cases. Therefore the court tends to be conciliating; it strives to affect a compromise acceptable to, and accepted by, all the parties.[29]

As against the community dimension guiding the judgment, the codified system would endeavour to prove that one party is right and the other wrong. The idea here is applying a particular rule to a specific conflict in order to arrive at a decision, which rewards the innocent and punishes the culprit. In a particular case, therefore, one party is just, while the other is unjust. In such a scenario, there is no scope for compromise and reconciliation (Hooker 1975: 65). The hatred and rancour between parties will continue when they go back to their villages. A new *modus vivendi* was not arrived at and hence the harmful effects of dispute may not have been completely erased (Bennett 1980: 213). The settlement, since it focused on the individual alone, is piecemeal and not holistic.

According to Hooker, another important consequence of codification is the silencing of indigenous local political institutions and loss of a good deal of their former powers. According to him, native tribunals lost out on financial help from government and lost their support in enforcing laws (Hooker 1975: 65).

Customary law is the repository of tribal culture. The culture of a tribal community is manifested and articulated in a special way in the customary law. The customary law gives visible expression to the values and ethos a tribal culture stands for. This is one of the reasons why many tribal communities all over the world have taken refuge in customary law in carving out and strengthening their identity (Svensson 2002: 4-5). Codification of these laws could harm the rich cultural heritage of these communities resulting in fossilization of their rich traditions.

The above discussion on codification of personal and customary laws in India and African countries has driven home its effect on customary law. While codification results in uniformity and certainty in the application of customary law, this is at a great cost of ossifying the flexible nature of customary laws. The other adverse effects such as silencing of self-governing institutions, loss of a swift, simple and economic conflict resolution system, erosion of a reconciliatory and holistic conflict resolution system and the freezing effect of codification on culture have been enumerated above.

Concluding Observations

The above discussion dealt with the various alternatives the modernization of customary law can take. Documentation of customary law has the benefit of recording them and preserving them for posterity. It may not serve the purpose of claiming legitimate political and economic rights like administration of justice according customary law, safeguarding and protection of communal property resources and a right of tribal communities to live in an atmosphere of multicultural ethos. This limitation of documentation can be overcome by giving the documented customary law state recognition as is done in Nagaland and Mizoram. But recognition has the risk of a romantic and conservative interpretation of customary law by the gerontocratic ruling elite of a community, which may result in discrimination against certain sections of society. Codification, while bringing about clarity and certainty, may have the chilling effect of freezing the spirit of customary law and converting them overnight into a statutory law system.

In the context of the Northeast, whether a customary law of a tribal community is documented or not, the first step is to recognize their customary law. Recognition will have the positive effect of bringing an end to conflicts centred on the denial of land rights and reducing the threat of cultural assimilation. This is integral to the peace process because it is also a sign of acceptance of their identity. Besides, with state recognition the customary law remains a living body of rules and norms open to ongoing interpretation and changes according to the social and political situation.

In other words, codification goes against pluralism which may exist even within the same tribe. For example, there are substantial differences in the customary law of the Kuki living in Manipur and in Assam because a law evolves from their life experience. As a result, commitment to their traditional laws changes according to the degree to which it applies to their concrete situation. Such flexibility can die if it is codified and a single interpretation imposed on the whole tribe. It would be much worse if the customary laws of several tribes were brought together into a single tribal law as is thought of in Nagaland. Any such leveling of the differences can cut at the very root of diversity and can become an attack on the identity of unique tribal groups. Instead, efforts should be made to evolve a system of recognition that provides for diversity and remains flexible.

Flexibility is required because customary laws need to evolve further. It means that while recognition is important, one has to do it in such a way that it lays the foundation of progressive changes in it. One such change required is gender equity. Though the social status of tribal women is higher than that of their caste counterparts, most of the customary laws have subjugated women by denying them the right to participate in their decision-making bodies and to inherit the ancestral property. So while according recognition to the customary law, the State has to create a situation in favour of gender equality. Otherwise in the name of their tradition and identity, men from these tribes may continue to deny women their rights. In the name of the same law they may also discriminate against persons from other tribes who inhabit their area. That can intensify ethnic conflicts.

The ideal would be for the tribe concerned to document its laws. While so doing it can initiate a debate on gender and class issues and introduce clauses that take them towards equality. That will be an ongoing process that protects their identity without stagnation or injustice to any section of society. This process of recognition with enough leverage to interpret the customary laws according to the changing context is possible because tribal cultures are organic, not static. So the customary laws should be allowed to exist in an evolved or evolving format in contemporary society and recognized as such by the State.

Road Map for the Future

The following suggestions could be discussed and deliberated upon by the Naga tribal communities as a road map for the future.

1. Customary law discourse in India in general, and in Nagaland in particular, is in an embryonic stage. It has not taken deep roots among academics, intellectuals and legal experts. Perhaps a statewide awareness drive on this could be encouraged through seminars and workshops by a competent body.

2. Not all tribes in Nagaland have compiled and documented their body of customary laws. The Angami G.B. Association has compiled Angami

Customary Law and the first edition was released in 1983. Two more editions of the same have been released in 1988 and 2000. Similar work needs to be done on a priority basis by all the Naga tribes.

3. The Government of Nagaland has plans for a single customary law for the state. Such a step, if implemented, will have a significant impact on the culture and identity of Nagas. Therefore, such a plan could be preceded by state-wide debate and discussion at various forums.

4. *The Rules for Administration of Justice and Police in Nagaland (Third Amendment) Act, 1984*, talks of constituting three classes of customary law courts, namely, Village Courts, Subordinate Customary Courts and District Customary Courts. This Act has received presidential assent in 1987. Such an Act, if properly implemented, could go a long way in strengthening and boosting the customary law system.

5. Customary law of most tribal societies has been discriminatory towards women. Customary law needs to be made gender sensitive in keeping with the requirements of human rights issues.

6. It is desirable that Naga culture and customary law becomes part of curricula in the school syllabus as well as in legal studies of the state. This is necessary because of the disappearance of the *morung* system.

7. Mention has been made of the limitations of customary law courts particularly with regard to personnel. This has resulted because of the appointment of GBs and DBs who are not sure of a proper interpretation of customary law. This in turn results in the public losing faith in these courts. Therefore, in the place of

morungs, which had the function of imparting customary law, some training program for customary law personnel could be developed and implemented.

NOTES

1. More on it may be found in the chapter of Dr. Christina Kekhrieseno in this volume.
2. During interviews with the Angami of Nagaland and the Garo of Meghalaya between August 2006 and March 2007, I frequently came across such an opinion. The tendency in the older among the interviewees was that customary law is relevant and vital for tribal communities and the younger lot found these laws a hurdle on the path of development.
3. Quote from the interview that took place in Jakhama, Nagaland, on Sept 11, 2006.
4. Raja Devasish Roy, 2005. *Traditional Customary Laws and Indigenous Peoples of Asia.* London: Minority Rights Group International, p.21.
5. E. I. Nwogugu, 1976. "Abolition of Customary Courts – The Nigerian Experiment" *Journal of African Law*, Vol.20, No.1, p.12.
6. During the fieldwork, I met quite a few *Apuotsas (elderly men)* and *Gaonburas* (village elders recommended by the khels but appointed by the government) who felt that women cannot be in the decision making bodies of the village because the Angami customary law prohibits them from participating in such political forums. While asked why customary law does not allow political participation for women, the answer was that women are meant to look after the domestic affairs of the family while men look after the affairs of the village.
7. In the interviews I had with the Angami women, most expressed their trust in customary law system and hence were very cautious in suggesting changes. While they stressed on making their voice heard in political arena, few suggested changes in inheritance rights.

8. Interview held in Kohima on Oct 4, 2006 with a prominent Naga woman who has been office bearer of many women organizations.

9. The interviewee went on to say that men folk in the village have ingeniously created women VDBs (Village Development Board) just to keep the women away from taking part in deliberations on policy issues concerning the village. "Most of the villages in Nagaland have introduced a new nomenclature known as VDB women secretary and that woman, what does she do? Her job is only to handle the few funds that come from the main VDB for women welfare which very often is not fourth of the funds. If you ask any women secretary how much actually is the annual fund for that year, she will not know. She will just receive the funds and they are quite happy with it. Secondly making separate women VDB has ensured that women will never be members of the executive council of VDB and never ever be its secretary. With all this segregation, women still have shown that they can do great things with the limited funds that have been allotted to them. The remarkable success stories only prove tell about women power."

10. Interview held in Phesama, Nagaland, with a youth leader on 7th October, 2006.

11. This interview took place in Dimapur, Nagaland, on 16th December 2006. According to this elder, "The members of the murdered family will come and kill the culprit. They can kill him with spade and *dao*. No one is allowed to save the culprit. If a person flees to another village and enters a house and says that he has committed mistake and asks the house owner to protect him. And if he is accepted and adopted by the house owner, then his opponents cannot kill him. But the culprit can never go back to his village. If he goes back to his village, he will be killed."

12. This interview took place in Tura, Meghalaya, on 11 November 2006.

13. Interview with a lecturer, Nagaland University.

14. One of the interviewees had this to say regarding the state of

Dobashi courts or customary law courts: "If you have a look at the *Dobashi* court you will realize that some of the *dobashis* are young and know mighty little about the customary law. They are not really groomed in that whole adage of what customary laws are and how they should be applied." Interview held in Kohima, on Oct 4, 2006.

15. In an interview with a lawyer in Kohima on 1 September 2006, it was mentioned that the investigation procedure does include maintaining of records and cross examination of witnesses. "Acutally see...in the village level or DBs court, they don't have to maintain any written records. After hearing the parties and then their witnesses they give the verdict. Say it is land dispute, there is no cross examination of the witness by the opposing party..."

16. Refer an anonymous comment in Kuknalim website, "Are you Kidding?" July 2006.

    http://www.kuknalim.com/modules.php?name=Forums&file=viewtopic&t=1026. The writer mentions how justice was sacrificed for the sake of inter-village harmony and the murderers, who killed an innocent boy, went scot-free.

17. In a seminar organized by the Nagaland University held in Kohima in 2004, a Naga woman participant stoutly defended the codification of customary law as a remedy to set right the injustice meted out to women in Naga society.

18. The Hindu Marriage Act, 1955, The Hindu Succession Act, 1956, The Hindu Minority and Guardianship Act, 1956, The Hindu Adoptions and Maintenance Act, 1956.

19. For an exhaustive discussion on the debate that took place on the personal laws of the Hindus in 1955 refer J. D. M. Derrett, 1968. *Religion, Law and the State in India*. London: Faber and Faber; refer also J. D. M. Derrett, 1957. *Hindu Law Past and Present*, Calcutta: A. Mukherjee & Co., Private Ltd.

20. J. D. M. Derrett, 1957. *Hindu Law Past and Present*, Calcutta: A. Mukherjee & Co., Private Ltd, p. 8.

21. J. D. M. Derrett, 1968. *Religion, Law and the State in India*. London: Faber and Faber, p.333.

22. J. D. M. Derrett, 1957., p.25.

23. Derrett has dealt with the codification debate surrounding Hindu Law elaborately in Derrett 1957., pp.38-41.

24. Cited in M. B. Hooker, 1975. *Legal Pluralism*. Oxford: Clarendon Press, p. 67.

25. Bernard S. Cohn, 2003. *An Anthropologist among the Historians and Other Essays*. New Delhi: Oxord University Press, p, 467.

26. Neeladri Bhattacharya, 1995. "Remaking Custom: The Discourse and Practice of Colonial Codification." in R. Champakalakshmi and S. Gopal, eds. *Tradition, Dissent and Ideology*. New Delhi: Oxford University Press, p. 50.

27. J. D. M. Derrett, 1957., p. 50.

28. Cited in Martin Chanock, 1985. *Law, Customs and Social Order*. London and New York: Cambridge University Press, p.27.

29. Max Gluckman, 1973. *The Judicial Process Among the Barotse of Northern Rhodesia (Zambia)*. Manchester: Manchester University Press. (first published in 1955), p.21.

REFERENCES

1. Allen, C. K. (1961). *Law in the Making*. London: Oxford University Press (first published in 1927).

2. Allott, A. N. (1984). "What is to be Done with African Customary Law? The Experience of Problems and Reforms in Anglophone Africa from 1950," *Journal of African Law*, Vol.28, No.1/2, pp.56-71.

3. Barooah, Jeuti. (2002). "Property and Women's Inheritance Rights in the Tribal Areas of the Northeast," in Walter Fernandes and Sanjay Barbora, eds. *Changing Women's Status in India: Focus on the Northeast*. Guwahati: North Eastern Social Research Centre, pp.99-113.

4. Bennett, T. W. and Vermeulen, T. (1980). "Codification of Customary Law," *Journal of African Law*. Vol. 24, No.2, pp.206-219.

5. Bhattacharya, Neeladri. (1996). "Remaking Custom: The Discourse and Practice of Colonial Codification," in R. Champakalakshmi and S. Gopal, eds. *Tradition, Dissent and Ideology*. New Delhi: Oxford University Press, pp.20-51.

6. Buxbaum, David. C. (1967). "Introduction," in David C. Buxbaum, ed. *Traditional and Modern Legal Institutions in Asia and Africa*. Leiden: E. J. Brill, pp. 1-8.

7. Cohn, Bernard S. (2003). *An Anthropologist among the Historians and Other Essays*. Delhi: Oxford University Press.

8. Derrett. J. D. M. (1957). *Hindu Law: Past and Present*. Calcutta: A. Mukherjee & Co. Private Ltd.

9. Derrett, J. D. M. (1968). *Religion, Law and the State in India*. London: Faber and Faber.

10. Driberg, J. H. (1934). "The African Conception of Law," Journal of Comparative and International Law, No 16.

11. D'Souza, Alphonsus. (2001). Traditional Systems of Forest Conservation in North East India: The Angami Tribe of Nagaland. Guwahati: North Eastern Social Research Centre.

12. Durie. (2006). "Legal Pluralism and Cultural Difference - New Zealand Perspective," Paper presented in Australian Law Reform Agencies Conference in Sydney in April, 2006.

13. Fernandes, Walter and Menon, Geeta. (1987). Tribal Women and Forest Economy: Deforestation, Exploitation and Status Change. New Delhi: Indian Social Institute.

14. Fernandes, Walter and Barbora, Sanjay. (2002). Modernisation and Women's Status in North Eastern India: A Comparative Study of Six Tribes. Guwahati: North Eastern Social Research Centre.

15. Fernandes, Walter and Bharali, Gita. (2002). *The Socio-Economic Situation of Some Tribes of Bishnupur and Palizi*. Guwahati: North Eastern Social Research Centre (mimeo).

16. Fernandes, Walter, Melville Pereira and Vizalenu Khatso. (2005). *Customary Laws in Northeast India: Impact on Women*. Guwahati: North Eastern Social Research Centre.

17. Gluckman, Max. (1973). *The Judicial Process Among the Barotse of Northern Rhodesia (Zambia)*. Manchester: Manchester University Press (first published in 1955).

18. Haksar, Nandita. (1998). "Law and the Self-Management of Tribal Societies in North-East India," in Bhupinder Singh, ed. *Antiquity to Modernity in Tribal India: Tribal Self-Management in Northeast India, Vol.II,* pp. 161-193.

19. Hooker, M B. (1975). *Legal Pluralism*. Oxford: Clarendon Press.

20. Human Development Report. (2004). *Cultural Liberty in Today's Diverse World*.

21. Kamkhenthang, H. (2005). "Status of Women and Customary Laws of the Paite with Reference to its Cognate Tribes in Manipur," Paper presented at the Seminar on *Status of Women and Customary Laws among the Tribal Population of Northeast India*." Guwahati: National Institute of Public Cooperation and Child Development, March 7& 8.

22. Kelhou. (1998). "Women in Angami Society," in Lucy Zehol, ed. *Women in Naga Society*. New Delhi: Regency Publications, pp. 55-61.

23. McLachlan, Campbell. (1988). "The Recognition of Aboriginal Customary Law: Pluralism beyond the Colonial Paradigm: A Review Article," *The International and Comparative Law Quarterly*, Vol.37, No.2, pp. 368-386.

24. Menon, Geeta. (1995). The Impact of Migration on the Work and Tribal Women's Status," in Loes Schenken-Sandbergen, ed. *Women and Seasonal Labour Migration*. New Delhi: Sage publications, pp. 79-154.

25. Nongbri, Tiplut. (1998). "Gender Issues and Tribal Development," in Bhupinder Singh, ed. op.cit., pp. 221-246.

26. Nwogugu, E. I. (1976). "Abolition of Customary Courts – The Nigerian Experiment," *Journal of African Law*, Vol. 20, No.1(Spring), pp.1-12.

27. Orebech, Peter et al., (2005). *The Role of Customary Law in Sustainable Development*. Cambridge: Cambridge University Press.

28. Our Correspondent (2005). "Law to Cement Naga Unity: Young Tribals Support Move, Elders Express Scepticism," *The Telegraph*, 10 February, Guwahati.

29. Pathak, Manjushree. (1991). *Crimes, Customs and Justice in Tribal India: A Teleological Study of Adis*. New Delhi: Mittal Publications.

30. Roy, R. Devasish (2005). *Traditional Customary Laws and Indigenous Peoples of Asia*. London: Minority Rights Group International.

31. Roy, Sripati. (1911). *Customs and Customary Law in British India*. Calcutta: Published by the Author, Hare Press.

32. Svensson, Tom G. (2002). "Indigenous Rights and Customary Law Discourse: Comparing the Nisga'a and the Sámi," *Journal of Legal Pluralism and Unofficial Law*, 47: 1-35.

33. Thong, Joseph S. (1997). *Head-Hunters Culture: Historic Culture of Nagas*. Tseminyu: Khinyi Woch.

34. Vijayakumar, V. (2006). *Traditional Futures: Law and Custom in India's Lakshadweep Islands*. New Delhi: Oxford University Press.

35. White, C. M. N. (1965). "African Customary Law: The Problem of Concept and Definition," *Journal of African Law*, Vol.9, No.2, pp. 86-89.

INDEX

■■■